ALTERNATIVE CURRENCY MOVEMENTS AS A CHALLENGE TO GLOBALISATION?

Ashgate Economic Geography Series

Series Editors:
Michael Taylor, Peter Nijkamp and Tom Leinbach

Innovative and stimulating, this quality series enlivens the field of economic geography and regional development, providing key volumes for academic use across a variety of disciplines. Exploring a broad range of interrelated topics, the series enhances our understanding of the dynamics of modern economies in developed and developing countries, as well as the dynamics of transition economies. It embraces both cutting edge research monographs and strongly themed edited volumes, thus offering significant added value to the field and to the individual topics addressed.

Other titles in the series:

The Sharing Economy
Solidarity Networks Transforming Globalisation
Lorna Gold
ISBN 0 7546 3345 4

China's Rural Market Development in the Reform Era
Him Chung
ISBN 0 7546 3764 6

Foreign Direct Investment and Regional Development in East Central Europe and the Former Soviet Union
Edited by David Turnock
ISBN 0 7546 3248 2

Proximity, Distance and Diversity
Issues on Economic Interaction and Local Development
Edited by Arnold Lagendijk and Päivi Oinas
ISBN 0 7546 4074 4

Creativity and Space
Labour and the Restructuring of the German Advertising Industry
Joachim Thiel
ISBN 0 7546 4328 X

Alternative Currency Movements as a Challenge to Globalisation?

A Case Study of Manchester's Local Currency Networks

PETER NORTH
University of Liverpool, UK

ASHGATE

Published by
Ashgate Publishing Limited
Gower House
Croft Road
Aldershot
Hants GU11 3HR
England

Ashgate Publishing Company
Suite 420
101 Cherry Street
Burlington, VT 05401-4405
USA

Ashgate website: http://www.ashgate.com

British Library Cataloguing in Publication Data
North, Peter, 1962-
    Alternative currency movements as a challenge to
    globalisation? : a case study of Manchester's local
    currency networks. - (Ashgate economic geography series)
    1. Local exchange trading systems - England - Manchester
    2. Local exchange trading systems
    I. Title
    332.4'942733

Library of Congress Cataloging-in-Publication Data
North, Peter, 1962-
    Alternative currency movements as a challenge to globalisation? : a case study of
Manchester's local currency networks / by Peter North.
        p. cm. -- (Ashgate economic geography series)
    Includes index.
    ISBN 0-7546-4591-6
    1. Local exchange trading systems--England--Manchester. 2. Local exchange trading
systems. I. Title. II. Series.

    HD3435.G72M366 2005
    332.4'942733--dc22

                                                                                    2005017280

ISBN 0 7546 4591 6

Typeset by Saxon Graphics Ltd, Derby
Printed and bound by Athenaeum Press Ltd, Gateshead, Tyne & Wear

Contents

For Beverley

Acknowledgements

There are too many people to thank for the production of this book and the research from which it was constructed. I would like to thank colleagues at the Universities of Bristol, Sheffield, London South Bank and Liverpool who have helped, encouraged and critiqued my work over the years: and in particular I would like to highlight Paul Burton, Colin Williams, Roger Lee and Irene Bruegel. From the world of LETS I would like to thank Liz Shephard, Harry Turner (sadly no longer with us – you will be missed), Nigel Leach, Angus Soutar and Michael Linton. They all got me thinking. From Manchester LETS I would like to thank everyone that I met with, including (but not limited to) Malcolm Allum, Jo Bend, Linda Bloomfield, John and Wendy Clifford, Marian Daltrop, Inland Driftwood, Bernard Ekbury, Spencer Fitzgibbon, Gilli Gladman, Siobhan Harpur, Kos, Steven Knight, Peter Gay, Karsten Jungnickel, Bob Kirby, Katrina Long, Alison Milner, Margaret Mansoor, John Piprani, Mike Scantlebury, Rose Snow, Storm Steel, Lyn Woolry, John from Withington Cycles; and Chris, Frazer, Andy, Kai and Kryshia from LETSGo.

"Where there is a need, there is a need to meet it."

CHAPTER 1

Introduction:
Money Only has the Value We Give It?

In September 1992 Britain was famously expelled from the European Exchange Rate Mechanism (ERM) when George Soros, amongst others, successfully bet that Sterling would not be able to continue to track the then hegemonic German Mark. Interest rates briefly hit 15% before the then Chancellor let the pound float, before (he later said) going home to sing in his bath that sterling had been liberated from what he saw as an unreasonable straightjacket. Others faired less well. The recession of the early 1990s saw the national unemployment rise from 5.2% in May 1990 to 10.4% by January 1993, with higher rates in poorer areas. The success or otherwise of the economy seemed to have no relation to the need: people's likelihood of getting a job or not seemed to be related less to their skills or whether there was any need for their services, but more to the amount of money in the economy and confidence. Nothing had changed between 1990 and 1993 in terms of the skills people had and the needs they had, but unemployment never-theless doubled. Unsurprisingly, people looked for solutions.

One solution to the coexistence of unmet need and unwanted skills was an attempt to reassign the status of money from a prerequisite of economic activity to a lubricant, or tool for measurement. Groups of people came together, often through their membership of green or leftwing groups or community associations to hear a claim that since the UK left the gold standard and began to use paper money unbacked by any commodity, all a pound note is is a representation, social construction, a collective agreement we all make to accept a certain form of meas-urement, store of value, and unit of exchange. We use money created by the state, but as state- validated money is just a piece of paper (rather than something of intrinsic value) it follows that if this money is unreasonably restricted we can, recognising that what we are lacking is just paper, make a collective agreements to issue and use other forms of money. They argued that saying that needs can't be met because there is not enough money to pay for it is like saying that a table cannot be made as there are not enough inches to measure it. If we see money as a social construction, then we should be able to create and use our own forms of money to fill the gap caused by a lack of state-created money. These forms of currency created from below became known as Local Exchange Trading Schemes, or LETS. After Black Monday, LETS schemes began to emerge in cities, suburbs, estates, towns and villages across the UK as people who felt that the economy was not working for them, who felt a need for more community feeling, or who were concerned about sustainability, came together to develop what they hoped would be an alternative to the 'money system'. This book examines their experiences.

1

WHAT IS LETS?

LETS schemes are essentially a network through which members agree to create a form of currency that they agree to accept from each other, which they back by their 'commitment' to earn, at a later date, credits from someone else. The network offers members an account and credit facilities, denominated in the local currency and managed on their behalf by someone keeping accounts on a personal computer. The currency often has a name that reflects the locality, for example Brights in Brighton, Tales in Canterbury or Olivers in Bath. The currency may be valued in relation to sterling, to an hour's work, to some notion of what is a 'fair' wage, or something else entirely – for example how highly a certain service is regarded or needed. The network operates by members listing the goods and services which they want to offer and receive, along with their telephone numbers. This is collated into a directory, which members use to contact each other in order to trade. Payment is then made either by writing a cheque in the local currency, or by registering the transaction with the accountant. The networks build on barter in that reciprocal exchange between partners for each trade is not required. For example, a trader can get another to fix his car, and earn the currency back by providing others with, for example, childcare and help decorating.

LETS was introduced to the UK at a meeting of The Other Economic Summit (or TOES) in 1985 (Ekins 1986) before being popularised in a book written in 1988 called *Beyond the Crash: the emerging rainbow economy*. The first schemes in the UK were in Norwich (established 1985), Stroud (1989) and West Wiltshire (1989). By 1994 there were thought to be some 200 LETS schemes in the UK. Some local authorities, noticeably in Greenwich (London), Liverpool and Leicester saw LETS as a way of generating local economic activity, helping people develop new skills, empowering communities, and meeting needs that could not otherwise be met. When New Labour was elected in the UK, the Government investigated the extent that these schemes could be new ways of building community and cohesion, and of helping people develop their skills and access work. By 1999 a survey undertaken by a team led by Colin Williams (Williams, Aldridge et al. 2001) found that there were 303 LETS. Some remained small-scale networks involving 10–20 people, perhaps in a small town or neighbourhood, while others grew into more substantial networks involving one or two hundred people (for example in Bristol, Brighton or Stroud). One scheme, in Manchester, grew to around 460 members.

Outside the UK alternative money schemes have emerged in countries as far apart as Argentina, Australia and New Zealand, Canada and the US, continental Europe, and Japan (for a review see (Dauncey 1988; Lang 1994; Douthwaite 1996; Croall 1997). They range from Time Dollars (USA), Green Dollars (New Zealand, Australia, and Canada), Grains of Salt (France) and 'Talents' (Germany, Hungary) and '*Redes global de Trueque*' (global barter networks) in Argentina.

THE EMERGENCE OF ALTERNATIVE FORMS OF MONEY

Of course, alternative forms of money have a long history which includes the labour notes developed by the utopian socialist Robert Owen and the stamp scrip, alternative money forms that emerged in the great depression in the US and Europe. The current wave of currency movements arose out of the Green movement in the countercultural 1960s. While many dropped out, joined communes and tried to live off the land, others, not wanting such a total withdrawal from society, set up skills share networks to enable members to share their skills without the use of money. Examples included the 'Really Useful Exchange' of Richmond, Virginia in the United States, Canada's Vancouver Community Exchange, and Vancouver Island's Widget Exchange (Weston 1992) and the Community Network in Palmers Green, London (established 1978, with 500 members by 1980). But these were all small-scale networks of people who were opposed to capitalist exploitation and technological modern society, wanting to exchange skills within smaller scale convivial communities without using capitalist money, but valuing an hour of each other's labour equally. They used notes denominated not in dollars or pounds but hours of labour. At the other end of the political spectrum, businesses used commercial barter networks both to save money and to break into new markets, such as the then communist bloc countries where currency exchange facilities were as yet undeveloped. These were big business, and efficient – but served no progressive function.

The innovation that led to the large scale use of alternative money networks, which made them different, perhaps more modern than the utopian socialist or hippie experiments of the past came in Comox Valley, Vancouver Island, Canada in 1983. Michael Linton developed a model for a computerised exchange network, hoping to marry the efficiency of commercial barter with the liberatory potential of the countercultural exchanges, in a beautifully simple concept called the 'LETSystem'.[1] The elegant LETSystem model caught the imagination, utilising the newly emerging personal computer technology to provide individual accounts in alternative forms of money that would balance currency issued by each issuer with that paid into the recipient's account. I pay you ten green dollars, my account goes down ten and yours goes up ten – the balance of the system as a whole is zero. It seemed a thoroughly twenty-first century variation on an old concept.

Linton's second innovation was to use a unit of currency linked not to the hour, but to the Canadian Dollar, the Green Dollar – meaning that users did not have to buy into the whole philosophy of equality to of labour time to join (an advantage in the 1980s when New Right ideas were dominant and equality seemed an 'out of date' hang over from socialism or the 1960s). Linton's LETSystem eventually grew to about 500 members, but died a death according to Linton when the three businesses in the system left "and people didn't have anything to spend their money on". Linton also ran up a personal debt of some 14,000 Green Dollars which he later felt to be bad practice and to be a contributory factor in the stagnation of the system. After this experience the importance of reciprocity was stressed. Members were encouraged to give to the network as much as they received, and to demonstrate this by periodically balancing their account. After a quiet period of a couple

---

[1] "LETSystem", one word, refers throughout the text to Linton's design. Other community currency schemes which differ in one way or another from Linton's design are referred to by the generics LETS, LETS schemes or LETS systems (two words).

of years the Comox system slowly picked up trading. Linton promoted LETS around the world and the idea spread to Australia where by the mid 1990s there were thought to be 164 systems and New Zealand (55) (Jackson 1995).

In the United States Edgar Cahn promoted a parallel concept, Time Money (Offe and Heinz 1992; Boyle 1999; Cahn 2000). Time Banks connected volunteers with people who need support and matched their requirements and skills, paying volunteers in Time Money based on a straight hour-for-hour swap, which cannot be aligned directly to any national currency valuation. These credits could either be used to pay for care and su___ ___ his or her time comes, or donated to a needy ___ ___nger volunteer. Time Money further diff__ ___r cheque book is issued: rather ___ administrative point whic___ ___its centrally on a comp___ ___nts to be returned to a ___ ___ilosophy of members co___ ___ rather than running in___

Another North ___ ___red considerable busin___ ___te between individuals ___ ___ Columbia) and up to 2___ ___r 1995; Boyle 1999; Greco 200___ ___nally high quality notes, produced ___ ___work is valued both in time spent and by re___ ___ that, for example, an hour's labour would equa___ ___ average wage per hour was ten dollars. Participating ___ ___dvert in 'Ithaca Hours' – a specially produced local newspa___ ___pants use to identify who accepts Hours, in return for which they re___ ___rst four Hours and then earn others through trading – no central recor___ ___ept beyond one of the number of notes printed. Hours cannot be spent until they are earned, although interest free loans are available. The Ithaca Hour project has been spectacularly successful in terms of involving the many countercutural and community-focused businesses that thrive in an upstate university town with a strong tradition of dissent – something LETS schemes in the UK have conspicuously failed to do (North 1996). In 1997, an Argentine NGO PAR imported the Ithaca hours model to Argentina where, as result of that country's financial collapse in 2001 (Primavera, De Sanzo et al. 1998; Powell 2002; Pearson 2003), and scrip notes took off at a level that dwarfs its usage everywhere else. From 2000–2003 literally millions of people would come to buy food, clothes, get their hair cut, their nails done and meet their neighbours in barter markets where they would trade using notes produced by the markets themselves. Until a crisis of confidence and a reviving economy hit barter in late 2002, it operated at a mass scale not seen since depression era scrip.

Other local currency innovations in the United States include those pilots developed by the EF Schumacher Society of Great Barrington, Massachusetts. Examples include 'Deli Dollars' circulated amongst customers at wholefood restaurants (Greco 1994:95/6, Solomon 1996:54–55). Customers bought 'Deli Dollars' in advance to pay for the refurbishment of a local delicatessen, to be redeemed once the refurbishment was complete through the purchase of food with the local currency. These innovations were expanded into 'Berk-Shares', discount coupons issued by local traders in one small Massachusetts town to a value of $1 for every $10 spent, and redeemed at the end of the summer at a rate of approximately 25%. In other words, an item costing $100 could be bought for $75 and 25 in local script. In the same state, farmers in Berkshire, Massachusetts traded their produce on 'Berkshire Farm Preserve Notes', a local script redeemable in the farmer's markets. Customers bought the ten dollar-valued notes for $9 in the winter when farmers are growing, providing them with income in the winter months. They then redeemed the note with that farmer, or with another grower in the programme, in the summer to even out annual imbalances in income. These notes were not connected to a recommended hourly rate in any way.

The Swiss 'Wir' model is the most successful example of a parallel currency involving business in levels of economic activity that have any significance to that businesses performance – just about all the other alternative currency networks that have emerged in the 1990s are restricted to trade between individuals, not businesses. 'Wir' was formed in 1934, its name combining two meanings ('wir – we' and 'Wirtschaftsring' or 'business circle'). Unlike similar contemporary experiments in Austria and Germany, the 'Wir' movement was not closed down by the Nazis and therefore offers considerable experience of the operation of a parallel currency involving over 70,000 small and medium business participants with a turnover of 2521 million 'Wir' units, equivalent to Swiss Francs (Douthwaite 1996:100). After making a cash deposit, participants receive a credit card with an interest-free credit of five percent of their deposit, and they can then trade these 'Wir' units, equivalent to Swiss francs in value, with other participants. Alternatively, they can negotiate further credits as working capital on offering sufficient collateral. Until the 1970s mortgages were available interest-free before a small interest charge was introduced. Wir involves businesses, and saves members money – but apart from the interest-free component, it is difficult to see it as in any way progressive.

The overall tone of academic writing on these new forms of money is to conceptualise them firstly as a response to social exclusion (Williams 1995; Barnes, North et al. 1996; North 1996; Williams 1996a, b; Pacione 1997). They are seen as an attempt by the poor and unemployed to gain resources and consumption opportunities, and money and credit primarily through the adoption of a new form of money that straddles domestic exchange and the money economy (Thorne 1996:1632), thereby providing access to new forms of work and livelihood (Aldridge, Tooke et al. 2001), perhaps also allowing those without work to access it (Williams, Aldridge et al. 2001). Secondly, alternative currency networks are claimed as a technology that builds community. They connect people who do not each other, so they feel less atomised and fragmented by rekindling a sense of capacity to make change, promoting economic inclusion through transparent financial relationships (Lee 1996:1380) or through regaining community control over work by recasting money as something that should enable needs to be met through what Polanyi called the re-embedding of markets within social relationships (Thorne 1996:1632–1634). Third, local currencies are seen as a way of imposing social regulation over the economic. Just as we require regulation over what forms of market exchange are deemed acceptable by banning, for example, slave or child labour, the unfettered discharge of pollution, and minimum labour and safety standards, so, through *local* currency networks like LETS, local people should be better able to control the means of exchange between each other to discourage that which is thought inappropriate. Following Polanyi 1944/1980, economies are seen not as given, natural, or an apolitical technical matter, but as social constructions with a morality that is negotiated, created and reproduced through economic activity. Against neoliberal forms of globalisation that assert that goods and services should be produced by those who do it best even if this means lower standards, more exploitation, burning fossil fuels to move goods around the world and the like, all goods that can be produced locally, should be (Hines 2000). Thus, fourth, they have been described as lifeboats against globalisation developed by the marginal in spaces suffering from uneven capitalist development (Pacione 1997; 1999) where money flows, often in irrational or over-exuberant ways, not where it is needed but where it gains the best return (Strange 1986). Against globalisation, LETS are 'locally defined systems of value formation and distinctive moral economic geographies' (Lee 1996:1377); as micropolitical challenges to capitalism (Lee 1999; North 1999), or as a form of sustainable local development which puts ecological values front and centre (Seyfang 2001). David Harvey, (Harvey 1996:237–238) mentions local currencies as an 'interesting example of a set of social practices ... to create a certain kind of money that embodies a different kind of socio-temporality than that experienced in the world market'. This is an economy that, it is hoped, run by slower, local, community rhythms, rather than those of a globalised market working according to Adam Smith's instrumental rationality and a global division of labour. People and communities should come first, and economies should be structured to build conviviality, community, and local control.

However, much of the academic writing undertaken to date has discussed LETS in its formative period. Much of it was undertaken when LETS was but two or three years old, in the period where, like many social movements, it was growing at a spectacular trajectory. Many of the claims made had yet to be tested. The positionality of 2005 allows a longer view to be taken: were the hopes and dreams of the LETS pioneers well founded, once academic interest had moved on the next big thing? Were they able to change economic rhythms? This book aims to fill that gap.

THE STRUCTURE OF THE BOOK

This book is an ethnography of one of the larger schemes, in Manchester, UK. Research has been undertaken over a twelve-year period, with first contact with Manchester LETS being made in 1993. In 1995–96 a nine-month period of fieldwork was undertaken, with follow-up visits made in 2001 and in 2005. It provides a detailed study of the inside life of members of Manchester LETS: what inspires them? Why did they join? What sort of economic life are they creating? Are they able to live the life they want, using the form of money they have created – and what barriers do they meet? What goods and services can they access, and what is beyond their reach? Are they able to create their new form of money for any length of time, or is the experience ephemeral? Given that large claims have been made for these schemes, how successful are they?

Chapter 2 discusses how we might theorise these alternative forms of money. It conceptualises alternative money schemes as social movements with criticisms of market economies. The chapter will review social movement theories from the American (McCarthy and Zald 1977; McAdam, McCarthy et al. 1988; Tarrow 1998; Tindall 2003) and European schools (Touraine 1981; Melucci 1989; Eyerman and Jamison 1991; Snow and Benford 1992; Melucci 1996) The chapter discusses how social movement theory and allied concepts such as Foucault's genealogical understanding of how systems of domination can operate with their own logics will be used to theorise the ethnographic discussion that follows.

Chapter 3 will review how we can study these networks, detailing the specific methods used for the bulk of this study, Sociological Intervention (Touraine 1981:150–183). The method consists of the construction of a programme of focus group discussions involving social movement militants who have taken part in action to an appreciable degree, but who are not leaders or representatives of particular organisations within the social movement. The latter, Touraine argues, are likely to want to speak 'on behalf of' their particular organisations, and simply reproduce the analysis of the movement without taking it further – in what can be a sometimes painful and rigorous process of discussion. The group should also, as far as is practicable, include militants from the full range of organisations, ideologies and tendencies within the social movement, so that all the tensions and potentialities within the movement are represented within the discussion. At the same time, the group should remain small enough to develop some collective identity. Touraine takes the group through a series of sessions on a guided journey of what he calls the 'self-analysis' of the social movement through a staged inter-action between participants, the researcher and critics of the movement. The chapter will discuss how this method was used in the field, and supplemented with ethnographic methods such as participant observation, interviews as conversations and more semi-structured interviews, and periods of action research with members of LETS wanting to reach out and encourage use of LETS to spread.

The final theoretical chapter will examine what social movement theorists would call the Political Opportunity Structure within which the LETS schemes in this study emerge – Manchester, a paradigmatic example of the problems and possibilities facing British Cities in the 1990s. It will examine debates about regeneration and social exclusion, and how community and voluntary groups might work together with government to address some of these issues. It discusses the frames around urban futures that shape the dominant regeneration script in Manchester, and challenges to it from the Green Movement: a movement that may provide allies for LETS and/or resources that it can access.

Part II of the book provides case studies of local money in action in the UK. Chapter 5 introduces the three LETS in Manchester that form the focus for this ethnographic study. Manchester LETS, which grew to be one of the UK's largest in the mid 1990s; LETSGo, an attempt to generate large scale use of alternative currencies by business, and a scheme on an outer housing estate, Hattersley LETS. Chapters 6 and 7 discuss the rationales for and agendas behind people's partici-pation in LETS, as identified through Sociological Intervention: the actualisation of alternative economic relations and livelihoods based on conviviality, ecological sustainability, free exchange, and unalienated labour. The chapters introduce competing visions of social change through LETS. On one side are those who see local currencies as an unproblematic rational policy innovation with the capacity to reform mainstream economic rationales towards free, humanised, ecological values. On the other, activists with more ecological, even anarchist values see local currencies as resistant or emancipated spaces which operate under their changed rules. Chapter 7 contrasts the competing strategies to examine the extent that alternative ecological values can be generated from below before structural limits are encountered in a discussion of the extent that members of LETS do see what they are doing as social movement activity.

Chapters 8 and 9 discuss how those that saw LETS as a policy reform that would be able to help businesses grow in ways that built sustainable local economies, and solve many problems experiences in inner city environments worked with local and national government agencies and businesses to promote LETS; and discusses why these proposals remained unfulfilled or did not achieve the hopes for goals in practice. The failure of New Labour to adopt LETS will be examined, along with the reasons for the success of Time Money in this regard. It will be argued that the resistant conceptions of LETS as a tool for building alternative economic values are not attractive to a government committed to managing the efficient workings of a capitalist market based on labour discipline, a commitment manifesting itself in a labour market policy based on disciplining the unemployed into work through the New Deal and active welfare. LETS was attractive to many precisely as it did not involve capitalist labour discipline – consequently it proved to be a poor tool for helping the socially excluded get work. The less resistant ethos of the co-production of public services, and on volunteering encapsulated by Time Money was far more attractive to government. Chapter 10 discusses how effectively those in Manchester LETS who saw LETS as an attempt to build a localised economy based on alternative conceptions of money and livelihood were able to achieve their goals. It argues that within limits set by the resources they were able to access through their own private networks, members of LETS were able to develop economic relations with each other based on their preferred conceptions of the role of money and what constitutes valuable work and ethical livelihoods in a localized economy.

The conclusion, Part III of the book, revisits Manchester LETS from the perspectives of 2001 and 2005, showing that half of the members contacted again in 2001 were still members. The conclusion will argue that the critiques of the role of money, its impact on livelihoods for those who are not successful according to a conventional market paradigm, and the need for radical alternatives to globalisation developed by activists are well met, but that the effectiveness on the ground of these projects is less clear. Radical environmentalists committed to an alternative to mainstream employment patterns do find that these networks operate as effective 'bonding' social capital – they connect people of similar political beliefs, enable them to trade with and support each other, and build networks of mutual aid making an alternative to the nine to five easier than if they did not know each other. This is a valuable demonstrator that the claim of neoliberal enthusiasts, that there is no alternative, is challengeable. Secondly, they do build community, connectedness and mutuality for those that join – again a function of bonding social capital. These systems do help smooth the changes by helping people to meet, solve problems and look after each other such that they do not feel isolated and abandoned. The recent success of Time Money in the UK builds on this strength. But for too many members the networks stay too small for significant levels of trading happen. LETS can therefore be best thought of a part of what emerged after Seattle as the counter-globalisation movement, putting forwards alternatives to globalisation that can be enacted in the hear and now for the most committed, especially if they see LETS as a way of carving out a new economic space that exists between the cash economy and the hoped for realm of pure co-operation.

PART I
CONTEXT AND
THEORETICAL
BACKGROUND

CHAPTER 2

Developing a Toolkit for Understanding LETS: Social Movement Approaches

If you want to know what God thinks of money, just look at those he gave it to.

Dorothy Parker

Groups of people have, from the early nineteenth century, got together and made claims about how money should be used, what is wrong with the money they have, and attempted to put into practice, alternative forms of money. We call groups that make claims about the imperfections of society and the economy, and proposals for radical change, social movements; and this book will investigate the extent that members of LETS, as a social movement, make claims about the way money is organised, and use forms of money they have created for themselves as part of their political action. This is not to assume, at the beginning of the book, that LETS is a social movement and that members do believe that they are making radical claims – they may believe that LETS is entirely unproblematic. The extent that the claims about money, work and community made *are* social movement claims is one to be uncovered as the argument progresses, not to be assumed. This way we can examine the normative basis on which alternative forms of money are created and the value system which is supposed to govern their usage (Lee 2002:339). But before we go on to explore LETS we need a theoretical toolkit to help us rigorously and logically discuss the extent that alternative money forms may – or may not – lead to new possibilities for social change, and what limits those practicing alternative forms of economic life through alternative forms of money come up against. In social movement theory, we have a substantial tool kit to hand from which we can conduct our analysis.

The elements of social movement theory which are of use in an analysis of social movements around money include the Resource Mobilisation, American or 'strategy-based' school, and the New Social Movement (NSM), European or 'identity-based' school influenced by post-modern theory. This chapter examines each in turn, looking first to see how an analysis of the processes of what McCarthy and Zald (1977) call 'resource mobilisation' has explanatory power for money-focused social movements. Secondly, it explores how the American approach only takes analysis so far. Resource Mobilisation Theory (RMT) explains *how* money-focused social movements develop but not *why*, and assumes a priori that advocates of alternative forms of money aim to win elites to their point of view. This is rectified by the NSM paradigm, which made a cognitive turn that concentrates on the self-production of political meaning by social movements within civil rather than political society. Finally, the chapter examines how the best elements of the two schools might be combined into a more convincing analysis (Cohen and Arato 1992; Diani 1992; Tarrow 1998). Ideas from postmodern theory, especially Foucault's interest in micro-politics and in 'local circuits of power' will also be employed in the analysis. These social movement concepts will be used as a theoretical construct around which the radical potential of LETS as a social change tool can be investigated in a structured way.

THE 'AMERICAN' SCHOOL: STRATEGY-BASED SOCIAL MOVEMENTS

What Diani (1992) calls the 'American School' or Cohen and Arato (1992) 'strategy-based' movements arose primarily in the United States as an attempt to understand the growing Civil Rights, Anti-Vietnam War and Women's movements (for the best review of the field see Morris and Herring 1987; Klandermans and Tarrow 1988; Della Porta and Diani 1998; Tarrow 1998; Schwedler 2002). The field developed from Robert Park's original conception of 'Collective Behaviour' and Olson's 'Rational Choice Model' which contrasted collective action as rational and purposive as opposed to functionalist accounts which focussed on crowd behaviour as irrational and of protest as 'deviant', 'pathological' or 'mob psychology' on one side, and on the other structuralist accounts which saw humans as mere embodied carriers of wider structural forces.

The American school conceptualises social movement actors as seeking to influence, change or overthrow political structures – i.e. with an articulation on political society. Tarrow (1998:1–2) seeks to examine why at some times people accept the status quo, perhaps one significantly unfavourable to them, while at others they challenge it. What makes the difference? Why do they challenge seemingly overwhelming odds, at some personal sacrifice? Secondly he notes that social movements are often 'fireworks' – they emerge spectacularly and disappear just as quickly – why do they emerge when they do, and is there some inevitability in this explosion followed by disillusionment? Thirdly, after the fireworks, do they have more long lasting ends? The tradition stresses 'hard nosed political realism' and a concern with integration into political society (Scott 1990:116). Social movements' 'success' or 'failure' can be measured in terms of long term success in success in gaining concessions from elites within political structures, in interaction with those political structures. For Costain, at its simplest the American school 'is based on the idea that successful movements acquire resources and create advantageous exchange relationships with other groups as they achieve success in fulfilling their goals' (Costain 1992:xvi, quoted by Foweraker 1995:16). While the school is broad and encompasses many concepts that we do not have space to go into fully here (see Tarrow 1998), this analysis will engage with 'Resource Mobilisation Theory' (McCarthy and Zald, 1977), and the 'Political Process' model (Tilly 1978). Both stress an analysis of the political process whereby populations with grievances are pro-actively transformed into social movement actors, rather than the analysis of grievances *per se*, the focus of the 'European' school that we engage with later.

Resource Mobilisation Theory (RMT)

McCarthy and Zald (1977) developed an organisational-entrepreneurial concept that held that 'a social movement is a set of opinions and beliefs in a population which represents preferences for changing some elements of the social structure and/or reward distribution of society' (1977:43). Their contention is that as in any given society there will always be grievances and/or deprivation, and that as grievances are more common than social movements, the key question is to explain why some social movements successfully mobilise while others fail to materialise out of observable grievances. RMT therefore concentrates on the processes that enable social movement mobilisation, in particular the role of organisations within the social movement and of outside supporters, rather than issues raised by the social movement itself.

McCarthy and Zald recommend a focus on three aspects of the social movement. Firstly they stress the centrality of what they call 'conscience supporters', actors outside the social movement who facilitate or support it but who are not direct beneficiaries of its success – such as northern liberals in the Civil Rights Movement. They hold that without this support the resource pool of potential supporters will be too narrow for the movement to meet its demands. Secondly, they articulate on political society (ie government, the local state, the United Nations, officials), but stress the role of the state in adjudicating between competing demands, pointing out that opponents may be changed into supporters. They argue that analysis of social movements should focus on the debate over which tactics are appropriate to change powerful opponents into facilitators of the movements' demands. Thirdly, while they agree that political society is the field the social movement swims in, they stress that the political environment may not automatically be oppositional. They argue that traditional theory has 'ignored ... ways in which movement organisations can utilise the environment for their own purposes' (1977:43).

RMT privileges the organising processes that lead to the development of social movement organisations (SMOs) operating within a social movement. They distinguish between a social movement as a current of opinion, which they call a social movement sector or SMS; and organisations that are created within the SMS (for example Greenpeace as an SMO within the environmental SMS). To illuminate the mobilisation process RMT stresses the effectiveness of the SMO in mobilising resources that enable it to achieve the tasks that it sets itself. In particular RMT would identify the money and labour power an SMO can call on, the extent of its organisational efficiency, and the existence of support from outside the SMO. A successful SMO would ensure that enough resources flow through the SMO for it to function effectively and that the costs do not outweigh the rewards of participation. Given sufficient resources, including the existence of other SMOs within the SMS, a network of organisations or social movement industry (SMI) will be created with the resources at its disposal to achieve its goals.

Thus the key to social movement success is the extent to which beneficiaries and conscience supporters of the movement can be mobilised by SMOs – and that the authorities do not intervene. Indeed, RMT stresses the role of the state in supporting rather than repressing a movement and sees successful SMOs as pressure groups rather than as resistant organisations. The extent to which an SMO will be able to operate as a pressure group will be constrained and channelled by the environment in which the SMO operates, and McCarthy and Zald

e existence or production of a 'dense network of pre-existing SMOs, a
nse SMI to which it is part' (1977:47) makes successful influence on
nore likely.

'Political process' approaches

Tilly (1978), McAdam, McCarthy et al. (1988), Eisinger (1973) and Tarrow (1998)
concentrate on the emergence of a favourable 'structure of political opportunities' (POS) that determines the likely success or failure of any social movement
(Tilly 1977:54–55). Tarrow describes the POS as 'consistent – but not necessarily
formal, permanent or national – dimensions of the political environment which
either encourage or discourage people from collective action', i.e. external to the
social movement.

Tilly's conception of the POS is the most constantly developed, encompassing
both how the movement and its opponents engage in processes of structuration
(see Giddens [1979] for his more sophisticated take on the mutually reinforcing
nature of structure and agency). For Tilly the POS within which the movement
operates 'corresponds to the process by which a national political system shapes,
checks, and absorbs the challenges that come to it' (Tilly 1984:312 quoted by
Foweraker 1995:71). An analysis of these features will illuminate the opportunities
and threats the social movement faces. Firstly, Tilly pointed to the analysis of
shared advantages and disadvantages likely to accrue to actors as a consequence of
participation in the movement and in interaction with other populations. A social
movement that does not benefit its participants in some way, he argues, is unlikely
to receive support from rational actors. Secondly he stresses organisation. This he
identified as being the extent of pre-existing common identity and unifying
structure among the population from which the social movement springs, or the
processes of increasing common identity and/or unifying structures. A social
movement that grows out of a strong social network, or builds such a network, is
more likely to be successful that one operating in a fractured environment. This
might explain the historical failure of attempts to build strong social movements
among unemployed people.

Tilly's third analytic category was resource mobilisation. This he defines as the
extent to which political actors have access to resources under their collective
control, the degree of collective control of resources they have, or the process of
increasing resources. These are factors favouring social movements with members
wealthy in time or well connected to social networks, or movements favoured –
perhaps funded – by the State. Fourthly, Tilly identified the extent to which actors
act collectively in pursuit of common ends, or that the movement's actions build
feelings of communal endeavour from which collectivities emerge. Social movements with members who have low levels of commitment to collective action will
be less successful than those with higher levels of commitment.

Finally, he stressed opportunity, which he defined as the social movement's
ability to recognise and negotiate its way through the Political Opportunity
Structure. This involved making judgements about the relationship between the
interests of the social movement, the interests of other actors, and the state of the

environment around it. Thus a social movement's interactions with the state may mean the state favours it above others if the movement's interests are in harmony with the state's, and as the social movement increases its power or loses influence it becomes more or less likely to be favoured. Conversely, there may be costs of collective action either to members joining an organisation and experiencing repression, as opposed to costs or benefits incurred by the state in repressing or facilitating social movements. Finally there will be costs and benefits incurred by the state, or the object of the social movement's protest, (local government, businesses, multilateral organisations), that make them more likely to have to meet the social movement's claims. These calculations all enhance either the social movement's ability to reach its goals, or the ability of the state to reduce the options open to the social movement. From an analysis of the Political Opportunity Structure within which it finds itself, the social movement selects an *'action repertoire'* – the range of collective actions it undertakes – that best enable it to take advantage of the opportunities offered it.

The contribution of the American school to an analysis of alternative currencies

The American school is a useful place to start to conceptualise LETS as a social movement. Many social movements do provide tangible benefits to their members. With its emphasis on rationality, the American school is well located in realist perspectives of politics, avoiding the 'naivety' of post-modern inspired European school conceptions (Scott 1990:116). In particular the school helps us understand that social movement organisations have a crucial role in turning anger or discontent into action, and that dense networks of social movement organisations make success more likely. An analysis of any networks and organisations that facilitated the development of LETS will help explain how perceptions of need were translated into action. Similarly, analysis of the organisations that developed out of these networks will demonstrate the effectiveness of activists in persuading elites of the appropriateness of alternative forms of money as a tool to meet elite policy goals.

However, the American school can only be the start of a journey towards a social movement analysis of money reform. Tilly's concepts of POS and action repertoire help to operationalise an analysis of money-focused social movements, whereby their action repertoire would be observed within its POS, together with the movements' success or failure in the light of the five determinants identified by Tilly. Unfortunately though, concepts of the POS and the action repertoire, unless grounded, lack explanatory power beyond an analysis of everything the movement does (action repertoire) and how others affect it (POS), and at the national level this can be meaningless. Consequently Gledhill (1994:123–150) recommends the use of anthropological method to ground the movement within an observable and capturable POS.

Critiques of the American School also concentrate fire on the school for drawing too heavily on Olson's (1965) conception of *homo politicus* acting simply to maximise benefits and minimise costs, which Scott (1990:118) calls an 'impoverished interpretation of human motivation which reduces it to instrumental rationality'. Olson's conception, Scott argues, is methodologically too individual-istic and a 'sociologically adequate theory of mobilisation would need to identify the sources of solidarity which are the prerequisite for collective action by accom-modating expressive, habitual and affective as well as instrumental orientations for action' (Scott 1990:110). Analysis needs to uncover the specifics of what 'costs' and 'benefits' are, as 'action may be its own reward' (Hirschman quoted by Foweraker 1995:17) and postmodern challenges would critique the whole project of 'rationality'. This is particularly important in our analysis given the fire and passion that inspire participants in social movements, and the esoteric, non-rational elements of some of the facets of their worldviews. To adopt a rationalist view would make us blind to their arguments and miss the finer points of their arguments – not to say downright disrespectful to people who work hard, at some personal cost, for social change.

The American School says too little about the content and context of collective action (Scott 1990:120) and decontextualises it in favour of an ahistorical cost/benefit analysis. Political actors have a history and culture (Foweraker 1995:17) that affect their cost/benefit calculations, and which may make their deci-sions seem irrational to the uninformed observer. In fact the school overturns its own attachment to cost/benefit analysis; McCarthy and Zald stress the need for conscience activists who do not benefit directly from the movement, and who cannot be conceptualised as operating narrowly from rational choice. Cultural considerations explain why there are more social movements than the free rider question would predict (Foweraker 1995:17, Scott 1990:118).

The school assumes that social movements are attempting to gain entrance to the polity. It has no explanatory power for social movements that make few demands on states, wanting only their own autonomous space, and ignores the whole raft of lifestyle movements (what Giddens and Beck call 'Life politics') whose benefits derive from the day to day lived experiences of the individuals participating in them rather than on changing government policy at some future date (Cohen and Arato 1992:509). The school similarly does not explain the emer-gence of 'hopeless' social movements, those ignored by government (Foweraker 1995:17), or those hidden. Morris and Herring (1987:164–165) point out that the emphasis in RMT on SMOs fails to identify the mass-based movements that are quietly emerging and that '(s)uch conceptual neglect in the 1950s allowed the mass movements of the 1960s to catch social scientists by surprise'. RMTs focus on elites, and inclusion, has explanatory power for interest or lobby groups, but cannot explain anti-systemic social movements.

Stressing resources does not address the question of exactly how 'poor' poor people's movements are, and why – if the poor are so effectively excluded – poor people's movements arise. Consequently it is limited in application to self-help movements. The RMT approach would suggest that unless advocates of money-focused social movements are able to gain conscience support – elite support or facilitation for money reform – the direct benefactors will be unable, on their own, to achieve their goals. It assumes that advocates of money-focused social move-ments are orientating themselves on changing elites or winning resources from them, and that money-focused social movement members on their own will be inadequately resourced to do that without conscience support. RMT might therefore be inappropriate as money-focused social movements mobilise without elite facilitation or support from the state.

That social movements aim to influence elites is challenged by Melucci (1989; 1992; 1996) who argues that social movements are about creating their *own* values and measures of success rather than adjusting their action to gain favours from elites. He values local micro-level struggles with locally set rules, not necessarily located at the state level, against power relations which might not implicate the state. An articulation on inclusion devalues radical or nonconformist strategies unlikely to win over supporters outside the movement, but which are likely to win local power struggles, or are internally coherent in their own terms. The identity school, drawing on postmodern critiques, would reproach the American school for doing violence to the heterogeneity of the social movement. The school implies that social movement actors are to be 'treated as an essentially asocial being *whose identity is given*' (Scott 1990:122, my emphasis) and postmodern concerns would emphasise the creative side of social movement activity, in what Touraine called the *production of knowledges*. Cohen and Arato (1992) criticise the school for assuming that a focus by a social movement on identity politics and local struggles (located in civil society) are symptoms of the movement's immaturity or lack of political sophistication, and will inevitably be superseded in a linear process by the development of more 'sophisticated' strategies aimed at securing inclusion into political society rather than resistance to it (Foweraker 1995:17). For Cohen and Arato a social movement may contain articulations on political and civil society simultaneously.

Given the inadequacy of the American school alone in developing a toolkit for an analysis of money-focused social movements, other schools must be taken into consideration: 'European critiques' of the American school, growing out of postmodernity. These focus more on 'why' social movements emerge, less on the 'how' of the strategy school.

THE COGNITIVE TURN: NEW SOCIAL MOVEMENTS (NSMS)

The NSM paradigm defines the central role of social movements as being about the *self-production* of values, strategies and ways of living – holding that social movements are what Eyerman and Jamison (1991) call 'Knowledge Producers' – rather than focussed on strategies to ask, persuade or force the state to grant their demands. They take the post-structural emphasis on the ability of a social actor to create their world rather than structuralist or functionalist emphases on social movements as being about demands that need to be met by the state.

NSM theorists envisage a postmodern society where the large decisions about what this society is going to mean are as yet undecided. In this new liberated, deterritorialised space, social movements are involved in a dynamic process of the self-production of meaning for this world. While the social movements of industrial society were concerned with gaining control of production or of attaining state power, in contrast *new* social movements (NSMs) are concerned with the way meaning is produced and with the control of images. The generation of new meanings is a constant process of contestation in which social movements are the vehicles and the sites of struggle over the meaning of society. Thus the goal of social movements is not primarily to achieve an end (currency reform by the state), but to define life *today* (how can we use new forms of money to facilitate freedom, unexploited labour, and value everyone's contribution?) As a result, participation is not a means to an end, to achieve a future goal, but *the end in itself* – as a sign to the rest of society of what form of society could or will be organised. Alternative money schemes should be seen as a demonstrator of what should be, not a tool for the state to take up.

The theoretical contributions we shall investigate here are those of Alain Touraine, primarily in *The Voice and the Eye,* and Alberto Melucci's work in *Nomads of the Present.* While these two authors do not represent the totality of the NSM paradigm, they capture the key contribution of the school.

The Voice and the Eye

The originator and perhaps still most comprehensive theorist of the NSM paradigm is Alain Touraine (Touraine 1981), who defines a social movement as 'the organised collective behaviour of a class actor struggling against his class adversary for the social control of historicity in a concrete community' (1981:77). In contrast to RMT he regards social movements as operating in the cultural as well as the political field and denies that social movements are aimed at the taking of state power (1981:80). They cannot therefore be confused with purely political action such as that of an interest group looking to change a policy. He locates their struggle in civil society, in the struggle for control over life, although this may well involve political action and certainly involves the identification of an 'opponent' as well as the identification of the 'stakes' in the struggle – what the struggle is about and what claims the social movement makes about how society should be organised.

Touraine's aim is the modest one of restructuring social theory around a conceptualisation of the self-production of society through social movements. Large claims are made, no less than that: '(m)en (sic) make their own history: social life is produced by cultural achievements and social conflicts, and at the heart of society burns the fire of Social Movements.' (1981:1). For Touraine modern society is moving through epoch making changes from 'Industrial Society' into what he called 'Programmed Society' – scientific and information based rather than industrially based. Programmed society is far more open and diffuse than industrial society, and in it social actors are able to self-produce (or programme) themselves and their world through struggle within the concrete situations in which they find themselves. Touraine distinguishes between two sorts of social struggle. In contrast to Marxist epistemology, he argues that social movements are not fighting for a temporally more advanced society (a socialism that will inevitably replace capitalism) which he calls struggle along a 'synchronic axis' – but simply *another* society, along a 'diachronic axis'. Thus he regards the future as both unwritten and its direction undetermined. The importance of social movements is their role in the construction of political meaning for this other society, to articulate new political questions and visions of an alternative, perhaps future society, and to construct new analyses of contemporary society. A social movement must be developing a *total* analysis of the ills of society and the nature of the society it would like to see, otherwise it will be little more than an interest group. Consequently, Touraine denies that most of the movements SMT theorists analyse are in fact fully developed social movements, and he seeks to identify whether a movement has developed a total analysis.

He agrees with postmodern critics such as Foucault that there is now no one single source of power. Power 'is not only political …. it is to be found wherever social behaviour is organised from a decision-making centre, and this holds true not only from manufacturing producers but for television services, hospitals, municipal organisations and universities' (1981:50). He would not go as far as Foucault in arguing that power lies everywhere, but holds that there is a multiplication of centres of power and as a result a multiplication and dispersal of conflict – 'the more self-producing society is, the more conflicts it experiences' (1981:51). Given the multiplicity of power locations, Touraine explicitly wishes to identify sites of contestation, and in what must be a dig at Foucault, he argues it is the task for analysis is to help identify the forces of change, not just analyse domination:

> It is not enough simply to denounce the order: one must show that it is not all-powerful, one must rediscover the spring hidden beneath the cement, the word beneath the silence, the questioning beneath the ideology. This is what is at stake: if we lose we shall have to give up believing in social movements and even in what we call society; we will have to admit that there are no longer any citizens, only subjects, no longer class actors, only victims.
>
> Touraine 1981:55

Rather than a web of domination, for Touraine society is a system of actors struggling to define the cultural orientation and social relations of the emerging programmed society during the transformation from industrial society; a 'type of society, more than any other, (which) should be thought of as a complex of social relations and movements, cultural products and political struggles'. Politics for Touraine is 'no longer carried out in the name of political rights or worker's rights but in support of a population's right to choose its own kind of life and in support of its political potential, which is often called *self management*' (1981:5, my emphasis).

In *The Voice and the Eye* Touraine argued that one pre-eminent social movement will emerge, which will in future take over the central role previously held by the workers' movement in industrial society provided, that is, that the social movement's analysis becomes sophisticated enough that it reflexively understands both the nature of the new information-based society, who it represents, and the nature of the stakes in the conflict. In other words, Touraine is looking to identify whether the social movement that has become aware of its historicity is, to paraphrase Marx, a *Social Movement for itself*, able to reflexively self-create its world (1981:84). It is this emphasis on a conscious recognition by the social movement of its historicity in programmed rather than industrial society that justifies the claim 'New' for 'New Social Movements'.

Touraine therefore argues that analysis of social movements should seek to uncover three key elements. If the social movement has developed all three, it is a mature social movement rather than an ephemeral protest. Firstly he looks to examine the extent to which social movement actors have identified an identity as historic actors, reflexively aware of their ability to make their world. This he calls 'the principle of identity'. Secondly, they will understand who their opponents are and how they disagree with their opponents – the 'principle of opposition'. Thirdly, if they have developed an analysis of what the social movement is struggling for and, in the recognition of centrality for the self-production of society of this struggle, understand what the stakes in their conflict with their opponent are, they will have developed the 'principle of totality'. This structure for analysing social movements Touraine represents as a triangle (1981:81):

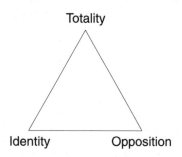

In *The Voice and the Eye*, the ecological movement is identified as the most promising candidate for this emerging central role in programmed society:

> The utopia of community appears at first to distance itself from the new social struggles, yet far often it is actually paving their way. It is the camp of the ecologists that has been most ready to lend a sympathetic ear to defend the appeals against technocracy, the concentration of power in giant systems, and the mystique of power itself ... one cannot yet know with certainty whether the ecology movement will become dissipated in contradictions, covering up the downfall of the old middle classes, or whether instead – as I am inclined to feel – it will tilt the scales towards the great battle against technocracy.
>
> Touraine 1981:20

Given the growth of what he called first 'post-industrial', then 'programmed', now 'information' society (Touraine 2001), the key focus for social movements is *self-management*. The self-production of society by new actors focussing on economic, social and cultural self-management, for Touraine, is as much at the heart of struggle for the heart of information society as was social justice for the worker's struggle, and political liberty for bourgeois struggle. Along with other social movement scholars such as Melucci (see below) and Castells, Touraine later moved from his search for one pre-eminent social movement seeking a total analysis into a wider concern for understanding which forms of social action best resisted to subjugation of social and cultural life to the economic, especially as globalisation began to be recognised as a new phenomenon which, the right claimed, limited prospects for change. This focussed on social movements struggling for cultural and social rights, and groups that enable oppressed groups to speak with their own voices and develop their own strategies for change (for example movements for the rights of and identities of gay, homeless or unemployed people, asylum seekers or immigrants). They fight not for any one particular future, but for cultural and social rights of individuals and minorities, for equality, for freedom. Social movement defence of the right of young Muslim women to wear their headscarves at school would be a prime example (Touraine 2001:52–53). This emphasis on the production of strategies for change by social actors themselves, in our case through reforming money to enable more liberated forms of work and livelihood, perhaps at micro-levels; and the centrality of self-management both to the contemporary movement for alternative forms of money and, more widely, as an organising principle for thinking the economy 'otherwise', contrasted with claims that globalisation is inevitable, must be central to our analysis.

Nomads of the Present

If Touraine's concern to identify the pre-eminent social movement and to identify its core essence – the stakes it argues for, on whose behalf, and against whom – Melucci (1989, 1992, 1996) imports postmodern concerns for heterogeneity and conceptualises social movements as diverse, 'fragile and heterogeneous social constructions' (1989:1). He analyses the resulting conflict within them which he sees as a process of self learning or reflexivity. For Melucci social movements are not nineteenth century 'heroes or villains' who win or lose political battles (and whose claims are to be accepted or rejected under some normative value system), but sites of conflict. He looks not at their political effectiveness, ideological coherence or explanatory power, but at the messages they pass on to society, which for Melucci amount to the redefinition of cultural codes:

> My claim that movements operate as a 'message' or a 'sign'…is designed to highlight the way in which they express something more than the particular substantive issues for which they are usually known. From their particular context, movements send signals which illuminate hidden controversies about the appropriate form of fundamental relations within complex society.
>
> Melucci 1989:207

For Melucci, society is more open than Touraine's 'programmed' society, where ownership of scientific knowledge is key. Melucci sees 'knowledge' – in a general sense – as pre-eminent in what he calls complex rather than programmed society, and this knowledge is contested. Consequently Melucci rejects the search for one unitary ideological essence, hidden potential or higher meaning, in favour of a conceptualisation of social movements as sites of contest over political meaning by social actors.

Being rooted in everyday life, social movements for Melucci are not to be found on the demonstration or the barricade. Rather they are usually private and invisible networks that only manifest themselves (to the outsider) when demonstrations make visible these submerged networks of reflexive life politics.

Melucci's aim is to explain why these private networks, ignored by RMT theo-rists, emerge as visible collective action and how they build collective identity from the contested nature of the stakes over which they argue. He identifies the site of the creation of social movements as the creation of *movement areas*, which he defines as multiple fragmented networks that act as cultural laboratories, which mobilise only rarely in response to specific stimuli. They are primarily 'exchanges in which information circulates, membership is multiple and involvement limited' (1989:58).

Melucci agrees that NSMs are 'New' as like Touraine, he does not see them as concerned with production. He rather puts a Baudrillardian spin on things, asserting that as information is key, NSMs are concerned both with the way meaning is produced, and with the control of image. Secondly, he agrees that social movements are not aimed at persuading governments to make changes, but with everyday concerns within the lifeworld – and consequently participation in the social movement is not a means to an end (achieving future changes), but an end in itself. The existence of a social movement, developing alternative meanings about how society should be organised, acts as a 'sign' to the rest of society; therefore, participation – creating that sign – is sufficient. Consequently, NSMs stress forms of organisation, the experience of living, or acting collectively rather than achieving their end. They seek to integrate the public and private, visible and hidden, political and personal sides of life so 'living differently and changing society are seen as complementary' (1989:40). Melucci's crucial contention is that social movements do not necessarily have the successful achievement of an end or agreement with a metanarrative of explanatory value in mind: they are *Nomads of the Present*.

Melucci therefore concentrates on the process of collective identity-building, which, he argues, proceeds along three continua which are the object of study. Firstly he examines questions as to whether the social movement aims to change the social structure or develop alternative cultural codes, seeking to analyse the capacity of members to develop such codes without being constrained by the social structure. Secondly he examines whether the social movement should work for institutional integration; or, if developing alternative cultural codes that are not accepted by the polity, accept radical marginalisation. Finally he seeks to explain debates about whether to orientate towards mass society or to strengthen internal solidarity, and whether the *form* of the group (building solidarity and alternative codes outside the polity) prevents an orientation towards mass society.

Melucci seeks to identify tensions between the movement being simultaneously supportive of the production of alternative codes, *and* of an orientation on offensive political action which breaks the limits of the existing system; and tensions within the processes whereby the social movement debates the value of these diverging and competing strategies:

> integration of defensive and transformative actions of an everyday ecology and a political ecology … is accomplished by the maintenance of two levels: intense but temporary mobilisations, and movement networks that produce information, self reflection and symbolic resources.
>
> Melucci 1989:69

Melucci feels that there are some types of collective action 'capable of affecting
the logic of complex systems', although he stresses a plurality of actions rather
than one preeminent. His emphasis on signs might be thought to preclude any
discussion of efficacy, but like Touraine, and unlike Baudrillard and the extreme
post-structuralists, Melucci does not see this negotiation over meaning taking
place in a void. He recognises that some political structures, power relations and
interests precede social movements and that politics 'does not take place on an
open field with equal chances' (1989:167), that there are limits to the political
game, and that part of the contestation of meaning is the collision of ideas and
structures. The capacity of social movements is limited by the structures and
Melucci agrees that resources enable the movement to grow.

Social movements, therefore, produce measurable results at three levels
(1989:75): *institutional changes* (political reforms or new processes), the selection
of *new elites*, and *cultural innovation* (new habits, dress, language, sexual customs).
But for Melucci the importance of social movements lies far less in measurable
change than in the nature of the resistant signs the movement produces. That is, in
the symbolic challenge that reveals the irrationality of the dominant, and that
operate at the *same level* '(information and communication) as the new forms of
technocratic power' (1989:78). He identifies three forms of this symbolic challenge: *Prophecy* (announcing alternative frameworks with the premise that the
present is not the only possible reality), *Paradox* (showing by exaggeration and
reversal both the irrationality of power relations in society, and that what society
feels to be irrational is not necessarily so) and finally *Representation* (again a
process of signification whereby the social movement shows society's contradic-
tions to itself, rather than attempting to speak on its behalf as a representative).
Melucci holds that social movements can have system-challenging features if they
make power *visible* as visible power is confrontable. Like Touraine, Melucci insists
that the dualism between structuralist and ideological conceptions of political
change is false, and that once power is made visible, structure and the challenges
to those structures (socially produced by conscious actors using the resources to
hand) interact in what he calls 'exploring the frontierland' between structure and
agency (1992:239–257). The task for research is to observe this process.

Frames

The production of new ways of thinking about the world can be operationalised
using the concept of 'frames' developed by David Snow and his collaborators
(Snow, Rochford et al. 1986; Snow and Benford 1992). Frame alignment opera-
tionalises the processes whereby knowledge and symbolic codes are produced
through Goffman's concept of the 'Frame', whereby by 'rendering events or occur-
rences meaningful, frames function to organise experience and guide action,
whether individual or collective' (Snow et al. 1986:464). Frame alignment
processes are 'the linkage of individual and SMO interpretive orientations, such
that some set of individual interests, values and beliefs and SMO activities, goals
and ideology are congruent and complementary'. They developed the schema as
they felt the RMT approach failed to address 'the interpretation of events and

experiences relevant to participation in social movement activities and campaigns' (1986:465). Also, they felt the American school tended to conceptualise willingness to participate in a social movement as a one-off decision, rather than a process whereby people can vary their commitment over time.

Snow and his colleagues identified four 'Frame Alignment Processes' that make these processes observable: 'Frame Bridging', 'Frame Amplification', 'Frame Extension' and 'Frame Transformation'. By 'Frame Bridging' they meant processes that link 'two or more ideologically congruent but structurally unconnected frames regarding an issue' (1986:467). Here the SMO attempts to reach 'ideologically congruent but untapped and unorganised sentiment pools' (1986:86) through marketing and networking. This goes beyond the existence of shared grievances, or the congruity of values, to analysis of the structuring of claims to persuade potential supporters to join the social movement. For Snow et al, micro-mobilisation is a bridging problem – a problem of connecting the unconnected – and analysis should start on how people persuade each other of the justification of their claims and rationalise their participation in the social movement. The next stage, 'Frame Amplification' is 'the clarification and invigoration of an interpretive frame' (1986:469) by the 'amplification' of values and beliefs that are held by potential actors, but which without amplification do not on their own inspire collective action. The social movement focuses, elevates and re-invigorates those values or beliefs that may have atrophied, fallen into disuse or been repressed. These may be general values such as 'freedom of speech', the 'right to protest', or beliefs such as 'capitalists are exploiters' which are built on. They identify five such processes of amplification: statements about the seriousness of the problem, the cause of the problem or of who is to blame, about who are the movements' antagonists and supporters, beliefs about the possibility of success, and finally statements about the need to 'stand up and be counted' (1986:470). The more these beliefs can be amplified, the greater the likelihood of participation in the movement increasing over time.

'Frame Extension' is the process whereby the social movement reaches out to potential supporters to 'extend the boundaries of its primary framework so as to encompass interests or points of view that are incidental to its primary objectives, but of considerable salience to potential adherents' (1986:472). The social movement aims to reach those whose values may be similar but not identical to those of the social movement's supporters, and attempts to explain why the values of potential supporters can be connected with the social movement's key values – for example the adoption into ecology of the values of social justice. For the movement to grow and participation to continue, regular 'hooking' (1986:473) to other value systems will be required. Finally, 'Frame Transformation' may be required when the frame developed by the social movement does not resonate with (or is even antithetical to) the values of potential supporters, and needs to be transformed in order to make it more attractive. This transformation may be a change in the perceived seriousness of the problem or of attribution of blame, and an example might be attempts by racist organisations to distinguish between patriotism and bigotry. They argue that these transformations can involve minor adjustment of belief or major transformations involving the abandonment of previously held metanarrative solutions. At the minor level, 'domain-specific' reframing involves small scale but significant changes within the way an issue in life (for example food, live animal exports) are framed, so that an issue once seen as unproblematic is reframed as an issue; and major 'global-interpretive' transformations of previously held metanarrative explanations (for example the acceptance of a new religion by a convert). Effective frame transformation can last well beyond the apparent decline of a movement. For example, Tarrow (1998:182) points to the resonance of the women's movement way beyond its membership in transforming language around gender into a new 'commonsense'.

Local analyses

Social Movement Theory is usually focused on large movements – the Civil Rights, Womens' or Peace movements for example. Can it also be used to examine smaller scale, more local phenomena, like LETS? An analysis of LETS conceived as micro-political resistance starts from the perceptions and analysis of members of LETS themselves – rather than from social movement theories – and emphasises their creativity in creating a political tool that addresses specific problems in society in ways that they, as political actors, feel appropriate. A micro-political analysis of LETS would be founded on an understanding of the possibility of the existence of multiple challenges to power relations, and an emphasis on the pro-active creativeness and dynamism of political action which makes other power relations visible, and then develops technologies and strategies to overcome them. Analysis would therefore be of the extent that LETS illuminates local power circulations, and is an effective local struggle against this local power, valid on its own terms. This provides more a effective conceptualisation either than Marxian dismissal of Owenite co-operation as 'dwarfish' in the face of hegemonic state power (Marx 1974) or uncritical McKay (1996) or 'naive' (Boyne and Rattansi 1990:39) boosterism of cyclical if interesting 'others' – new social movements that nonetheless fail to produce real collectivities and social actors with the system-changing potential of the proletariat of Marxist praxis (Harvey 1992:54; Geras 1990:86; Callinicos 1989:85). Rather that either a 'laissez-faire, "anything goes" market eclecticism' (Harvey 1992:42), or an a priori dismissal based on the experience of similar historical experiments, a heterotopian analysis follows Foucault in valuing 'autonomous, non-centralised kind(s) of theoretical production, ... whose validity is not dependent on the approval of the established regimes of thought' (Foucault 1980:81).

A second concept from Foucault's work that holds explanatory value for this analysis is that of the 'heterotopia', or the coexistence of an 'impossible space' of a large number of 'fragmentary possible worlds' existing in the same space simultaneously (Harvey 1992:48). Rather than the social movement producing any meta-narrative or recipe for a more perfect organisation of society of use to us all, LETS may be 'impossible' as it simultaneously contains many visions and aspirations of the 'good life' – which are contradictory, mutually exclusive, and unsustainable in the traditional political analyses developed in response to previous local currency and communal expacrementation. Following Foucault, LETS conceptualised as 'impossible' challenges unitary concepts of liberation, of a unified history moving forward towards one 'free' or 'liberated' condition. The concept of heterotopia therefore envisages the development of multiple spaces in which different political relationships can exist side by side, neither privileged, nor any less or more real. Heterotopia values politics as process rather than as end, and located not in political society (the state) but in the lifeworld. Heterotopia means the death of a unitary end-state vision (a single utopia being by definition repressive over other possible visions of the good life), and therefore political actors should not discipline and focus themselves and their actions to achieve any future goal but concentrate on localised resistance to power relations – 'micro-politics'.

The concept of heterotopia is, understandably, itself heterogeneous. LETS conceived of as a heterotopia would be firstly a space in which multiple claims about money and livelihood are raised and which then knock up against each other: in other words, as a hetero(genious u)topia. In this case LETS would be a struggle against specific, local power relations that results in multiple outcomes – contrasting values held by different participants within the network, with no single value-claim being successfully imposed on other network members in what is a heterotopia as multiple space. Secondly, LETS could be a heterotopia in that attention to the power held by participants illuminates the extent that network members are able to deploy this power within the structure of opportunities they find themselves, ie, through interaction with other actors in this heterogeneous utopia. Heterotopia here stresses the extent of creativity of LETS: the extent that this is a new technology that creates new, fecund forms of liberatory technology rather than a passive reaction to dominant and constraining power. It could be a space through which LETS as a new liberatory technology enables alternatives to be created alongside the mainstream (one of many possible lifeworlds) rather than going beyond or replacing it. Here this heterotopia might be a resistant space that operates for a sustainable length of time by these changed rules – heterotopia as temporal space. Heterotopia might then mean the existence of multiple, temporally lasting alternative economic spaces, alongside each other, living by different rules.

However, if boosterism is to be avoided, a third form of heterotopia might be the best theorisation of LETS as micro-political resistance. In this case, if the transformed codes that members create are realisable only fleetingly, then LETS is a temporal, cognitive heterotopia. LETS would be what Bey (1995) called a 'Temporary Autonomous Zone', a momentary effervescence structurally limited in its implementability and suggesting the need for meta-narrative solutions rather than micro-solutions. LETS would be unable to create its own values outside its network of traders who support its aims, unable to impose its values on others, and, as members do not themselves have the resources to establish a 'socialism in one LETS Scheme', unlikely to last. It therefore operates as a tactic of resistance rather than a strategy for power likely to be achievable for any length of time within the mass of society (de Certeau 1984:34–39 quoted by Pile and Keith 1997:15). In this case, heterotopia is an effervescent space: a fleeting liberation, effective only 'below the threshold where the systematic imperatives of power and money become so dominant' (White 1991:67, quoted by Harvey 1992:54). Fourthly, above that threshold, LETS becomes heterotopia as an 'impossible space', a declaration of resistance to the rules of the game set by the powerful operating at the level of information, a Baudrillardian sign, a vision of an alternative, unrealisable yet inspiring 'mobilising utopia' – a utopian space. However, in this case, LETS would reinscribe Marx's pessimistic dismissal of the co-operators of his day, of the 'dwarfish forms to which individual wage-slaves can elaborate it, by their own individual efforts', relegating co-operative experimentation to the mere demonstration of the possibility of a 'republican and beneficent association of free and equal producers' (Marx 1863, in Fernbach (ed) 1974:90).

A third Foucauldian conception would be useful for an analysis of LETS: his local conception of power. For Foucault (1980:98), power circulates within a decentered net or grid in which actors are simultaneously entrapped and resisting. Rather than theorising power as hegemonic, held by some (who have it all) over others (who have none) for Foucault power is found in all relations, and is anonymous and all-pervasive (1980:89); found in multiple, local, decentered forms of subjugation (1980:96), in an all inclusive 'capillary' flow (Gledhill 1994:150). Foucault wishes to understand power and domination so they can be fought, and to analyse power 'where it is in direct and immediate relationship with that which we can provisionally call its object, its target, its field of application ... where it installs itself and produces its real effects' (Foucault 1980:97). Foucault's conception of power can be strengthened by the work of Deleuze and Guattari as they stress resistance over domination. In contrast with the tone of Foucault's work, which tends to envisage actors caught, fly-like, in a spider's web of domination, struggling vainly to escape all powerful systems of control, discipline and surveillance (Best and Kellner 1991:96–97), Deleuze and Guattari emphasise the identification of creative 'lines of flight' – what they call positive reterritorialisations of unconstrained and undominated territory through creative local political action (Best and Kellner 1990:101, Callinicos 1989:84). Innovative political action enables actors to create their futures, going past resistance to pre-existing and constraining power relations (Callinicos 1989:84). In collaboration with the Italian Autonomist Antonio Negri, Guattari calls for 'a thousand machines of art, life and solidarity to sweep away the stupid and sclerotic arrogance of the old organisations!' (quoted in Best and Kellner, 1990:93). LETS will therefore be seen as a creative effervescence, as a technology of liberation, rather than a defensive resistance to a Foucauldian system of overarching domination.

As Gledhill (1994:123–150) cautions, however, the unproblematic valorisation of local struggles and of interesting 'others' is inadequate without grounded research identifying the nature of the resistance and the domination it opposes, and an understanding of the capacity of the actors to, in Marx's evocative term, 'make history'. While LETS may be one of Guattari and Negri's 'thousand machines of art, life and solidarity', grounded analysis of the creativity of LETS as nomadic micro-politics will uncover the capacity it has to make the changes it seeks to make. The task is to observe the extent to which the benefits LETS claims it can deliver are realisable from day-to-day participation on a micro-political basis; and the extent to which the local rules by which LETS works are internally consistent, thereby allowing alternative lifestyles to be lived irrespective of the actions of elites. This would be captured within an identifiable time and space within an observable 'structure of political opportunities' (Tilly 1977), or identifiable structure of allies, resources, enemies, opportunities and resistances, expected and unexpected, that advocates of LETS work their way through in pursuing their objectives.

The contribution of the NSM paradigm to an analysis of alternative currencies

The NSM paradigm is useful in taking an analysis of social movements away from an identification with changing elites and gaining access to the polity, and emphasising that social movements are proactive producers of knowledges and cultural codes. Melucci especially is helpful in indicating that social movements can be about life in the 'here-and-now', although as Cox (1996) points out he also privileges movements that are anti-systemic over those that only seek to develop countercultural codes. An analysis of money-focused social movements would not seek to *a priori* privilege either, but to analyse the effectiveness of each strategy on its own terms. Foucault is also useful in challenging a tendency within the NSM paradigm of an articulation on social movements as knowledge producers rather than as struggles against power relations – the metaphor of battle rather than of language. While Melucci and Touraine see social movements as actors struggling within structural limits to self-create society, their concentration on the actor as knowledge-producer needs to be tempered with Foucauldian analyses of power as restrictive web, or society may then be conceived as completely open to whatever claims the social movement may make (taking analysis back to a pluralist position).

Analysis of money-focused social movements will focus on what Touraine calls 'the principle of identity' – who joins the social movement and the extent that participants feel themselves to be engaged in a collective endeavour. In line with his epistemological concern to identify the 'prime social movement' for the post-industrial age, Touraine then called for the identification of what he called the 'principle of totality'. This is an analysis of whether or not the movement had developed a consciousness of its historicity. However, a break will be made with Touraine here as his search for the prime social movement, with what he calls a 'total analysis', is predicated on acceptance of his project of identifying one type of movement with one type of society, as well as a prime social movement for programmed society. This, for Pickvance (1995:127), is arbitrary. Worse, it is de facto evolutionism, which Touraine says he rejects. Key to any consideration of Touraine's contribution to an understanding of money-focused social movements must be the contentious issue of whether society is in transformation from industrial to programmed society (see Harvey 1992:121–201). Touraine's thesis of the centrality of the Greens to social change depends on acceptance of the thesis of post-industrialisation. Hence if we are not yet in programmed society, either the centrality of the Greens must be doubted, or we again have de facto creation of another monolithic metanarrative (Scott 1990:5). Given these shaky epistemological grounds, this analysis shall limit itself to the far less totalising search for 'the stakes' (what claims the movement makes about why it struggles, over what, and the opposition or support it receives). Consequently, Touraine's triangle will be retained with the substitution of 'stakes' for 'totality'.

Touraine remains the guide, thirdly by identifying the 'principle of opposition' – an analysis of who the social movement conceptualises as the enemy (if any).

However, given Tarrow's objection that the NSM school does not explain why some collective actors explain at some times, not at others, the Political Opportunity Structure within which Melucci's new knowledges and local networks operate will be added to the equation. To what extent actors produce knowledge that they are able to actualise, and whether they have the resources to achieve their goals? Given that neither school adequately explains both 'how' *and* 'why' movements emerge, we need to understand how insights from schools can be blended for a more nuanced analysis, including an understanding of the influence of processes of structuration that explain 'when' movements emerge (Tarrow 1998:83).

PUTTING THE SCHOOLS TOGETHER

Understanding of social movements has suffered from the bifurcation into the American and European schools (Tarrow 1998). In an effort to synthesise the two approaches, Diani (1992) attempts a combined definition of social movements as:

> Networks of informal interaction between a plurality of individuals, groups and/or organisations, engaged in a political and/or cultural conflict, on the basis of a shared collective identity.

Diani identifies points of commonality between the two schools in that they both involve networks of people, organisations and groups, which develop a common specific collective identity for political challenge – which may be political or cultural struggles, at the systemic or non-systemic level.

Tarrow (1989:423) characterised the American school as concentrating on organisational factors, and the European school on the relations between structural changes and social movements on one hand (Touraine), and the individual construction of political frames on the other (Melucci). This, he argued, left a space in which the concrete political process whereby structure and agency dialectically interact, falling 'between two stools'. This deficiency could be remedied by analysis of the Political Opportunity Structure in which the social movement operates. However, Tarrow argued that by drawing more heavily on RMT implications, it fails to differentiate whether the POS is regarded as objective and determining in the last instance; or as subjectively perceived or constructed, bringing analysis back into the field of the NSM paradigm.

Tarrow therefore calls for comparative work using insights from both schools triangulated with each other, perhaps over a number of countries and social movements (Tarrow in Rucht 1991:392–419). He then builds on his work with Klandermans on the POS and calls for a temporal analysis of a social movement's trajectory. This would make use of the European school to explain structural reasons why participants are mobilisable, and therefore why social movements may arise, American conceptions to show how members are aroused to participate, Melucci's work to show how networks and putative organisations then create their identity, and Tarrow's work to see how they begin to involve themselves in struggle through their POS. Melucci addresses this problem with a call for complete intellectual break from dualist conceptions between structure and agent, and for an analysis of how agents construct knowledges within the limits of systems (Melucci 1992).

Cohen and Arato break the impasse by sidestepping the differentiation between systemic and non-systemic, and political or cultural struggle. They hold that struggles go on at both levels simultaneously within a given social movement, and 'within both civil society and the polity for autonomous social action'. The task for the analysis of social movements, they argue, is to unravel this complexly inter-twined struggle 'to ask whether a new twentieth century action repertoire is in the making' (1992:509). This again suggests that, like Touraine, they are heralds of the post-1989 dawning of post-industrial and post-socialist society. Consequently Cohen and Arato advance social movements for the role of advancing their project, inspired by Habermas' concept of 'communicative rationality', of the reconstruction and deep democratisation of civil society. This democratisation of civil society, the space between the system and the individual lifeworld, they call a 'self-limiting radicalism' that 'is a self-understanding that abandons revolutionary dreams in favour of radical reform that is not necessarily and primarily orientated to the state' (1992:493).

Cohen and Arato are helpful in indicating a conceptualisation of alternative currencies systems contested spaces. Analysis of modern social movements around money can be used as a testbed to investigate the limits of micro-political politics as an anti-systemic micro-struggle against specific power relations around money, work and livelihood illuminated by these social movements. Following Tarrow, a range of concepts will be deployed to illuminate different aspects of money-focused social movements, while Foucault's conceptionalisation of power as web will be used to go beyond an articulation on the state through the American school, and to show the limits of such micro-politics and the role of structures in limiting participants' abilities to self-produce their own world. However, before we move on to our analysis, we need to sketch how we operationalised these concep-tions through an examination of method.

CHAPTER 3

Investigating Social Movements

Having identified research questions and a body of theory with which to investigate LETS, the next task is to identify suitable research methods.[1] As a discussion of what I did as a researcher, this chapter will use the first person where appropriate. The first task is to consider methods developed by Touraine and Melucci, who advocated intensive focus group work as the prime arena for an interaction between the social movement and the researcher. There then follows a discussion of how Touraine and Melucci's approaches were adapted and evolved, to take account of instrumental considerations related to field conditions; to the ethos of LETS and by ethical considerations about how I as the researcher wished to relate to the social movement actors studied. This involved the blending of ethnographic and focus group method.

An ethnographic approach would methodologically involve a focus on the knowledges self-produced by members of LETS. These knowledges would be observed through participant observation as frames produced and then deployed by members of LETS, and which would resonate to various extents with other actors. This process of frame production and alignment would be observed in the field by varying degrees of passive-then-active participant observation, field interviews-as-conversations recorded through fieldnotes, semi-structured interviews, and analysis of documents created by the LETS systems under study. This process would be observed in one location for a relatively long but discreet period of time. These ethnographic considerations supplement Touraine and Melucci's focus group approach, enabling both triangulation of methods, and a safety net should field conditions mean that focus groups do not provide a complete picture.

The chapter discusses how methods were adapted as field conditions changed (primarily involving the use of semi-structured interviews), and various methods were triangulated against each other. In conclusion, the chapter shows how the documents, notes and transcripts collected in the field were organised and analysed into this book, and how informant review techniques were used to authenticate findings.

SOCIOLOGICAL INTERVENTION

Touraine devised a specific methodology for his quest to find the pre-eminent social movement for programmed society, which he called 'Sociological Intervention' (Touraine 1981:150–183). The method consists of the construction of a programme of focus group discussions involving social movement militants who have taken part

---

[1] This chapter is aimed at students of social movements interested in methodological issues: the lay reader can safely skip it.

in action to an appreciable degree, but who are not leaders or representatives of particular organisations within the social movement. The latter, Touraine argues, are likely to want to speak 'on behalf of' their particular organisations, and simply reproduce the analysis of the movement without taking it further – in what can be a sometimes painful and rigorous process of discussion. The group should also, as far as is practicable, include militants from the full range of organisations, ideologies and tendencies within the social movement, so that all the tensions and potentialities within the movement are represented within the discussion. At the same time, the group should remain small enough to develop some collective identity. Touraine takes the group through a series of sessions on a guided journey of what he calls the 'self-analysis' of the social movement through a staged interaction between participants, the researcher and critics of the movement.

This journey to self-analysis starts with the group being a *witness group* proclaiming its identity as a social movement; members talk about action they have been involved in and create some shared understanding and identity. Touraine then introduces 'interlocutors', opponents of the social movement whom he gets to argue with the group about its claims. In what develops into a process of reflexive self analysis, the group then becomes a *confrontation group*; in which it answers criticisms, defines what the stakes in the argument are, and who are friends and enemies. The group slowly begins to explore debates between different opponents and different parts of the movement.

The researcher acts as referee ensuring that all sides can speak, that neither side breaks under the pressure of opponent's arguments, and that neither side turns in on itself and refuses to engage in debate. By being confronted by opponents, participants shift from safe ideological protection to self-analysis of the social field in which they operate. This Touraine calls the process of *flexion* – 'the self-criticism of the groups' ideological language' (1981:167). During this process, the group should move from unreflexive transmission of its' ideology to the discussion and analysis of the political choices it faces, reasons for taking the political actions they have, and finally to an analysis of the success and failure of its political action – as a result of interactions with other actors.

The first flexion is the confrontation with the interlocutors, and the second is reflexive discussion of these confrontations as the witness group becomes an *Image group*. During this stage members of the group take on the various positions of the social movement, and the questions the group evades are those also evaded by the movement. In other words, the group moves from being a witness to the values of the social movement, to an image of the contradictions and arguments within the movement. From the second flexion, the group should move to the third flexion, *Conversion*. The group begins a process of exploring its potential in the social situation it finds itself, the possibility of overcoming barriers, or of attaining a higher level of mobilisation. In other words, the group starts to grapple with its Political Opportunity Structure. The final flexion is a *mixed group of self-interpretation*, during which the researcher and the group together discuss the researcher's unfolding analysis, with the researcher effectively part of the group. Touraine looks to conduct his intervention preferably during a period of struggle. About three months of intensive group work is followed by a year during which the researcher and what are by now social movement co-researchers develop and discuss the research findings.

The researcher helps this process by *reminding*: setting before the group the problems it has thrown up so that it must come up with a coherent response to them; by tape recording meetings for playback, providing typed minutes, topics for discussion, statements on flip charts (historical quotations, comments from opponents, charts), or video clips to help people view their own actions from a distance; and examining and analysing earlier statements by viewing them again. The researcher analyses the self-analysis that evolved in the interaction between researcher and social movement actor-analysts, and the finished work is then an analysis of the intervention.

MELUCCI'S METHOD

Melucci (1989:235–249) builds on Touraine's method, which he regards as the basic building block for the construction of a method for studying social movements. However, as he objects to Touraine's attempt to identify the 'principle of totality' – an underlying 'higher' meaning that can only be uncovered through Sociological Intervention (1989:237) – he wishes to understand the interplay between the various simultaneously competing meanings the social movement produces, without attempting to valorise one above the others. He avoids suggestions that the researcher can be in some way 'outside' the group and communicate its 'true' meaning at the end of the intervention – a mission Cohen (1983:216) calls 'barely concealed Sociological Leninism'. Melucci therefore attempts to avoid a 'missionary spirit' that 'increases the risk of confusing research with political agitation' (1989:237–239). He is concerned that the group may intentionally or unintentionally conspire to provide some 'mythical higher meaning' in order to 'please' the researcher.

For Melucci, Touraine confuses the struggles and conflicts that go on in his unnatural focus groups for real struggles in the real world. Consequently he argues that the relationship between the researcher and the actors is not a problem 'external to the research' (1989:239), but that the study of a social movement should be of the analysis that the interaction between the group and the researcher produces. The relationship between the researcher and social movement actors should be made explicit in the form of a contract in which the researchers bring "a research hypothesis and (research) techniques which cannot be verified or utilised without the participation of the actors" and actors who want to reflexively analyse what they are doing 'to help them increase their potential for action' (1989:240). Melucci makes the laboratory explicit by working with pre-existing groups, and by a strong emphasis on video analysis of non-verbal forms of communication (which contextualise the statements actors make to capture the totality of the interactions between the group). The study of the non-verbal communication processes that contribute to the construction of the analysis the group produces, will, in Melucci's view, compensate for the un-naturalness of the focus group setting.

The process the focus group adopts follows the first two stages of Touraine's method, with the same emphasis on reflexivity but without attempting to achieve convergence. Instead of a witness group Melucci calls the first stage a *'who we are'* group focusing on memories of previous events, self representation (in which the group is encouraged to do role plays and games to illustrate the multiple identities within the group), and finally a 'how' phase which focuses on the construction of definitions of the movement. There is then a playback of video material, followed by a *'who you are'* phase using video film of statements by allies, opponents and journalists about the movement, again followed by a playback of the footage. The research product is an analysis of the processes by which the actors constructed their political understanding, captured on video.

ADAPTING THE MODELS TO THE STUDY OF LETS

Before entering the field it seemed that a method modelled fairly loosely on Touraine's seemed appropriate. Not only did it follow logically from the body of theory being employed; it was methodologically rigorous in the confrontation between interlocutors and group participants. A balance was, however, taken between criticisms of Sociological Intervention that claim that the method relies too much on the researcher confronting participants in what could be for them a quite stressful and upsetting experience (Pickvance 1995), and Melucci's (1989:238) view that it is patronising and moralistic to try to protect emerging social movements from rigorous discussion and engagement with complex questions. However, while Melucci's claim that research should not be an attempt to find a preeminent social movement but to make clearer the stakes and conflicts within LETS (1989: 237), his attempts to make use of video to overcome the artificiality of the focus group seemed misplaced. Rather, a clear contract and understanding of the context of the focus group in relation to the wider social movement were held to meet his worries about substituting the focus group for the movement. Consequently the method adopted for an analysis of LETS would borrow from both theorists: using focus groups involving the use of interlocutors in the manner suggested by Touraine, but with the goal of illuminating the stakes in the social movement rather than a misplaced attempt to find a principle of 'totality'.

Adoption of this method was risky (Melucci 1989:236). Sociological Intervention would require considerable commitment from participants over some time. As LETS is a fairly new social movement, participants might not be sufficiently well versed to carry out self analysis, and this task might fall back on the researcher. The group might not turn out to be confident enough of its position to confront interlocutors, and LETS might not be sufficiently well known and understood by potential interlocutors for a useful confrontation to take place. In social movement terms, LETS might be too immature to have identified enemies and to have developed a clear understanding both of the claims it made, and of the stakes in any conflict with enemies. Identifying interlocutors would be time-consuming and this, when combined with the logistics of convening a number of focus groups over some time, and might prove to be difficult in the field.

However, until research was underway it was impossible to know how achievable the method would be. All that could happen was a hopeful embarkation towards an unclear destination with no map! Consequently, and with a full appreciation of the risks, the challenging but risky project of attempting a variant of Sociological Intervention coupled with ethnography was adopted. In the absence of focus groups it was felt that ethnography would provide an abundance of data – although the vital process of self-analysis between social movement actors in a dynamic process of discussion with each other (and preferably with interlocutors) might be lost unless participant observation provided opportunities to observe real confrontations between advocates of LETS and other actors. Interactions between actors observed in the field could then be analysed using RMT and Frame Alignment approaches, although self-analysis by the actors themselves in group work would be more authentic.

Choice of method was further informed by ethical questions in relation to the style of research I personally wanted to adopt politically, as a researcher, and as a human being, and that I would also have to adopt for utilitarian reasons if I was to successfully gain access and rapport with members of LETS. Concerns that the 'personal is political' – that the way things are done are as important as what is done – were strongly reflected in the ethos of LETS, and early contacts to nego-tiate access indicated the need for considerable sensitivity. Participants in LETS often expressed themselves unconvinced of the need and value of academic research. Some systems expressed themselves 'researched out', having been bombarded with surveys.

Research design had to be clear regarding the power relations between social movement actors and the researcher, and here ethics were crucial. LETSGo, a national development organisation, wrote on the 'econ-lets' discussion site 'here, our work is our research. We learn from our work. I have not read a single piece of research into LETS which has told me anything that was useful to me in a devel-opment role – and I've read several' to which Michael Linton, originator of LETS, replied: 'much of the research has probably been useful to others new to the field, or valuable in establishing credibility in certain circles. But with respect to devel-opment, the work is far ahead of the research, and probably will be for the next few years ….(as) the LETSystem design itself is to all intents and purposes complete.'

Research design therefore had to balance the contradictions between 'the researched hav(ing) power and knowledge which the researchers need' and the charge I wished personally and politically to avoid, of 'bumming off the movement' (Stanley and Wise 1993:32–33), through unpaid LETS activists providing infor-mation to a funded researcher in an unequal financial power relation.

Ethnography would also be crucial instrumentally to the development of rapport, since the actors I spoke to strongly indicated that they felt that partici-pation in LETS was crucial to effective research. One said – only half jokingly – that she did not listen seriously to comments from people who had not traded six times 'either way' (i.e. received and provided six services), as she did not feel that they could fully understand LETS without having experienced it. Without first building rapport through ethnographic participation in the day-to-day activities of LETS, it seemed unlikely that I would be able to attract participants for Sociological Intervention. Ethnography would therefore be used to identify potential focus group members, the range of organisations, tendencies and ideologies within LETS, and to design topic guides for discussion. Ethnographic method would also be crucial to get behind the front door into the backstage, hidden world (Goffman 1974). As social movement actors producing frames, activists in LETS could be quite sophisticated in presenting LETS in an exceedingly positive light, and a method relying just on interviews with activists would not fully illuminate the backstage debates and tensions within LETS.

Consequently, the aspirations of the project were towards the ethics of feminist research methods as advocated by Stanley and Wise (1993). A successful research project would for me be one of participation, in which the research questions would be of mutual interest to both research subjects and researcher. In developing a methodology I therefore used a collaborative approach, in which I asked social movement actors what they themselves felt were the important questions, and solicited their comments on my research design. I looked upon the participants in LETS as what Gramsci called 'organic intellectuals', 'the thinking and organising element (of a social movement) distinguished less by their profession, which may be any job characteristic of their class, than by their function in directing the ideas and aspirations of the (social movement) to which they belong'. (Gramsci 1971:3). Touraine calls them 'Movement Intellectuals', in the same vein.

However Stanley and Wise (1993:159), and Melucci (1992:237), alerted me against adopting an uncritically participatory style that conflated differences between the researcher and the 'researched'. I recognised that I was a 'foreigner' separate from the values of the social movement actors with whom I was involved, and with my focus on LETS as a social movement. I tried to be explicit about my research questions and my role as a researcher in all discussions with members of LETS, making clear the right of anyone I interviewed not to 'be researched' at any point (unfortunately some interesting people exercised their right!). I made my own political position clear and saw my research as an interaction between the field and myself (Burgess 1984:37). As we shall see below, I adjusted the emphasis of the research in the light of changing field conditions (Hoggett, Jeffers et al. 1994).

SAMPLING THE POPULATION

Having adopted a method I needed to identify the location for field research. I identified Manchester by knowledge from research obtained for my Masters dissertation, when I gained an understanding of where interesting developments in LETS were occurring. This was updated by the national body LETSLink UK's 1993 survey of the then existing LETS systems, which elicited a response from 50 LETS systems. This enabled me to identify the population and diversities within LETS, and issues, problems and opportunities offered by respondents. The survey was supplemented with exploratory conversations with LETSLink UK, with members of various LETS systems at conferences and events organised by them, and discussion groups dedicated to LETS on the Internet (see bibliography for details).

In further narrowing down the sample to one or more sites for field research, a number of conditions needed to be met. Firstly, the LETS system should be well established, with enough active members with experience of trading to talk authoritatively in group work about the quality of the experience of participation in LETS, rather than of what could be. Secondly, the system should be urban in order to test LETS as a policy for urban regeneration. Thirdly, in order to test the American approach to social movements, the LETS system should be one that was in some way interacting with its Political Opportunity Structure by talking with other actors about developing wider applications of LETS (for instance, attempting actively to involve businesses, or talking to local authorities). Finally, in order to take a constructivist approach, the system should be engaged in debate about the nature of LETS. The simplest way to do this was to see which systems set the value of their currency to the pound and which allowed debate, as it would be likely that systems which left the value of the currency to members would have a greater diversity of members than those that tied it to sterling, or set an hourly rate. Guided by Melucci, I wanted to observe internal conflict over the values of the social movement.

From these considerations a typology of LETS systems was developed which helped focus down to the eleven LETS systems that formed possible locations for research: Stroud, West Wiltshire, Bristol Bishopston, Lancaster, Brixton, Drumchapel (Glasgow), Manchester, LETSGo and Hattersley (Manchester), Calderdale (West Yorkshire), and Totnes (Devon). The sampling process indicated that a focus on the conurbation of Greater Manchester would enable research into three systems. Manchester LETS, LETSGo, and Hattersley LETS could all be studied within an identifiable Political Opportunity Structure – the city of Manchester:

1   *Manchester LETS*. A 'traditional' system with approximately 500 members with a wide variety of perspectives on LETS, a wide range of available services and some business members. Members valued the currency in different ways. Manchester LETS had received a local authority grant of £10,000 and has activists of national prominence engaged full time in development activity. At the time, the system was the world's second largest (the largest being the Blue Mountain System, Sydney, Australia).
2   *LETSGo*. A Manchester-based demonstration project led by LETS originator Michael Linton which aimed to kick off large scale use of LETS in a particular city in a 'big-bang'. If significant levels of participation are achieved, including business, participation, the wider possibilities of LETS will be demonstrated more quickly than can be achieved through the slower, organic, grassroots approach favoured by most advocates of LETS in the UK. Given the depth of economic crisis, Linton argued, the grassroots approach was too slow.
3   *Hattersley LETS*. A small LETS system on a local authority outer estate in Greater Manchester.

NEGOTIATING ACCESS

I met activists from Manchester when I was exploring LETS through work in 1993, and made contact again at a conference during the first year of the research. They indicated that research in Manchester would be possible, and I followed with a letter to the Manchester LETS Core Group suggesting that I move up to Manchester to study. The Core Group agreed that they would be happy with this so long as I joined the system to trade, and that they saw a copy of what I wrote. Peter Gay, the Core Group facilitator, agreed to become my guardian and mentor on behalf of the Core Group and rented me a bedroom for the duration of the research. I moved to Manchester in January 1995, and stayed until August for the first period of research. Short follow up visits to Manchester were made in 1996, 2001 and 2005.

Access to Manchester LETS was easily achieved. This was due to the Core Groups' libertarian ethos, which affected the research process in a way that was not clear at first. The Core Group did not see itself in any way as the 'management committee' or 'government' of LETS, but as a group of people who get together to see that the system is administered effectively for the members. In their view, as long as I joined Manchester LETS it was up to me to do with it what I wanted, and up to members individually to decide if they wanted to take part in my research. Consequently I thought I had been given access, while the Core Group did not feel that access was for them to give or withhold. As the research unfolded I became increasingly aware that I had to renegotiate access with every individual participant, as if there was no organisational gatekeeper.

I did not attempt to formally negotiate access to LETSGo and Hattersley LETS before I moved to Manchester. I was already on good personal terms with Angus Soutar, the leading British LETSGo activist, and a quick phone call reestablished contact. However the main body of the LETSGo project had taken place before I went to Manchester so there were few opportunities for ethnographic observation, and LETSGo were unwilling to take part in focus groups. Consequently, research on LETSGo consisted of a retrospective evaluation relying on triangulation (see Burgess 1984:144–146) between one-to-one interviews with former participants, documents produced by LETSGo, and comments from other actors whom LETSGo had met.

Access to LETSGo was problematic as a result of the exceptionally vituperative nature of the debate they inspired within the community of advocates of LETS in the UK. LETSGo's approach, radically different from that operated by just about everyone else in the UK community, effectively split activists into supporters and diehard opponents of the LETSGo approach (the latter led by LETSLink UK, the West Country-based NGO that saw itself as the peak body for LETS). Consequently, the remaining activists on the LETSGo project were understandably suspicious of outsiders, who they felt would contribute to the attacks on them, and it was only my personal friendship with Angus, combined with continued protestations of independence and openness that gained me the level of access that I did achieve. I took the approach that, while I did not support the aims of the LETSGo project, I did support their right to do what they saw fit. I made it explicit that I believed that alternative approaches to LETS development were healthy, enabling LETS advocates to see through practice what works and what doesn't. I attempted to facilitate dialogue between the two sides. However, further into the research process the relationship deteriorated. Some supporters of LETSGo felt that as a result of participation in a research project associated with LETSLink UK, I had become too identified with their detractors, and I was denied access to a conference on the LETSGo approach to urban regeneration which would have yielded valuable data.

Differences in approach between LETSGo and just about everyone else provided the first clues in a social movement analysis that contrasts approaches aimed at political society, with those of filling out civil society from below might be appropriate. I began to develop my understanding of these differences in more detail as the research process unfolded. However, the difference in power relations between the two groups – LETSGo feeling isolated, attacked and marginalised – was reflected in problems of access and during the writing up of the book it became clear that information on LETSGo was not as complete as it might be. Considerable (and sometimes personal) criticisms of LETSGo were being made. Out of human consideration and for completeness I needed to give Michael Linton the chance to meet some of these criticisms. LETSGo's UK activists were so close to what they had done, and so hurt by attacks, that the plain logic of why they had adopted the strategy they had, and why they used the language they had became difficult to fathom given high emotional tensions. Distance was required.

I as yet did not fully understand why, from the actor's perspective, LETSGo adopted such a controversial strategy. In particular I wanted to get a feel for the culture, politics and economy of the POS in which LETS had been conceived, and strategies for development designed – strategies imported unreflexively and dogmatically into an alien POS. Consequently a short research visit to Vancouver Island, Canada, was organised in May 1996 to interview Michael Linton and others involved in the early development of LETS. This visit gave Linton the chance to explain in considerable detail the origins and concept of LETSGo, and engage in critical reflection about his experience one year on. He was also able to give useful informant review of the first draft of the book. After 1997 I was also able to observe how LETSGo's approach evolved through participation in work-shops in Brighton and London, while the reaction of a group of Hungarian LETS enthusiasts to a workshop run by a LETSGo supporter in 2000 showed that they retained their commitment to their approach, critique notwithstanding. A final interview was undertaken with a key LETSGo informant in Manchester in 2001 which suggested that no concrete progress had been made towards realising the 'big bang' approach. By 2005 this continued to be the case.

Access to Hattersley LETS was not attempted until I had been in Manchester for one month. As I had no previous acquaintance with any of the activists a cold approach had to be undertaken. I carried out an interview with two activists and was joined during the afternoon by local economic development workers who were able to offer their views on the system as a contribution to solving urban problems. They informed me that Hattersley LETS had never got off the ground and that again there were few opportunities for ethnographic exploration. A focus group about the reasons for the failure of the system was held, which also discussed the possibility of relaunching the system. Comments from the manager of the local community centre were obtained through later correspondence. Hattersley was later included in a wider study of the experiences of developing LETS in inner city environments funded by the New Economics Foundation (North, Barnes and Walker 1996) which enabled experiences on that estate to be put in a wider context.

A CLUMSY ALIEN GETTING STARTED: ETHNOGRAPHY AMONG MEMBERS OF MANCHESTER LETS

On arrival in Manchester, I started by using ethnographic method. I first concentrated on developing a taxonomic understanding of who the actors were and the way they organised and categorised each other (Burgess 1984:212, Spradley

1979:132–154). This was carried out during early participant observation in Manchester LETS and through long conversations with my gatekeeper and flatmate. Through such close and regular conversation I was able to gather together such local knowledges fairly quickly. I had to start to make decisions about what to regard as data. For the first couple of months I kept unprescriptive fieldnotes of conversations, trades, Core Group meetings and social and trading events I attended, and methodological fieldnotes in which I reflected on the research process and discussed emerging findings. Thus I developed method-ologies for interviews and focus groups reflecting local conditions as they evolved (Burgess 1984:167–174). I put my social movement focus on one side until I was sure that that approach was the most appropriate, and attempted to be adaptable and open to new information from the practitioners in designing my programme. I was guided by Chambers' description of fieldwork:

> ... the fieldworker cannot anticipate the developments in the field which will inevitably guide the course of his investigations. Hypotheses formed without regard to these considerations may turn out to be trivial if not banal ... What most fieldworkers do is to go into the field with a grounding in the theory of their discipline, especially of the sub area of their interest, and with as much knowledge of the region as can be derived from secondary material. The field then takes over, and the outcome depends on the interaction between the fieldworker and the field.
>
> (Chambers 1990)

I collected documents and newsletters produced by Manchester LETS for content analysis, trading records to allow for a quantitative evaluation of the levels of participation in the system, strategies for the regeneration of Manchester produced by other agencies for identification of possible grounds for alliance or conflict with LETS, statistics on socio-economic conditions in Manchester and relevant newspaper articles, and leaflets from other green social movement organisations. I attended meetings organised by Greens identified from the noticeboard of Manchester's radical bookshop (the first point of call for any student of social movements!).

I joined Manchester LETS and started trading, using the opportunity to have conversations with LETS members, to observe the process of trading, and the opportunities for social interaction that trading provided. I went to the two "Social and Trading Events" (STEs) organised during my stay, met members in social settings such as parties organised through LETS, at music events and on political protests unconnected with LETS. I was explicit that I was researching and rarely felt that people were anything other than happy to talk endlessly about LETS. Most importantly from an ethnographic perspective, I did get a feeling of the hopes and enthusiasms of new members that I did not get from the concentration on activists suggested by Touraine.

Crucially, and as I had hoped, trading was an important vehicle for me to gain acceptance and credibility as well as a method of accessing the 'backroom'. Interviews with LETS members with whom I had traded seemed to provide richer, and more honest, data than those with members of LETS who had not met me previously. Trading helped me move 'from clumsy alien to friendly stranger' (Fried

1968 quoted by Burgess 1984:11). As my own experiences grew, I felt the same annoyance as my new friends when I called a member to trade and got no reply or was not phoned back, when the person could not do what I wanted, or when I did a trade and saw no-one all day. I also got the joy and acknowledgement of training someone to use the basics of word-processing, helping them with their MA on ecological fiction, sorting out an old couple's garden, renting a boat and getting an academic article translated from German. The experience of trading in a large and established system complemented my experiences of setting up a new system in Bradford. I could see my some of my early hopes, and fears, realised.

I attended meetings of the Core Group and took detailed notes of discussions, beginning to identify issues and stakes, actual or hidden conflict, and watching the way members interacted with each other. I accompanied activists to 'start up talks' to groups interested in the possibility of setting up their own LETS systems and attended meetings of Manchester's Local Agenda 21 process, which gave an opportunity to study interaction with the Political Opportunity Structure in a natural setting. However, the density of links with other actors was limited and as the research process continued it seemed that increasingly fewer opportunities would present themselves to study how LETS interacted with its environment. Opportunities for participant observation were further limited by the individual and hidden nature of most trades, the lack of community-organised trades where members got together collectively, and Manchester LETS' unfortunate (for me) decision not to centrally organise Social and Trading Events. No STEs were organised during the second half of the research process, which meant that participant observation opportunities became less regular. Consequently the method needed to evolve away from an early emphasis on participant observation to the next stage – Melucci's and Touraine's focus group approach.

However, this early theoretical openness directed me towards literature I had not previously examined. In particular LETS members suggested I look at psychoanalysis. This I did, leading me to consult Reich and Fromm. They also mentioned conflict resolution, community building, alternative therapies and the politics of 'New Age' lifestyle and 'positive thinking'. One key member was a Humanist. I had to grapple with (to me) alien concepts of 'responsibility', 'acting from abundance', 'being in community' and 'acting with love'. However, during this early period of ethnography, the nature of the stakes became clearer and I understood that a social movement analysis was generally on the right lines. As I began to fill out conceptions of what the stakes were, I began to design topic guides for focus group work from this developing understanding.

INTO FOCUS GROUP WORK

Ethnography the informed development of topic guides for a series of four focus groups. Inspired by Melucci, I decided to hold focus group discussions firstly on 'who we are'. This would be followed by three discussions suggested by an ethnographic understanding of what the stakes were likely to be. The second focus group would be on 'the politics of LETS' (discussing what the political stakes were and whether or not members had identified any opponents – Touraine's 'principle of opposition'), the second on 'trading on LETS' (to discuss the extent that LETS empowered participants), and finally 'community building and LETS' (to discuss the development of collective identity). The last two focus groups were inspired by Melucci and designed to discuss the effectiveness of LETS in the day-to-day life-world. I hoped these four focus groups would then develop into a series of confrontations with these interlocutors.

LETS' 'statement of accounts' (in LETS, a statement of everyone's trading balance is regularly produced, so it was a simple matter to use this to identify active LETS participants). I wrote to 30 of the 'highest traders' (who were not also Core Group members). This I hoped, would provide 10 participants who reflected the conflicts and differences in LETS, identified during ethnography. In particular I wrote to three 'bob-a-jobbers' – members who valued the Bobbin as one job rather than as one pound and who did not necessarily have high turnovers, but who are active LETS traders. Of these 30, 14 agreed to attend and three of the planned four focus groups were run, taped and transcribed. Eight participants attended the first focus group, four members the second, and the third with was held with three. The fourth and final focus group proved impossible to convene at a suitable time. A decision was made that enough data was being obtained from participant observation on LETS as a 'community', that I did not press for a meeting.

As expected, Touraine's method did prove exceptionally difficult to organise logistically. Participants were willing and able to come to one session but had other commitments that kept them from coming to the series. As the discussions progressed, I judged from the level of conversation that participants were not sufficiently confident to be able to engage in serious conversations with interlocutors. There was also a strong current that what was important was to develop LETS irrespective of what other people thought, and a reluctance to engage in what were regarded as irrelevant conversations with opponents. Consequently the group did not reach the stage where interlocutors could have been introduced. In this it reflected the level of development of Manchester LETS (recall that for Touraine the questions the focus group avoids are the questions the social movement avoids).

Despite their small size the focus groups also yielded an abundance of data not obtained through participant observation. Participants were enthusiastic, and the group engaged in considerable periods of self-analysis in which it became what Touraine (1982:168) called an image group, reflecting and engaging with the debates, uncertainties and conflicts within Manchester LETS. Consequently no serious efforts to boost the membership were made which would have disrupted its developing collective identity. However, the size of the group did become a problem in that beyond the first two meetings it ceased to be an image group, but became instead a *'resistant group'* which reflected people excluded from the dominant ethos of keeping the politics out of the administration of Manchester LETS and the administration lean. Many members did not want to attend meetings to discuss the politics of LETS, but wanted to get on with trading. Consequently they were uninterested in my offer of a space for discussion, and an important constituent of Manchester LETS was not reflected – the group that do not want to 'talk politics'. Those who attended were more politically motivated, and emphasised the need for a social element in LETS, rather than a perception of LETS as a purely trading network – nothing more. They were people like myself, with similar interests in politics, people who had joined LETS for the same reasons as me, people I made friends with during the research, and people who held a similarly resistant view of LETS. They did not have a voice until I provided a suitable forum for oppositional voices to organise.

This outcome resulted from the decision not to invite Manchester LETS main activists to the focus group. While within the group they might well have simply reproduced the frames produced by the social movement and dominated less confident fellow members, they would at least have been confident enough to engage with interlocutors. However, ethnography had provided opportunities for observation of real engagements between LETS and its opportunity structure. In these cases, self-analysis was obtained through interviews-as-conversations after confrontations, and in formal sessions later into the research process.

Once this became apparent I recognised the extent to which I as a researcher with definite (and expressed) political views had become a player in the drama who attracted allies. To an extent, my research had become one of the stakes and rallying points in discussions about LETS. I began to see my focus groups as a space that was being colonised by resistant voices in LETS, rather than being an external appendage produced only for the purpose of research. As Melucci predicted (1992:236), but Touraine does not theorise, the focus groups became part of the action repertoire of Manchester LETS, and my research was appropriated into the discussions about the future of LETS. I became not researcher but player – or action researcher.

Naturally I was delighted to have hit this rich seam of submerged resistance to the prevailing ethos that I heard articulated through the core group. However, at the same time I was both concerned and disappointed that as I was getting only one side of the conflict, the focus groups were not reproducing the totality of the internal conflict about the future, ethics and values of LETS. Consequently, I did not feel that I was pulling off a piece of successful and hygienic research, faithfully following in the footsteps of Touraine and Melucci – and it seemed more like personal failure than a predictable event and data in itself. However, I was simultaneously clear that while the focus groups verbalised the submerged, other voices also needed to be heard – those with less of a political approach to LETS. After about five months in the field, I carried out more formal semi-structured interviews, and in my dealings with LETS activists, I moved from a passive to a more active research style. As members of LETS adjusted to my change in style this caused some problems – and yielded results.

THE FIELD TAKES OVER: REFLEXIVE ADJUSTMENTS TO METHOD

Aware of the partiality of the focus group, I decided to collect more voices from the next cohort sample of active traders, to supplement the innumerable ethnographic interviews I had undertaken, and would continue to undertake, during trading and participant observation. I decided to contact traders who had traded between 300 and 400 Bobbins, business traders, and low traders. Again my concern was to contact people who had been active in LETS for some time and who would be able to comment on their experiences rather than their as yet unfulfilled hopes. My worry was that a random or a geographical sample would throw up too many new or inactive members, unable to provide the level of information I required in the short timeframe and given limited resources. Sampling by trading records provided a self-selected but still random group of people who had chosen to trade. I carried out ten interviews with medium traders without too many problems, and eight who had joined Manchester LETS in the previous 12 months but not traded. Finally, I identified the five members trading using business addresses. Of these, two had ceased trading, and three were interviewed (one over the telephone). These interviews supplemented those with individuals who were trading small-scale business services, and whose problems and successes are little different to those of individual members. The relative paucity of potential interviewees empirically reflects the lamentable record of LETS in attracting and keeping business members that is in strong contrast to the claims made by those who see LETS as making a major contribution to economic development.

THE RESEARCHER-AS-ACTOR AND THE ACTOR-AS-RESEARCHER: TOWARDS ACTION RESEARCH

From the beginning of the research process, I attended the bi-monthly meetings of the Manchester LETS Development Agency (LEDA) – a Social Movement Organisation (SMO) aiming to work with local authorities and others, developing wider uses of LETS, and helping other groups develop LETS. At early meetings I simply observed, but as I became more familiar I began to offer (hopefully) constructive thought and comment about the debates that LEDA members themselves raised. As the research continued I became more proactive as I got more involved with LEDA's activities. In particular I helped LEDA develop a strategic plan and define its objectives, and initiated ideas for developing processes for accountability and communication between LEDA and Manchester LETS. I combined my focus group on Hattersley with an input from LEDA to help members of Hattersley LETS to restart the system, and I took part in the Local Agenda 21 process as a researcher and representative of Manchester LETS. In return, LEDA at many times functioned as a natural focus group on development issues that very nicely contrasted with the (increasingly) dissident views coming from my focus groups.

In partnership with Peter Gay, my flatmate, I helped to organised a 'Members Forum' replicating one we had observed being run by Lancaster LETS. Manchester LETS members were invited to come and discuss LETS' successes, failures and their views of its future, over a shared meal provided for local currency – Bobbins. Within the Core Group and LEDA there was some discussion over what the role of this forum should be, which reflected differing conceptions of what LETS was. I was drawn into these discussions (which at times were fairly robust), and again felt that I was being identified with one side of the dispute. However, the forum attracted 35 LETS members, which again provided the opportunity to take more views, assuaging my doubts about the partiality of discussions I had had in the focus groups. Once ethnographic interviews, focus group participants, formal interviews and forum participants were added together, I had a rich sample.

By this time (June 1995) I had also become part of the LETS community (what ethnographers call 'enculturated'). I was drawn into disputes between members of the Core Group and LEDA about accountability and decision-making in Manchester LETS, interesting (and illuminating) social dramas. The dramas reflected differences in members' perceptions about what the stakes are in Manchester LETS, but the fact that dramas happened in my presence reflected my growing involvement, the extent that I was able to access the 'backstage', and that I had become a player. A LEDA member said 'Sometimes I think you say things as a researcher and sometimes I think you are saying things as a LETS member'. Indeed some people felt I encouraged these dramas as a way of illuminating LETS ('What you've done is set up a series of experiments on LETS to see what happens'). I don't believe that I did do this, as I was by now able to observe a natural social movement of which I was now part, and therefore did not mind these dramas. However, their existence did alert me to the need to gain some distance and time for reflection.

By the end of the fieldwork period the field had well and truly taken over and I was, at the time, unclear as to the extent and richness of the diversity of methods I had undertaken. I had overemphasised Sociological Intervention, and was disappointed by the small number of people able and willing to take part. However, that had been expected, and (although I did not see that quite so clearly at the time), I had undertaken a rich variety of methods over the eight months which I could triangulate. Consequently I completed the first stage of the research and left Manchester in August 1995.

'THE CRUNCH': ANALYSIS

Whilst ethnographic method emphasises the constant development of an evolving analysis in the field (Hammersley and Atkinson 1983:175), once I had left the field I came to what Fielding (1993:154) calls 'the crunch' – the process of analysing the data. Inspired primarily by Atkinson's 'The Ethnographic Imagination' (Atkinson 1990) I began to construct my personal narrative of LETS.

Using social movement theory as the tool kit to pull apart LETS, I combined data gained from ethnographic observation, and focus group work with theoretical constructs from social movement theory. I first identified themes around which I might organise the data, and who the competing actors were (those articulating of political society and those articulating of civil society). These themes emerged firstly from how members of LETS categorised themselves; secondly from a description of the stakes as raised by members; and thirdly from ethnographic observation of local actors' capacity to implement their political action. I cross-referred the insights gained from the different methods and data sources, using what Denzin (quoted in Burgess 1984:144) called a process of 'methodological triangulation', or Burgess 'multiple strategies', to produce what Atkinson called a 'plausible' and Burgess a 'valid' and 'reliable' account, suitably rich in original sources. Participant observation notes, transcripts, newspaper and magazine articles, and documents produced by the three systems were woven into what Ditton (1977, quoted by Burgess 1984:182) calls a 'theorised ethnography'.

Tapes of interviews and focus groups were transcribed and coded using the concepts derived from social movement theory, and related literature read before fieldwork ('theory-generated categories'), categories I had observed in the field ('observer-identified categories') and actors' own concepts ('folk categories') (Hammersley and Atkinson 1990:178). Once coded, information was sorted using mind-map techniques to brainstorm and then organise (and re-organise) chapters in large mind-maps (which eventually covered a whole wall of my home!). Producing the book as a giant mind map produced a visually striking representation of research themes, quickly organised data, and enabled it to be quickly and visually rearranged in a way impossible with data held in purely electronic form. Mind mapping also allows visual connections between datasets to be made in a manner impossible with either linear representations or electronic data storage methods – enabling the researcher to be nomadic in method, working across themes while quickly enabling the structure of the book to emerge from the data. By this process, chapter outlines were constructed from the mind maps.

INFORMANT REVIEW

Touraine's method puts strong emphasis on the researcher and the group together developing a shared analysis (Touraine's *Mixed Group of Analysis*). However, logistics (myself being based 200 miles from the field) would preclude such a collaborative approach. Consequently I aimed to ensure the validity of the account by using social movement theory to illuminate the fit between data gathered in the field and written up, and theory in providing a robust and plausible analysis of LETS as a social movement. Field data 'should serve as evidence that the claims made … are valid' (Hammersley and Atkinson 1983:185). The project therefore goes further than pure ethnography (illuminating another culture, as a baseline for the production of 'grounded theory', or for content analysis) on one side, or simply a report of a Sociological Intervention on the other. To adequately illuminate the capacity of LETS to operate as a social movement in a concrete local setting, it should pass both ethnographic tests of validity (Fielding 1993:166–167, Atkinson:1990), as well as putting the data through the social movement 'gymnasium' (Melucci 1992:239). I decided to adopt the method of 'Informant Review' of my own findings (ie, by the LETS members to whom I had spoken) as a further validation of the book beyond the utility of social movement theory in illuminating LETS, rather than engaging in further lengthy group work.

I therefore sent a copy of each chapter as written to the Manchester LETS Core Group (who advertised in the LETS Newsletter that the information was available to any LETS member who wished to read it), to LETSGo, and to Michael Linton. In addition I carried out a final series of structured interviews and a final focus group with informants to get their comments on the draft and reflections on the research process.

In view of the healthily contested nature of the debate on LETS, it was not expected that all LETS members would agree with every last conclusion of the analysis of LETS as social movement – which is in the last instance my personal analysis as the researcher – and they didn't. They would have to be in agreement that the analysis was not illegitimate, inadequate or fatally flawed. They may have motives for not agreeing with the researcher's analysis which would need to be made explicit. They may be uninterested in reviewing sections of the report which do not relate directly to them. If my analysis as researcher is not the only possible analysis of LETS, similarly no individual LETS member's analysis is privileged (Hammersley and Atkinson 1982:195). But hopefully competing analyses are internally consistent, backed by data, and plausible, whilst also forming another dataset for triangulation on the analysis (from a later period in the fieldwork). The comments gathered tested the 'correspondence between the Sociologist's and the members view of the member's social world by exploring the extent to which members recognise, give assent to, the judgement of the Sociologist' (Hammersley and Atkinson 1982:195). By and large, they did.

Leaving Manchester in 1996, I also joined and traded in Bishopston LETS in Bristol, and Brighton LETS. In 1997 I joined the Management Committee of LETSLink UK, and remained a member until 2000. In 1997 I carried out a short research project for the New Economics Foundation, which looked at LETS in Caia Parc Wrexham, Drumchapel Glagow, Adamsdown Cardiff, Brandshome Hull, and Hattersley: all areas suffering from social exclusion (Barnes, North and Walker 1997). I was able to examine LETS in Hungary, New Zealand, Argentina and the United States. Finally, in 2001 I revisited Manchester LETS and re-interviewed as many of the respondents from the 1996 study, and carried out a final series of interviews in 2005. By 2005 it was felt that the story of Manchester LETS was ready to be told. The hopes and dreams uncovered in the first phase of fieldwork had been worked through, and analysis undertaken in 2001 and then 2005 enabled a more complete analysis to offered. But before we engage in that analysis, the political opportunity structure in which LETS in Manchester developed needs to be set out.

CHAPTER 4

'Dirty Old Town':
Urban Change in Manchester

... in Manchester, English manufacture finds at once its starting point and its centre ... The effects of modern manufacture upon the working-class must necessarily develop here most freely and perfectly, and the manufacturing proletariat present itself in its fullest classical perfection. The degradation to which the application of steam power, machinery and the division of labour reduce the working-man, and the attempts of the proletariat to rise above this debasement must likewise be carried to the highest point and with the fullest consciousness.

(Engels 1844).

Reporter: *'Frederick Engels ... he sort of changed the world ... Karl Marx's mate ... he used to be big in Russia'* ... like he dwarfs Simply Red, Take That, Ryan Giggs and Morrissey in the Manchester fame stakes. Not that you'd know it ... Council Representative: *'Yes, Frederick Engels made a major contribution etc ... There will be some sort of commemoration ....'*, but will they be getting the banners flying from the town hall? *'The banners are for mass participation events, for instance the Milk Race,'* he says. *'I wouldn't say this was in the same league.'* The Milk Race verses fifty-odd Engels inspired workers revolutions?

(Manchester Evening News on the centenary of Engel's death, February 1995)

Our first task is to introduce the Political Opportunity Structure (POS) within which LETS in Manchester emerged and grew (Tarrow 1998:71–90). It will be recalled, following Tilly (1998) that the POS is 'the process by which a ... political system shapes, checks, and absorbs the challenges that come to it' (Tilly 1984:312 quoted by Foweraker 1995:71). It is an environment within which an emerging social movement finds allies sympathetic to it, powerful actors who might facilitate it, or actors who have resources that the social movement could access. Are others making arguments that the social movement can align its frames with? Does the environment mean that people joining the social movement will gain advantages from so doing, or will the environment penalise them in ways that outweigh the advantages? Do more powerful actors check the social movement's advances, or does the environment allow the social movement to make the most of its opportunities and minimise the actions of opponents? In other words, we focus here not on the actions the social movement itself makes, but the more structural factors that exist before it and independent of it, external to it. Through acting in certain ways, taking advantage where possible of opportunities and avoiding barriers, the social movement can affect its POS, but it does not create it (Tarrow 1998:18). The interaction between a POS can, of course, change over

51

time as the situation becomes more fluid or open, or opportunities are closed down and offers of support withdrawn, or new political cleavages change the nature of the POS. As the argument developed in this book progresses we will see how the POS also changes.

Tilly was thinking of a social movement operating at a national scale, but the concept can be deployed more locally: as we have argued before, processes that operate at higher scales are often experienced more locally. If you want to understand globalisation, then observing the effect of changing primary goods prices on peasant economies can be as illuminating as any other method, as globalisation really hits home when peasant farmers are observed receiving less money than they need to live from coffee production and decide to switch to cocoa (Gledhill 1994:123–150). A more local conceptualisation of the Political Opportunity Structure also has the advantage of being more precise. As Della Porta and Diani (1998:223–224) point out, when looking at national or international mobilisations the number of variables that would need to be drawn into any analysis of who a movement's allies and enemies are and how they check or advance it would be so large that analysis would be impossible. Secondly, we cannot assume that an actor's intended impact on a social movement has the desired effect as social movement actors may perceive an action in a completely different way to that desired. For an example, an actor may perceive themselves to be sympathetic to a movement and act in ways that they feel will advance the movement, while the social movement actors are suspicious of that actors intentions and avoid engagement, or react in ways that are unexpected. Consequently, a more fruitful approach would be to focus more tightly on cognitive liberation, the identities of actors and the arguments they develop, without attempting to engage in analysis of structures since, structural constraints beyond those in physical form – say the Berlin Wall – are cognitively experienced (Gamson and Meyer 1996). A local analysis will enable, through close attention to what happened and discussion with actors to find out how they experienced what happened, will enable some of these variables to be teased out in a more convincing manner. Thinking of a POS as 'framed' rather than completely structural, objective and 'out there' need not reduce its conceptual usefulness: analysis can focus on what the framings are and how social movements align and transform their frames in competition to the other frames, or scripts, produced by other actors, before proceeding to examine what happened as the result of the deployment of those scripts.

The object of this book it to study LETS in an urban context. What therefore follows is an analysis of the city of Manchester and of the frames or scripts of that city. How did other actors frame the city's problems, what the solutions could be, and what the 'good city' could be? What was their conceptualisation of what Urban Social Movement theorist Manuel Castells called the 'urban meaning' developed as the city is "made, transformed and experienced by people" (Castells 1986)? Three frames for three Manchesters are produced by other actors which compete to frame the Political Opportunity Structure within which the three LETS systems must operate: the 'Labour Manchester' of the urban left, the 'Entrepreneurial Manchester' of local boosters, and reflexive, culturally heterogeneous 'Madchester'. We will examine these in turn.

LABOUR MANCHESTER

'Labour Manchester' is the industrial Manchester that was the cradle of the Industrial Revolution, the city of which Engels wrote one of the first great political analyses of capitalist cities, decrying the hypocrisy of a city producing great wealth and great poverty, side by side (Engels 1844), and the city whose 'Manchester Men' developed the ideology of free trade and economic liberalism that we now call 'globalisation'. It is the city of protest against the horrific conditions of industrialisation, the home of the first trade unions massacred at St Peter's Fields in what is now central Manchester (but try in vein to find any memorial). It was the home of the Rochdale Pioneers who established the worker owned and run co-operative store from which the modern co-operative movement grew (a tradition within which Manchester LETS still stands). It was the city in which Ewan McColl 'kissed my girl by the gas works wall' and 'dreamed a dream by the old canal'.

In the early 1990s when Manchester LETS emerged, Manchester was still a 'dirty old town'. Labour Manchester had suffered over the 1970s and 1980s losing 50,000 full time jobs between 1971 and 1981 (Tye and Williams 1994:31). Between 1971 and 1997, England as a whole saw total employment growing by 5%, while Manchester employment declined by 38%, hitting male, full time employment particularly hard with a decline of 43% (Giordano and Twomey 2002:55). Manchester City Council's third poverty report (1988) found that 30,000 Mancunians lived in homes without essential heating, 20,000 homes were damp, and half a million residents couldn't afford a week away. Unemployment rates in the city varied from 34% to 35% in north and east Manchester, to the relatively more prosperous middle belt (Didsbury 9%, Chorlton 16%) (Source: Manchester City Council 1994) with an average male unemployment rate in 1993 of 18%. In 1993, 46.1% of unemployed men and 32.2% of unemployed women had not worked for 12 months. Even after economic recovery, things did not look so good. Employment was more readily available, but 94% percent of all job centre vacancies and 89% of all jobs paid less than the benefit rates for a couple with two children in 2002. For middle-aged working class men, the new jobs generated did not replace those lost and economic dislocation is still a major problem. Even female, part time employment has not grown as the rate it has elsewhere. Only Liverpool has done worse in terms of generating jobs to replace those lost in manufacturing (Peck and Ward 2002:16).

Labour Manchester had been one of the Municipal Socialist authorities of the early 1980s that attempted to improve the city's economic problems in the face of what they saw as a hostile Conservative government that did not understand urban problems and saw the heartlands of Northern cities as enemy territory. Under the slogan 'defending jobs, improving services' Manchester council, like its allies in Sheffield and London (Albery 1979; Boddy and Fudge 1984) attempted to construct an alternative urbanism to the market-led approaches of the Conservatives which argued that cities like Manchester should adapt to the changing global division of labour, accept that the manufacturing jobs lost since the 1970s would not return, and reinvent itself as an 'entrepreneurial city' competing with others to win inward investment to provide new jobs in the service sector. It should move from a city managing services for citizens to one acting like a business, ensuring its profitability in a global marketplace where no city can sit back and assume its future is assured (Harvey 2001). Rejecting this view, Manchester City council argued that central government support for cities should reflect the problems they have to deal with, and they awaited the election of a Labour Government in 1987 that would surely look upon them more favourably. They therefore stressed equality, community development, and work with ethnic minority and women's groups, with, from 1984, Council Leader Graham Stringer emerging from a 'rainbow coalition' to run a leftist council (Quilley 2000; 2002).

Manchester's municipal socialist vision was not as well developed as those in Sheffield or London who, through what they called 'restructuring for labour' developed a range of radical economic development approaches that attempted to intervene against structural forces, in particular against job losses in manufacturing, to promote employment that specifically benefited local communities. The municipal left in the UK and, to some extent in the US (Clavel 1986; Clavel and Kraushaar 1998) sought to promote investment in viable enterprises facing immediate difficulties who would in some ways be model employers. Alternative plans for industrial sectors were developed with trade unionists that promoted industrial democracy. The left attempted to ensure that businesses tendering for council contracts were equal opportunity employers and offered 'fair' employment and that councils purchased property to facilitate the development of plans conceived of by local residents such as Coin Street on London's South Bank. Community organisations were funded and supported in opposing developments that residents did not feel met the needs of local people – for example in Docklands or on London's South Bank (Mackintosh and Wainwright 1987). Militant-led Liverpool Council's more 'workerist' conception of local socialism was more overtly concerned with defending municipal jobs and building council homes, which it did with considerable success, and with battling the Conservative Government for a more favourable financial settlement than with developing alternatives (Parkinson 1985; Taafe and Mulhearn 1988; Parkinson and Bianchini 1993).

Manchester's local socialism was less strongly developed than those of the GLC or Sheffield, and less overtly confrontational than Liverpool's. Manchester's trade unions, with a strong Communist presence, preferred to defend their interests through industrial action rather than through political links to the Labour Party. The result was that activists schooled in the social movements of the late 1960s and 1970s quickly found a home in a weak Labour Party, drawing inspiration from the wider anti-racist, women's liberation and community-based protests of those heady times rather than, as in Liverpool or Sheffield, trade union struggle. The urban left grew through a community-based anti-cuts campaign, with the result that when, in 1984, the older leadership was deposed, the new council had a strong emphasis on internal democracy and equal opportunities. Powerful equal opportunities and anti-racist committees were established in 1984, which stressed the building of daycare centres, improving disabled access to council buildings, and the attempts at decentralisation of council services to local offices in order to work more closely with local residents and empower them to make more decisions locally (Wainwright 1987:114–126). But while from 1984 business grants would be conditioned on equal opportunities and there was an explicit focus on helping workers facing redundancy, there was not the strong connection with industrial policy that was a feature of London or Sheffield, or the workerism of Liverpool.

In any case, there were a number of problems with municipal socialism (North and Bruegel 2001). First, while the urban left went far beyond an understanding of the forces that led to urban problems to the designation of programmes to provide an alternative to the market-led deregulation approaches undertaken by the Department of the Environment of the early 1980s and typified by the Urban Development Corporations and Enterprise Zones, the left could only see itself as piloting approaches that would inform a left orientated incoming Labour administration working at a national scale. They looked to use the local state as a vehicle for overcoming the power imbalances that meant that communities were always on the receiving end of economic resources by widening community involvement and decentralising power, but they could only promote these polices when they had the resources to do so. Given that they were opposed by an unsympathetic central government that was reducing funding, that their residents were often poor and paying little or no local taxes yet needing high levels of support, and given that the focus was more on fighting contractions than on growing the economy, without the election of a Labour government the urban left would be unable to afford to fund its services. This 'cavalry' was expected in 1987, but failed to appear – leaving the left to face some hard choices.

Secondly, the strategies developed by the metropolitan authorities were built on the experiences of the sit-ins, occupations and alternative economic plans of more heady times. While appropriate for the period of heightened economic struggle that gave them birth, they did, it seemed later, prove to be inadequate as serious counter cyclical interventions and limited as a serious response to economic restructuring. The reality was that left Labour local authorities spent much of their time simply defending existing resources in the face of central government hostility. Their more long-term plans floundered on an over optimistic understanding of levels of trade union and community support. Alone, the local state was never seriously expected to be able to counter to destructive economic forces. As Mackintosh and Wainwright put it:

> While they would mainly describe themselves as socialists of one stripe or another, they had no serious illusions about being able to 'plan' their local economies, whatever the titles of some of their fancier publications. The best that could be done was to try to understand what happening and look for points of intervention to halt decay, to redirect some types of development, and to support the regeneration of self organisation among their constituents. The 'socialist' content of their work, where people thought it existed, was probably chiefly in the last point.
>
> (Mackintosh and Wainwright 1987:17)

The urban left were at their most effective when they acted to support and facilitate struggle from below. The local state could make a difference to local struggles by devolving power by, for example, funding community resource centres that employed local people rather than planning professionals; purchasing land for communities to put their strategies into effect, or providing alternative forms of technical advice. The urban left could not act alone, for where there was not a groundswell of support for their actions 'the policies tended to flounder or become captured by establishment thinking' (Mackintosh and Wainwright 1987:3).

Communities also came to recognise that in a polity such as the United Kingdom where troublesome local authorities can be centrally abolished, or where community organisations themselves can be incorporated, there was no alternative to self-organisation by grounded and localised community organisations (Bennington 1986). While they might get valuable support and resource from a local authority and indeed, had a right to such support, action at the level of the local state could not substitute itself for action from below. But by the 1987 election the levels of community action that had inspired Manchester's urban left were past their peak, and the environment seemed less than favourable.

The cavalry not having arrived in 1987, Manchester council changed track completely. Municipal socialism was dropped, and Graham Stringer, council leader, began to recognise that:

> Cities, like sprinters, can't stand still. They have to make progress or go into decline. The great days of heavy industry won't return. We have to find new ways forward. And that's where the Olympic Games come in. Our bid for the 2000 games is no town hall fantasy. It's a calculated move capable of transforming Manchester.
>
> (Graham Stringer in 1993 quoted by Quilley 1999)

Whether the more co-operative spirit of Labour Manchester lived on past 1997 is a topic that this book will explore in more detail later. For Hacienda DJ Dave Haslam it survives in Manchester's cultural industries. He writes:

> often ways of working in Manchester seem to reflect the history of the city. The city's role in the early days of trade unions and the founding of the co-operative movement just down the road in Rochdale are just two markers on the road to cooperation. In the music business this has extended to a degree of cooperative work between clubs and bands that you don't get everywhere: make a phone call offering somebody a part in a project and they don't often ask 'what's in it for me?' Mark Rae at Grand Central makes a point of nurturing a collective spirit: 'For me, the most important thing is people working together. Whatever your talent – as a programmer, a great musician, if you have ideas, or are a good singer – its about realising those talents. Its not about using people, its about working with people. It's the right attitude that matters.
>
> (Haslam 1999:266/7)

ENTREPRENEURIAL MANCHESTER

Labour's defeat in 1987 led to the transformation of Manchester from bastion of municipal socialism to the paradigmatic 'entrepreneurial city' where local movers and shakers 'get things done' (Peck and Tickell 1995). Having twice waited in vain for 'the cavalry to come to the rescue in the form of a Labour Government' (Randall 1995:51), local business people 'got together with the City Council and began to say let's stop dabbing our eyes at the loss of these manufacturing industries and see whether we can't do something to get to terms with what Madam called the enterprise culture' (Quilley 1994). Political pragmatism, boosterism and partnership became the new orthodoxy, and 'going for gold became synonymous with going for growth' (Peck and Tickell 1995).

'Entrepreneurial Manchester' was the Manchester of the Central Manchester Development Corporation, the Olympic bids' Sir Bob Scott, council leader Graham Stringer, and the Northwest Business Leadership Team: on first sight a traditional 'growth machine' worked as an amalgamation of property-based interests and local government officials that looked to secure growth (Logan and Molotch 1996; Hall and Hubbard 1998; Jonas and Wilson 2000). Unlike Labour Manchester, it was a Manchester that 'wins public investment by advertising its growth potential rather than its poverty-strickenness' (Peck and Tickell 1995:56). This Manchester was advertised as '11th out of 165 European Cities in Economic Importance – ahead of such cities as Copenhagen, Hamburg, Stuttgart, Rotterdam, Lyons, Turin and Geneva', 'the UK's most important financial centre outside London' and a place where 'it is possible to eat in a restaurant of a different nationality every night for a month' (Central Manchester Development Corporation 1995). It was a Manchester that was the City of Drama 1994, of the Velodrome and the Hallé Orchestra, a Manchester that, entreated by changes to the council's slogan, is now 'making things happen' rather than 'defending jobs improving services'. The revival of Manchester city centre after 1997, the growth of city centre living and the jewel in the crown – the 2002 Commonwealth Games – epitomised Manchester's change from industrial decline to post-industrial revival. Entrepreneurial Manchester had five aims:

- Repopulating the city centre and bringing in a high spending population to revitalise the city's culture.
- Capitalising on the city's reputation for sporting prowess to win major sporting events.
- Creating a consumer base in the city through the encouragement of the arts, restaurants, clubs and cinemas.
- Development of a high tech base with the universities.
- Developing Manchester airport as the city's global gateway. (Robson 2002:37–38).

Manchester's City Pride document summed up the strategy of attracting high-profile events to the city: 'Manchester aspires to be a world city. This requires active participation in world class organisations and events and recognition from agencies that can bestow world class status on the city', such as the Olympic bid which hit the headlines with attempts to create in Manchester 'an Athens of the North' (*The Guardian*, 6th September 1993 quoted in Randall 1995:46). The strategy was pursued with 'an enthusiasm bordering on messianic zeal' (Randall 1995:44), and although Manchester failed to win either bid, it won the status of 1994 City of Drama, as well as the 2002 Commonwealth Games (for which it was the sole bidder). Participation in the *Euro-96* football bonanza would later be disrupted by a massive IRA-planted bomb that devastated much of the city centre. Unlike Birmingham, the Olympic bid was represented as being new money, not coming from council budgets, so there would be no accusations that the education budget was being redistributed to pay for it (Cochrane, Peck et al. 1996:1130) even through significant central government funding would be necessary.

Manchester also attempted to host the follow-on of the Rio Earth Summit, Global Forum '94. It had grand plans for an international community and NGO-led festival that never came off (and became known locally as 'Global Farce'). Global Forum was designed as attracting 200,000 visitors, delegates from all over the world, and a major environmental festival. With a lead in time of only nine months, it needed £7 million, which was expected to be raised entirely from commercial sponsorship. Consequently, there were initially no environmental groups on the board and little communication with environmental NGOs. Business participation failed to deliver the hoped-for sponsorship, and the event was hastily reconfigured to an international academic symposium (Randall 1995). We will see below how Global Forum affected plans for LETSgo.

However, failure to win the Olympics notwithstanding, the city's uneven track record did result in the city being one of three invited to bid for City Pride funding in order to draw up an agreed vision of Manchester's long term future. What became known locally as Post Olympics Trauma did not affect the continued prominence given to partnership and the development of a shared agenda (Williams 1998:124), and partnership continued to be centre stage. Randall (1995) and Quilley (1994) described these partnership strategies as the 'business' or 'entrepreneurial' agenda when contrasted with the municipal socialist agenda of the eighties, but the efficacy and hegemony of such partnerships is challenged. Peck and Tickell (1995) took issue with such descriptions of a neo-liberal conspiracy by business leaders to outflank the elected town hall through unelected quangos. They argued instead that Manchester demonstrated the existence of an effective vacuum in policy-making beyond adherence to 'wish-lists' of uncon-tentious urban regeneration strategies ('business politics of the lowest common denominator', 1995:76), or advocacy of individual (if high-profile) development opportunities which do not add up to a coherent business strategy for Manchester. Beyond the presence of the same well known local power brokers from business on the plethora of local quangos, they argued that 'business discourses and business appointees are being used, both 'offensively' by the local state and 'defensively' by the local state' and that 'Contrary to local perceptions, business leaders seem neither to be in control not exercising their own agenda' (1995:63). For Peck and Tickell, the real 'movers and shakers' were still the City Council, and in particular Council Leader Graham Stringer.

There were limits to Entrepreneurial Manchester. Much of the success was down to the very effective rebuilding of the city centre after the IRA bomb, much of it publicly, rather than privately, funded. And the legacy of Manchester the 'dirty old town' of Ewan Macoll lingered. Haslam argues:

> Manchester has been fixed in the international mind, entrapped in its history, condemned to live forever in its landscape of rusting iron bridges, rivers the colour of lead, rain pouring down on derelict canal wharfs, and red brown back-to-backs. The potency of Manchester's grim, rather than glam, public image remains, with out-of-towners especially happy to roll out the ready made preconceptions. When the bids to host the 2000 Olympics were being made, the fight to prove that Manchester wasn't rainy, grimy and half-derelict was too much for the spin-doctors. The winning city, Sydney, commissioned a damaging, unsubtle video which contrasted Manchester's empty warehouses and derelict, rainswept wastelands with a film of Sydney harbour and glinting downtown Sydney skyscrapers.

(Haslam 1999:11)

In many ways, Manchester's revitalisation comes as much from its hidden, subversive side than from attempts to sell the city, a hidden side that emerged as the Madchester of the Happy Mondays, Oasis, a Guy Called Gerald, The Stone Roses and the Charlatans.

'MADCHESTER'

Entrepreneurial Manchester focused on winning high profile events, but also capitalising on Manchester's culture. 'Madchester' was the cultural centre of the North (Haslam 1999). A city of four universities and 20,000 students, the famous Hacienda club of the dance scene, the 'Gay Village' in the city centre (see Quilley 1994, and Rusholme's 'Curry Mile' (an Asian Restaurant sector). This was the city that the early 1990s dubbed 'Madchester' on account of its world-class renown for dance and pop music. However, Madchester was not just linked around youth culture, but was framed as the post-industrial city 'articulated into a wider "re-imagining"'... around the familiar themes of European style cafes, pedestrian streets and arcades and a central role for leisure and cultural activities' (Quilley 1999). This is the soft city (Raban 1974) in which cultural diversity is reflexively created, and different cultural lives can be lived in different spaces. Madchester frames a liberated plural Manchester in which diversity is not necessarily subversive – but encouraged – in a strategy of developing a post-industrial service and culture-based economy. Alternative consumption choices such as the dance scene and gay scene have financial clout as citizens-as-consumers make their individual consumption choices through participation in the market (Randall 1995).

Madchester often clashed with entrepreneurial Manchester. While culture was to be supported, this was more an attempt to create a city-centre café culture and support the Hallé orchestra rather than community cafés in Withington, drum and base from Hulme or reggae from Moss Side. Cultural Manchester felt that entrepreneurial Manchester was too top down, too bureaucratic, not putting local culture centre stage and what became known as the 'McEnroe Group' reacted to what they regarded as crass and poorly constructed, top down advertising messages with the comment 'you cannot be serious'. On a website, they slammed entrepreneurial Manchester's slogan 'we're up and going' with its red, white and blue logo as "dull, mediocre and worthy of a cycling proficiency badge" (Ward 2000). Secondly, the vibrant dance scene led to a crisis of city-centre governability. Clubland was inevitably contaminated by turf wars between rival drugs gangs and security companies claiming that they are the only ones able to keep the peace, and Madchester became 'Gunchester'. Northern British working class drinking habits did not create the hoped for Barcelona café culture, and Haslam (1999:262–265) reports one local wag saying 'It's certainly very continental out there, but less like Paris, more like the Somme' as late bars and inner city life clashed 'as the excitement of living in a 24 hour city wanes after a few weeks of sleeplessness'. By late 1998 designer stores found themselves regularly ram-raided as those excluded from the designer city forcibly took a piece of the action, and the council argued that the police were unable to police drunken revellers in the city centre. Nearby 'unruly' spaces in Moss Side and east Manchester found themselves the subjects of renewed surveillance and control (Ward 2003) .

FOR A SUSTAINABLE MANCHESTER

If for Peck and Tickell the stage is more open and the business strategy is not hege-monic, were other challenges observable to local boosterism and partnerships of the 'lowest common denominator'? Entrepreneurial Manchester felt it was hege-monic, arguing that opposition: 'is fantastically small. You actually have to search for opposition to Manchester's bid in Manchester. You may find scepticism, because we are a very sceptical race ... But actually, the consensus is very positive.' (Cochrane, Peck et al. 1996:1330). But a local attention to the frames produced by other actors suggests that given the decline of the municipal left, the observable challenges to local authority-led boosterism came from greens, who counterpoised discourses of sustainable development.

Manchester's green community was the archetype of Melucci's sometimes hidden, sometimes visible, sometimes active, sometimes latent networks. The community consisted of sudden and ephemeral alliances followed by fragmen-tation (the word 'network' indicating a coherence that is not always observable). It included some organisations without membership lists (Manchester Earth First!), political parties (the Green Party), and events such as the 'Critical Mass' cycling campaign. It extended to allies or fellow thinkers in the town hall (Labour Party dissident and Local Agenda 21 chair Arnold Spencer and his Sustainability Unit). Some participants saw themselves as part of a network, while others maintained loyalty to their own organisations. They had very different strategies, but they all shared a concern with Manchester's trajectory – with a critique of growth, prestige developments and winning events, and a concern for sustainability.

Perhaps they seemed invisible as they had no agreed understanding of what the greens were *for* beyond what they were against: Olympic bids and car culture. The ephemeral green network stressed Manchester's position in league charts as being the most polluted city in Britain. In this they were backed by the local press, with the *Manchester Evening Post* (18th January 1995) headlining 'Choker! Traffic Fumes turn Manchester into the blackest spot in Britain'. They complained about the city's lack of an integrated transport policy and unwillingness to do anything that might make the city less attractive to car drivers (Manchester Evening News, 8th July 1995). Spencer contrasted the city with fellow successful boosters Birmingham, arguing 'all the big European cities are taking action. We pretend to be world leaders but we are not' (Manchester Evening News, 18th January 1995). He argued that the adoption of a new design code for the city

> has guidelines for multi-storey car parks. You don't give guidelines for multi-storey car parks unless you are going to build more – and the last thing Manchester needs are multi-storey car parks. It also talks about parking as a way of reducing car spread and curbing crime, but we should not be encouraging cars, we should be discouraging them.
> (Manchester Evening News, 23rd January 1995)

A poster in Hulme, spoofing a city council announcement, read:

> Madchester City Council: Update! We have democratically decided that your homes are not important. Big business and yuppies have offered us large amounts of money to have offices, posh shops, car parks, wine bars etc in Hulme. One or two of you paid the Poll Tax.

We have a few flats to offer you in Wythenshaw.[1] You will not be able to come to the city and spoil our chances of attracting big business and the Olympics. For you scum who pay no poll tax or are too young or too old to be bothered with we have a wide selection of park benches and cardboard boxes to offer you as accommodation. We apologise for any inconvenience.

Cutting Jobs. Destroying Services. Selling Your Home.[2]

(Reproduced by Quilley 2002:85)

However, such critiques had been excluded from the mainstream debate from the Olympic bid onwards, as 'one of the unpleasant sides of the Olympic bid hype was the intolerance of dissenting voices. Not so much my country right or wrong, but my city's Olympic bid right or wrong' (listings magazine *City Life* quoted in Randall 1995:49). Continuing to criticise the growth strategy, the increasingly marginalised Spencer commented 'It could be the end of me but if it carries on like it is doing, I no longer wish to be associated with it.' (Manchester Evening News, 5th May 1995). Eventually he was stripped of his position as chair of planning after the 1995 May local elections (Manchester Evening News, 10th May 1995).

Spencer saw the opportunity for getting issues of sustainability onto the agenda through the Local Agenda 21 process, whereby local authorities were required to draw up a vision of a sustainable city in partnership with their local community. A 'Sustainability Team' was established within the local authority to co-ordinate the Local Agenda 21 process, conscious that 'green issues are not taken so seriously by Stringer' (Interview with council officer, February 1995). The team did, however, have a commitment to a participative process involving local community representatives and organisations to develop an agreed vision for a sustainable Manchester. As the Local Agenda 21 process developed, so did the extent to which the critique of the contradiction between the City Council's advocacy of sustainability and its growth policy would become clearer.

Outside the Town Hall, green critiques of the growth strategy began to proliferate over 1995, in particular over the city's failure to balance its growth policies with an integrated transport policy giving alternatives to the car. A network of environmentalists stood in the May 1995 local elections as 'Fresh Air Now' (in wards the Green Party did not contest). 'DIY counterculture', that did not engage with the debate around Local Agenda 21 (except to protest against developments they opposed), was eminently observable, as any visit to Manchester's alternative bookshop or the One World Environmental Centre would show. This counter-culture ranged from Friends of the Earth through Manchester Earth First! to radical businesses to 'Critical Mass' 'go-slow' cycle demonstrations which met during rush hour each month. In the Sunflower Project, a group of young people who were raising money to establish an alternative cultural centre like Brixton's Cool Tan, ran gigs that brought the network together.

The campaign against the Criminal Justice Act brought greens and the parts of the urban left together into 'Manchester Defiance Alliance' (co-organised by Rusholme's one time Militant Labour councillor and Earth First!). It linked across to the 'deranged anarchist spirit' of pre-City Challenge subcultural Hulme where families moved out and punks moved in to a squat mecca. Up the road in Darwen the M65 anti-roads campaign drew many environmental activists to direct action. Outside radical environmentalism, gentler alternative networks formed the resource pool for LETS to draw upon for members and for allies, and formed competition for the resources (time, money, commitment) of potential members. Some members of these networks joined LETS – others criticised it, for reasons we explore below.

CONCLUSION: CONTESTED CITY?

The vibrancy of the challenge to the business or entrepreneurial orthodoxy that was now represented by the various shades of green opinion – rather than by the urban left – stood out in Manchester. The public debate in Manchester was no longer over the business city contrasted with the municipal socialist vision, but contested conceptions of what a sustainable Manchester would look, like from the Local Agenda 21 process within the local state at one end to ephemeral green networks within civil society at the other. Both were counterposed to the unfocused emphasis on growth promoted by the local authority (Peck and Tickell 1995). The new bifurcation was between the values of Graham Stringer and Arnold Spencer rather than between Margaret Thatcher and Ken Livingstone.

What Robson (2002:39) calls the 'Manchester model' of regeneration achieved dramatic success in completing the physical rejuvenation of Moss Side and Hulme through City Challenge, the redevelopment of the city centre after the IRA bomb of June 1997, and, to some extent, in developing the necessary infrastructure for the Commonwealth Games. However, there is less evidence that ordinary Mancunians have benefited from this impressive physical renewal. Community development was no longer one of entrepreneurial Manchester's priorities although with the election of New Labour in 1997 Manchester, wishing to avoid being seen as a creature of the previous administration, quickly developed a Social Forum to add a social dimension to its City Pride strategy. This prefigured many of the strategies later developed by the Governments Social Exclusion Unit (Robson 2002:47).

The Political Opportunity Structure seems a mix of barriers and opportunities. On the positive side there was the existence of potential grievances for a social movement to capitalise on (unemployment and poverty, low wages and part time employment for those in work, pollution and car culture, and a city elite committed to growth); a pool of potential members given the legacy of the urban left, the new greens, and a pool of cultural workers committed to the DIY ethos of Madchester. Obstacles included the 'growth coalition' – a major obstacle, but potential allies could be found in Spencer's Sustainability Unit and, after 1997, a New Labour administration that was more friendly towards local authorities and committed to social inclusion. The discussion of the political opportunity structure ended with the observation that the POS is cognitively experienced: so we now move to an analysis of the actors than experienced it.

NOTES

1   A large social housing estate in south Manchester.
2   A play on the 1980s municipal socialist Manchester Council's slogan 'Defending Jobs, Improving Services' later replaced in 1987 with 'Making it Happen'.

PART II
MANCHESTER'S
ALTERNATIVE CURRENCY
NETWORKS

CHAPTER 5

LETS in Manchester

This chapter starts analysis of LETS allowing the actors to construct their opening frames through an introductory narrative about Manchester LETS, LETSGo, and Hattersley LETS. We then proceed to uncover in more detail the social movement identities constructed by members of the three LETS systems, before moving on to an understanding of the extent that they conceptualised what they were doing as in some way oppositional. This begins our social movement analysis of LETS that unfolds in the following five chapters.

MANCHESTER LETS

Manchester LETS was founded in November 1992 with 120 members and, according to LETSLink UK's (1993) survey, quickly grew to be one of the largest LETS systems in the UK. Its early success was the result of growing interest in LETS across Manchester amongst four interconnected networks of individuals who came together. One group were friends with Andy Rickford and Georgeanne Lamont who first initiated Manchester LETS, and who in turn were also well connected to social networks based around Quaker meetings and the Labour Party. At the same time, members of Manchester Green Party were discussing LETS, and the two networks met and decided to combine resources, with Green Party members connecting to a fourth network of people interested in the various DIY ('Do It Yourself') projects. 'DIY politics' is a generic term for a myriad of single-issue social change and protest projects associated with radical (i.e. non-Green Party electoral) green and anarchist circles such as 'permaculture', anti-roads protest, food co-operatives and communal housing experiments (see (Berens 1995; McKay 1996; Carter and Moreland 2004). These networks spread out into 'Alternatives to Violence' conflict resolution projects, 'Community Building in Britain' (based on the work of the American social change theorist M. Scott Peck), circle dancing, and co-counselling.

Thus, unlike many LETS systems which are initially based around a limited social network or in a particular part of a city, in Manchester one city-wide system across all of Greater Manchester was established. Combining resources from many networks (as members put it, to 'go where the energy is'), Manchester LETS sprang from those 'hidden' social networks that, for Melucci, social movement mobilisation makes visible. However, whilst large, the majority of members were located in one part of the city (south Manchester) Manchester LETS expected to have a wider coverage of the whole city before breaking up into smaller more local systems.

Manchester LETS was also different from many LETS systems in that from the beginning the network around Rickford and Lamont had a core ethos that LETS should present itself as a serious, competent and efficient organisation with high standards. They did not see LETS only as part of the alternative milieu, but wanted to be taken seriously as an addition to the local economy, and this ethos became the dominant one in Manchester LETS. Therefore, a premium was put on members taking responsibility for ensuring they did what they agreed to do, and care was taken to produce, from the start, a professional image and a directory of some substance. As part of its effort to be taken seriously trading, did not start until a large community of prospective traders had been established and a high quality desk-top published directory had been produced; with the intention of ensuring that prospective members had something concrete to join. A high-profile launch meeting was then held, followed by a formal pilot and self-evaluation after six months. Like most LETS systems, it organised without any financial support from local government at first, but later obtained a local authority grant of £10,000, which it decided to treat as a loan to be repaid in local currency over 10 years.

The core ethos described above was developed in the early days, but this only came after some debate. Coming as it did from one of the founder networks, it was not shared by all members of Manchester LETS and came close to alienating members of the green networks. They wanted a more explicitly countercultural focus that did not put so much emphasis on a professional and mainstream image, and on personal responsibility. Members of the DIY networks did not want to base the value of the local currency on the pound, but wanted to value everyone's contributions equally by some accepted hourly rate. Others wished simply to share their skills with others without using local currency. Some wanted to be able to acknowledge other people by paying them local currency but not receive any themselves, while yet others wanted to charge simply one unit per job.

It was decided to reconcile these differing conceptions of LETS through the development of an essentially libertarian core ethos to guide policy and form an unofficial 'charter of basic values' for Manchester LETS:

> The vision was, and is, one where LETSystems remain 'light' in their administration and avoid becoming organisations themselves. The focus of a LETSystem is its trading. The administration of a LETSystem is only there to facilitate the trading activities of its members by the provision of accounts and the directory. If we keep things light, then all sorts of initiatives can happen from within the network, like the 'LETS get together', and local trading events, or imaginative community development ideas.
>
> (Internal Document, Harpur 1/4/95)

Primarily, this ethos manifested itself firstly in its organisational structure, and secondly in the way it named and then refused to set a value for its currency. Organisationally Manchester LETS saw itself as nothing more than what it called a 'free association' of members. It did not have elected officers, a written consti-tution, or any formal system of accountability. There was no formal management committee or ruling body, but a monthly meeting called variously the 'Core Group', the 'business meeting', the 'administration meeting', or even 'the not-the-core group', which oversaw administration of the system (ie, the twice-monthly delivery of account statements and directories to members), which was open to any member. The libertarian ethos defined LETS simply as a 'tool' that in itself was little more than an accounting package and directory. As little as possible should be done centrally except deliver this 'tool' to members, putting the responsibility on members to use the 'tool' as they saw fit. The implication of this ethos was, therefore, that LETS was not a social movement with a specific set of values but a value-free tool which people with different values can rub up against each other.

A libertarian analysis was similarly applied to the unit of local currency – the 'Bobbin'. The name Bobbin was chosen,

> because of the historical connection of Manchester with the textile industry ... (but also as) ... The expression 'it's Bobbins' is sometimes used locally to mean 'it's of little or no value' or 'it's worthless'. We considered if this might be a drawback, but decided that it is accurate since the Bobbins themselves really are worth nothing – it's the talents and resources of the members that matter!
>
> (Internal document, 'Manchester LETS policy')

In other words, Manchester LETS chose a name for its currency that made it clear that it had no value in and of itself, and the value to be given to the Bobbin was left to individual members to decide for themselves. Instructions on using LETS in the System's Directory encouraged people to innovate with value:

> What's a Bobbin worth?
> It's entirely a matter for you and the person you are trading with.
> Businesses usually opt to treat one Bobbin as equivalent to a pound sterling because it's easy for them to administer. The people who work for LETS usually claim 6 Bobbins an hour. People for whom social contact is an important part of their trades might charge a flat rate of 1 Bobbin for any job.
> Each trade has its own unique characteristics. No single exchange formula is satisfactory for everyone. You can try out one of the methods above or have fun trying out your own ideas. Feel free!

Thus members were free to decide how to value their work, how to value the Bobbin, and how much Sterling to charge, and individual members with differing sets of values were left to interact. The Core group 'decid(ed) to give no guidelines or restrictions, since the heart of LETS is to encourage people to take control of their economic life' (Internal Document, 'Manchester LETS Policy'). As membership of Manchester LETS was heterogeneous from the start, this diversity was managed by a libertarian ethos that left individuals to decide their own statements of value.

If administration and policy were kept light, nonetheless a fairly complex organisation was required to keep the LETS system in operation. Organising Manchester LETS involved some forty people and some 150 hours of work every two months. Members were paid six Bobbins an hour for administrative tasks which ranged from receiving cheques from members and inputting them onto a computerised account system, producing accounts, collating 'offers' and 'wants' into a 44-page directory of services; to printing, sorting and delivering accounts and directories to the approximately 450 members.

In addition to the Core Group, Manchester LETS had a development arm known as the LETS Development Agency (LEDA). This was a company which focused on developing the idea of local and alternative currencies more widely, helping new LETS schemes to set up, and working with organisations to see how they might be able to adapt the core insight of LETS – that organisations as well as states can create their own money. This outward development contrasted with that of the more inward looking focus of the Core Group, which wished to concentrate on running Manchester LETS. It is impossible to clarify here the exact nature of the relationship between Manchester LETS and LEDA, as this relationship was itself unclear – and the source of many of the conflicts discussed later, which illuminate a conceptualisation of Manchester LETS as a contested social movement. Here LEDA can be identified as a social movement organisation (SMO) that will be analysed as an attempt at resource mobilisation, of widening uses of LETS through an engagement with the local state.

Outside the core tasks of administration and development, Manchester LETS undertook other initiatives aimed at encouraging members to use the system, the majority (but not all) of these being organised by individual Core Group members. This included a network of neighbourhood contacts – members whose task was to induct new members, to ensure that they understood how the system works, and, more crucially, to support new members in starting trading. Initially, the Core Group centrally organised Social and Trading Events (STEs) at which members met, put on stalls to display their trades, and socialised. This practice, however, was discontinued and responsibility for running STEs was placed on ordinary members. Some single members wanted to get together for purely social events (with an eye on possible romance!) and set up 'LETS get together' which met monthly in people's homes. A couple of Core Group members set up a LETS tool hire agency, and other members organised a childcare party to establish a childcare network. Others used the network to organise and market a myriad other events from circle dancing to Permaculture, walking weekends and parties, all advertised in the directory.

Thus Manchester LETS was a vibrant and successful system. It had large numbers of members (approximately 550 at its height) and a system turnover of 183,842 Bobbins in the three years to October 1995. Of the 550 members, 142 had a turnover of over 160 Bobbins, and the highest individual turnover was 4886 Bobbins. It had a hands-off approach, that put responsibility for use of LETS firmly with ordinary members who would use the tool as they would. It contained a diversity of members who formed a spectrum of political opinions, all knocking up against each other, with valuations of the Bobbin that varied accordingly. In LEDA it had members who were more experienced and committed to LETS development.

LETSGO

LETSGo Manchester was a development project initiated by the founder of LETS, Michael Linton. He designed LETSGo essentially as a short term initiative to kick- start LETS in a particular city (not necessarily Manchester), in order to demonstrate the possibilities for rapid growth of the use of LETS than could reasonably be hoped for from unfunded organic growth. LETSGo Manchester was the third city in which Linton attempted to implement his design after Vancouver (in 1987) and Toronto (in 1991).

LETSGo Manchester had *big* ambitions whereby high profile development of a MultiLETS Registry (known as Greater Manchester LETsystem Registry) would provide nest or a network of linked local money systems for 20,000 people and organisations – including businesses – in a timeframe of months rather than years. For example, the MultiLETS registry might provide accounts for members of LETSystems based on networks of businesses, or churches, schools and other organisations, for NGOs, or for local districts. He expected people would want to open accounts that served whatever networks they were involved it: a businessperson would have one account for trade with other businesses, one linking her with other parents at her children's school, one for the district she lived in, and one across all of Greater Manchester. Within five years Linton expected that 30 to 40% of the trade of a city would be carried out using local money and most citizens of a city would have an account with a MultiLETS Registry. In accordance with Linton's original design, LETSGo used the 'Manchester Pound' at parity with Sterling, and looked to the experience of the successful development of commercial barter networks as the model for LETS development. As evidence that LETS is part of a new technological wave, Linton also cited the growth of non-cash alternatives such as Mondex (a cashless payment system using smart-cards which participants charged up with electronic money from their bank account themselves), supermarket loyalty cards or air miles, and business barter systems.

The LETSGo model differs from that adopted by just about all other LETS systems in the UK in several ways: in terms of its timeframe and vision of LETS, its advocacy of large-scale business use, and in its commercial outlook. Firstly, LETSGo advocated a 'big bang' development strategy to kick off large-scale use of LETS in a particular city, literally in a matter of months. They would gather together a team of experienced activists who would develop materials, establish a Registry and train another 200 local youngsters in all aspects of LETS. This team would then 'blitz' a city by putting on a series of street theatres, games, talks to community organisations, businesses and local authorities. They would use a theatrical approach designed to "move minds in a playful and pleasurable fashion (as) the core ideas (of LETS) can often raise considerable anxiety, since they are utterly dissonant with peoples' unexamined central assumptions about money" (internal document). This process was expected by LETSGo to generate such a sky-high media profile that awareness of LETS would reach previously unheard of proportions, and large numbers of people would take out accounts with the Registry. The figure of 20,000 accounts was quoted, derived from a forecast that foresaw each activist recruiting two account holders a day.

In contrast, most LETS systems in the UK saw themselves as organic, community-based organisations that grow slowly and steadily. For Linton, this process was and is too slow and unimaginative. Linton was concerned that many LETS advocates did not see the full possibilities of LETS, particularly for businesses, or the vital need for urgent action given the scale of what he identified as a looming ecological and economic crisis:

LETS get down to business. LETSystems for small subsets of society may be warm and cosy, but they won't do much to protect us when the great economic meltdown comes along. We need changes in the mainstream economy if we are to survive at all. And we are only going to make the necessary difference in how the economy works when a major proportion of the local population is involved. The general public will only take interest when they can buy groceries, clothes, dental services, restaurant meals etc in the local money. So we need to bring business into LETSystems.

(Internal document)

Key to this approach is that large-scale business use of LETS is essential for the local economy to be developed to its full extent. Therefore, participants in LETSGo 'should be comfortable that businesses will join' and that 'every business worth considering will be using local money' as 'there is really little impediment to this. After all, money that comes back when you spend it is as attractive to any business as to any individual.'

Local businesses were seen as the engines powering the growth of LETS through what was called a 'community support cycle' whereby the large numbers of businesses that open an account would pay what was called a 'contribution to community'. Essentially they would pay a registration fee of £50 Sterling and 50 local units to the Registry to run their account(s). This would normally be passed on to a community organisation as a charitable contribution – but with a difference. In Linton's scheme, the local organisation would use this local money to resource its own activities, its workers using the local money they are paid to spend again in the local businesses which have joined the system. The cycle sees completion as the units are again donated back to community organisations.

Businesses, then, are at the heart of the process, rather than being merely the optional extra that other LETS systems might tolerate within what is primarily a community organisation. The LETSGo approach was organised on commercial lines as a business, offering a service to businesses that they expected businesses would wish to purchase. Accounts were overseen by a trustee who has formal responsibility for the registry, rather than by a core group (although the individual LETSystems using the registry might well be managed by a core group). Manchester LETS called itself a 'free association', while LETSGo called itself a joint venture company.

However, LETSGo Manchester differed from Linton's design for the community cycle that could be replicated elsewhere, once piloted in Manchester. LETSGo Manchester was conceived as a one-off development project, which would use the business contributions to community as a way to fund and demonstrate the viability of large-scale development processes. LETSGo described itself as a 'privately funded joint venture', based initially on sweat equity from participants who worked full-time for the short explosion of growth, and private finance. Wary of the possibility of burnout, volunteers worked in expectation of future payment once the 'community support cycle' was established, and an element from the 'contribution to community' netted off into a separate development account. This expected payment would be redistributed through a process called 'LETShare', whereby participants filed a statement of the time and expenses they had incurred in the project. When the project achieved a certain amount of revenue through contribution to community (and when the development project was wound up and administration of the registry was handed over to local people), the group would then collaboratively discuss how the proceeds, in the development account, should be divided up.

As LETSGo expected large numbers of businesses to join during the 'big bang', participants expected that they would then be as rich as other entrepreneurs in what later became known as the 'dot.com boom' (or bubble). Consequently, Linton advertised LETSGo to participants as an opportunity to make money. LETSGo was therefore a for-profit, commercial organisation for which Linton seeks private-sector investors. The expectation of wealth came from their identification of LETS development with the trajectory of commercial barter networks such as *The Bartering Company*, which paid commissions of £120,000 to 16 franchises between 1992 and 1993 (Imeson 1993:6). Linton and his supporters in LETSGo believed that LETS had the commercial potential to undercut the barter networks (which charge a handling fee), in contrast to LETS, which levies no transaction charge beyond the individual membership fee. As it was felt to be only a matter of time before a possibly unscrupulous entrepreneur saw a market niche, urgent development of LETS on ethical principles was required to pre-empt exploitation of design work by the private sector:

> All involved should be aware of the scale of the opportunity, and the potential for substantial profit, and operate on that basis.
>
> Thus, it is not a question of how can we scrape together the resources to address this task, but rather what means need be adopted to ethically manage revenues which are potentially excessive.
>
> Those that do not appreciate this distinction should expect to be quickly overtaken by others that do – quite possibly, by people who see the opportunity for personal profit on a grand scale, and have little or no concern for ethics or community. While such profiteering is likely to lead to its own end, and appropriate systems will eventually assume the territory, the level of confusion generated in the interim will not be useful.
>
> (Internal document)

The *LETSystem Design Manual* (written by Linton and Soutar, the manual for the LETSGo approach) therefore stressed the need to develop an open and participative style which demonstrated LETSGo's aspirations towards participation:

> Enthusiasm and talent is widely available. It is much easier to recruit that talent in a framework which emphasises participation and reward.
>
> Open participation is achieved by a group which operates as a collective of independent individuals, each free to act as they choose. Work done on behalf of the group must be acceptable to the group as a whole.
>
> (Internal document)

Manchester was identified as the site for the LETSGo project as in Manchester LETS, LETSGo identified a possibly well-established ally which had done considerable ground work in promoting LETS to the local media. Consequently, the level of understanding of LETS in Manchester was felt by Linton and his British colleagues to be higher than elsewhere. Secondly, a push in Manchester was felt to be timely, as Global Forum '94, originally conceived as a high profile festival aimed at NGOs and the community, provided 'a unique opportunity to focus attention on LETSystem ideas, within Manchester itself and to delegates from around the world. Organisers of the events are showing interest in our participation' (internal document). Thirdly, Manchester City Council was felt to be supportive.

Consequently, LETSGo came to Manchester in May, 1994. Linton invested an inheritance in the project, and temporarily moved from Canada to be joined by his closest British colleague, Angus Soutar. He invited others to take part in his business venture. Soon advocates of LETS from across the UK, together with individuals who paid their own fares from as far away as Australia and Canada, came to Manchester and set up shop in a managed workspace on an industrial estate off the Rochdale Road in central Manchester. Over the summer of 1994, forty to fifty volunteers were working out of the office, undergoing training on LETS, writing materials, and modelling the MultiLETS software. Meetings were held with businesses, community organisations, the media and local representatives. An unscheduled meeting was held at Global Forum, when organisers refused formal permission to give a paper. Theatre was planned. LETSGo planned a major foray into Manchester's Political Opportunity Structure although, for the reasons explored in chapter 7, the hoped for 'big bang' did not occur.

By the autumn of that year, the ability of LETSGo Manchester to balance its commitments to democracy, ethics and participative processes, with its hopes of making money and getting large-scale use of LETS off the ground was quickly resolved. The majority of the volunteers left the project by the winter, when the bulk of LETSGo's 'big bang' orientated activity was over, and Michael Linton returned to Canada. When I first visited them (January 1995), the team was down to a hard core of five or six who, their prophesy having failed, were examining their experiences and exploring other opportunities in the now burgeoning dot.com world. Over the spring of 1995, LETSGo reconstituted themselves into a long-term development project aimed at fully establishing the Greater Manchester LETSystem (they had attracted approximately 150 accounts, of whom approximately 100 were active by January), in preparation for the time when they could 'go round the loop again' for the 'big bang' and their eventual financial reward.

As a SMO, LETSGo identified different stakes from other LETS systems: in its advocacy of a short 'big bang', its vision of MultiLETS Registries, its advocacy of large scale business use, and in its commercial outlook that concerned that small LETS systems were cozy but inadequate. In that, it drew created considerable criticism from other members of the LETS community in the UK – criticisms expressed in a manner that quite belied LETS' self-advocacy as vehicles for creating community harmony based on peace and love! For a student of social movements though, LETSGo was unique. The LETSGo experience illustrated parts of LETS as a social movement which more community based systems, like Manchester LETS, did not raise. Other issues were raised by the third system studied in Manchester, Hattersley LETS.

HATTERSLEY/TAMESIDE AND GLOSSOP LETS

Hattersley estate is a large early 1970s, low-rise relocation estate in the Pennine foothills outside Hyde, Greater Manchester, built to take residents from inner city clearances from Moss Side and Hulme, in Manchester. It is one of five such relocation estates built on the outskirts of the Greater Manchester conurbation, and is managed jointly by Manchester City Council and the authority in which the estate is located – in this case Tameside MBC. Hattersley is a typical outer housing estate, located physically on the outskirts of a city, but with inner-city problems and a poor reputation amongst people from surrounding areas. When visited, the physical structure of housing on the estate was good, green spaces were well maintained, and graffiti and vandalism were not obvious (as a result of recent renewal). While the shopping centre contained many void and boarded-up shops, the estate had a health centre, library, church and community centre. Hattersley boasted a popular credit union, and was felt by members of Hattersley LETS to be a place that is unfairly labelled – but at heart 'a place like any other'. Unemployment was 27%, 46% of the residents were under 30, and there was a high proportion of single parents (source: Tameside MBC).

Two local residents and community activists who had been involved in Manchester LETS, established Hattersley LETS in mid 1994 with early support from workers at Hattersley Community Centre. Originally the system was aimed at the estate alone, with a currency called 'Hats'. The inspiration for setting up just on the estate was a reaction to the perceived middle class nature of Manchester LETS ('with their vegan walking boots!', as a founder member put it). With support from LETSGo, Hattersley system was computerised from the start, and also linked its currency to the pound (as advocated by the Linton model). However, before launch supporters of LETS who lived in Glossop (a Pennine town on the borders of the conurbation) became known. The reconstituted system called itself as 'Tameside and Glossop LETS', covered much of east Greater Manchester, and used the Bobbin as its unit of currency – although it maintained a strong focus on the estate. Of the 45 members, 20 lived or worked on the estate, and membership included Hattersley Community Centre and High School.

Hattersley LETS never really got off the ground. Two directories were issued but trading was virtually non-existent. The member who set up the accounts programme got a job, another set up a food co-operative, and the supportive worker was told that she could not support development of LETS not focused exclusively on the estate. Consequently, the LETS system focused on Hattersley was stillborn, and attempts to develop a wider system did not raise much enthusiasm.

While Manchester LETS is an example of a successful large-scale LETS system, and LETSGo is a particular development strategy, as such they are less than typical of the overall experience of LETS development in the UK. In a discussion of Manchester LETS and LETSGo it is important to remember that Hattersley is perhaps more representative of the side of the experience of LETS that receives less attention from LETS advocates – a system that did not take root. Hattersley also demonstrates some of the problems and opportunities in developing LETS in communities which perhaps stand to benefit most from them – residents of outer housing estates.

CONCLUSION

Manchester LETS, then, emerged from the quite dense networks of older ex-urban left activists and of younger, Green activists to form, quite quickly, the UK's largest LETS scheme, centred around south Manchester. The Political Opportunity structure there seemed helpful, perhaps even helping understand why Manchester LETS grew so quickly. The legacy of the urban left meant that resources could be quite quickly mobilised: a grant of £10,000. Even the discourses of 'Entrepreneurial Manchester' helped crystallise these diffuse networks. They could not agree what they were for, and did not have a coherent strategy, but, in LETS, they did have a project that inspired them and helped pull the network together, making a hidden network visible. A final helpful element of the political opportunity structure was need: the existence of poverty and deprivation, and a lack of jobs. However, the same lack of jobs and presence of unemployment and poverty did not lead to the development of a vibrant scheme in the eastern part of the city, or on Hatterley estate. The reason for this needs to be explored in more detail, but this reinforces the perspective of the RMT approach that as the existence of discontent does not mechanically lead to the emergence of collective action, we need to explain why it emerged in some places and not others. Certainly, members of Manchester LETS were not wealthy: Williams (1996) survey found that 43% of the membership in 1995 were unemployed and 63% of them had degrees or postgraduate qualifications. He therefore calls these members of Manchester LETS the 'disenfranchised middle class'. They were poor, but were they socially excluded? Did they seek access to the market, or, by joining LETS, were they seeking an alternative? Analysis will have to uncover this. If so, it might explain why members did join Manchester LETS and not Hattersley: Hattersley did not have what people on the estate wanted. Again, we will need to examine this further. Finally, the political opportunity structure was not so kind to LETSGo. There were activists in Manchester, but they were not convinced on LETSGo's business orientated strategy, of the viability of the 'big bang' or of the ethos of the LETSGo approach. It could be that this is as the strategy cut against the ethos of Manchester LETS members: but this is moving ahead to quickly. We need to examine what the political perspectives developed by members of Manchester LETS were before we can make such judgements. And it is to the political identity of members of Manchester LETS that we now turn.

CHAPTER 6

The Politics of LETS

Flectere si nequero superos, Acheronta movebo – If I cannot change the powers above, I shall set the Lower Regions (*Acheron*) into motion.
(Vergil's *The Aeniad* quoted by Draper 1992:245)

We are the little folk – we! Too little to love or to hate. Leave us alone and you'll see, How we shall bring down the State! … Mistletoe killing an Oak! Rats gnawing cables in two, Moths making holes in a cloak – How they must love what they do! Yes – and we little folk too, We are busy as they – Working our works out of view, … Watch and you'll see it some day! … How we shall bring down the State!
(Kipling, 'A Pict Song', as sung at a LETS conference social in Wales, 1995)

The Greater Manchester LETSystem: the way forward to New Customers, More Sales, Extra Profits.
(LETSGo leaflet, Manchester 1995)

The task now is to use Touraine's method to examine why people participate in LETS – the political questions they felt needed to be raised and that they thought LETS could solve. If members of LETS made statements and claims which challenge the logic of industrial society, claims about how they believe society *should* be organised (perhaps claims that they can enact through their membership of LETS in the here-and-now) – then LETS can be regarded as a social movement. Further, if LETS raises claims about how society should be organised which critique the mainstream, and the mainstream cannot incorporate these claims and there is a struggle over these claims then they should be regarded as what Touraine (1981) calls 'the stakes', over which the social movement struggles – or what Melucci (1992) calls the 'why?' of collective action. This chapter will argue that following Cohen and Arato (1992), LETS can best be conceptualised as a heterogeneous social movement, a contested space. Within the social movement two trends can be identified. Firstly, there are those I call the 'Transformers' – those concerned to transform the mainstream with an articulation on political society through elites changing policy, and using LETS to develop a community economy alongside the mainstream. Transformers regard LETS as a policy innovation that will subtly humanise those that use it for purely instrumental, rather than overtly political ends. Secondly, there are those who articulate on changing civil society through the development of what urban social movement theorist Castells (1986) called alternative urban meaning – revaluing the relationship between work and leisure, alternative work choices, revaluing money, gaining access to organic food, and developing sustainable lifestyles – and I call them, following Foucault, the 'Heterotopians'.

They are clearer that LETS represents a political challenge, and as a result is a social movement. This chapter analyses the differing stakes the two identify, as they work their way through the implications that their contrasting plans have for the development of LETS.

THE CLAIMS

This section analyses the claims LETS participants make about what the stakes in the struggle are. It examines the extent to which participants in LETS see what they are doing as political, and if so, what political claims they make. This is achieved firstly through an examination of the public statements participants use, both in their written documents, and in public presentations observed through participant observation. Secondly, an analysis will be made of the claims partici-pants in LETS made during focus group research, and of how they themselves carried out self-analysis of their actions.

THE CORE CLAIMS: MONEY, EMPOWERMENT AND COMMUNITY

The discussion will commence by examining what a potential LETS participant would hear, through an examination of public statements which advocates of LETS make in public presentations in which they give the rationale for LETS, explain how it works, and argue that certain problems can be solved using LETS. In particular, we examine the way in which they attempt to connect with the values of potential participants using frame alignment processes (Snow et al. 1986). In 1992, when interest in LETS in the UK was mushrooming, advocates decided to co-ordinate the nature of the presentations they would give to ensure consistency, and what has become well known as the 'start-up talk' emerged. A transcript of one such start-up talk is reproduced below (Extract 6.1). This was given to local authority officers, councillors and residents on an outer housing estate in Bury, Greater Manchester, which I observed in February 1995. This will be analysed, and the frame transformation processes adopted will be illuminated in order to identify what claims are made for LETS; in particular the processes of frame alignment (Snow et al. 1986). We shall examine processes of *frame bridging* (linking advocates' values with the audiences' values), *frame amplifi-cation* (amplifying those beliefs by providing a reason why LETS can solve them), and *frame extension* (reaching out from networks of primary supporters to recruit new ones).

Extract 6.1 A LETS start-up talk, given by a LETS activist

I was reading a local paper in Leicestershire just the other day, and I was intrigued to know that in Leicester City 12,000 houses were unfit for human habitation and in need of renovation, according to the newspaper article, but the council haven't got the money. What a shame I thought, then I turn the page over and I see that builders are going out of business. So you've got substandard houses and unemployed builders, and you all lose out. And I thought, what a perfect example of the need for LETS.

So what's the miracle idea to square this circle? What are the problems of money?

- It's scarce – there's not enough of it about.
- It moves: out of the community to wherever it can get the highest rate of interest.
- It comes from *them*: to pay for packaging from elsewhere, for goods from around the world.

In every civilised country in the western world, there is a central issuing authority for money, they control how much money is in circulation. If there's too much money in circulation you've got inflation, if there's not enough there's no activity, so the job of the Chancellor of the Exchequer is to keep it scarce so that it has a value. If you could wade out down Bury New Road knee deep in £20 notes, money would have no value. It would just be litter. The only thing that gives money value, is our agreement (it's an agreement we all make from the time we are born) to *give* it value. You can't eat a £20 note, it has no intrinsic value at all, you can't wear it, you can't shelter under it. It has no value, only the value we give it.

And the problem with money is that it is scarce, it moves mostly away from us, and more particularly away from our communities, and it's always produced by somebody else…not us.

So let's explore that a bit more at a personal level. If you imagine your own supply of money … (the presenter draws a barrel). This is my personal barrel or purse of money. If you can imagine I've got various sources of income that flow into this barrel. It might be benefits, it might be income from work, it might be presents, it might be tax relief, whatever … but various source of money coming into my barrel.

But, the problem with my barrel, and you might have a barrel like mine, is that it has holes in it. And what happens with the holes, well all sorts of bits of money tend to leak out: my payments for rent, my payments for food, my payments for presents for the people who give them to me, and income tax or whatever. Now my role if you like in controlling my own personal money supply is to always try and maintain my level of money above the holes, ok, so I'm always trying to maintain that there's enough in there, enough coming in to cope with the holes going out, and that's the challenge that each of us have to cope with individually, but if you take that analogy to a local authority, it's probably exactly the same, trying to balance the income and the expenditure, it's always a struggle, and if you take it up further to the state level …

Spending money is always competitive. You are always maximising the amount coming into the barrel and minimising cash going out of it, so you are in conflict with those who give you income and try to strike the hardest bargains with those you are paying. That's the nature of money, it creates conflict. We are all like Cedric Brown trying to get as much income as possible and to spend as little as possible. You try to get it and not give it away.

So we need a money that's – what's the opposite of scarce? Plentiful. Opposite of moves? ("circulates around the community?") Do you mind if we say "stays"? All right. Opposite of from them – from us. So what we've got is a money where there's always as much as you need – always – stays, and I'm in charge of it.

While advocates themselves see this as a simplistic and populist version of their claims, they are made over and over again in presentations. They are the core claims about money, made by LETS:

Money is *limited*.	LETS is *enough*.
Money *leaves* our community.	LETS *stays*.
Money comes from *them*.	LETS from *us*.

Firstly, in a process of frame bridging the frame is produced that money is limited, that there is not enough of it about, and consequently needs are not met. To rectify this, a call is made for there always to be 'enough' money. Secondly, the problem is framed as one of control. We do not control money (and 'we' – they people in the room – is bridged to a more universal 'us', or, specifically, 'the community'). Money is controlled by 'them', 'others', 'away from our community'. To rectify this a claim is made for control: it should come from 'us', not 'them'. Third comes the frame that 'we' should have 'enough' money in 'our community'. It should stay, and, like a barrel, it flows out to 'somewhere else'. So, three frame-bridging processes are made, linking statements that there is not enough money to a call for enough; that we can't hold on to money, to a call for it to stay; and a statement that we don't control money, to a call for community currencies.

The final frame-bridging process is a claim for community self-reliance in which the community is all of us – local authorities included – who lose our money to elsewhere should stop the leakage. Trade outside 'the community' (implicitly a *local* community, not a more global community of interest) is framed as a problem (it leaks out of the barrel, and you have to pay for 'transport, packaging, whatever') and *we* are all used to money leaking out of *our* pockets. The holes should be stopped up and the community made more reliant, if not autarkic. In this analysis, the community is untheorised as an inclusive 'us', and the flowing of resources to others (who will also think of themselves as an 'us') is a problem.

There then follows a process of frame extension. The frame is advanced that no-one benefits from the money system as organised. If no houses are built, and builders go out of business 'we all lose', and an inclusive 'we' all benefit from LETS, while 'they' are not defined. 'We' are all victims of a financial system which ensures conflict, by paying out as little as possible and earning as much as possible so that 'we are all like Cedric Brown' – another attempt at bridging through the then unpopular 'fatcat' chairman of British Gas. While framed as someone not to be emulated, he is not framed as benefiting from the financial system, but as a person forced to be greedy by a design fault in the money system. Consequently he is as much a victim as anyone else.

The frame is then extended to one in which running a local authority, or even the state, is similar to the task of managing personal income (a claim famously made by a Grantham shopkeeper's daughter!). An inclusive 'we' all know what it is like to not have enough money, and we all need a solution. The frames are then amplified and a solution provided: create your own money. The claim that money does not have value in and of itself, and of itself is valueless, is amplified into a claim that money is hyper-real, a floating signifier with no reference to a signified (to frame the argument in Baudrillardian terms). Consequently, if money is hyper-real, of no value except the value that we give it – the claim is made that it is possible to assign value to a community-created currency. A hyper-real currency becomes real if we assign it value. Once you see the trick – you can break out of it. Money becomes a Baudrillardian simulacrum.

We can summarise the stakes currently illuminated in Extract 6.2 (below):

Extract 6.2 The problem with money

1   The mainstream financial system prevents needs being met and people working.
2   We do not control money: someone else issues it.
3   Money has no value in and of itself: just the value we give it. Therefore we can create it ourselves.
4   The way the money system is currently organised benefits no one. We all lose from its failure.
5   The conventional money system causes conflict. This is no-one's fault, but is inherent in the design of the money system. In contrast, LETS designs in co-operation.
6   Money leaving our community is a problem.

In addition we have two more claims:

7   LETS empowers people by valuing their skills, ingenuity and resourcefulness.
8   LETS strengthens local communities.

These are the frames as produced for a wider audience. To illuminate further stakes, more detailed claims need to be discussed, as produced by ordinary members, rather than those produced by leaders.

'TRANSFORMERS' AND 'HETEROTOPIANS': CONTESTED VALUES

In order to organise these discussions, four alternative value bases have been identified which inform varying conceptions of the role of LETS in social transformation, as a social movement. They were developed through Sociological Intervention and explored further through in depth interviews. Firstly there is the claim of 'transformation' – that LETS is an outwardly *value-free*, non-political financial innovation of use to mainstream institutions that nonetheless subtly, subversively but uncontroversially *humanises* the economy. Secondly there is the more explicit view that LETS is a *green* initiative. Thirdly there are the values of those with more explicitly *anarchist* views who see LETS as an alternative to the mainstream, either as an island or utopia within it, or as a beacon or metaphor back to society.

At one end of this schema are those who wish to see wider, mainstream, use of LETS, and we call them the 'Transformers'. They articulate on changing political society. Extreme Transformers see LETS as value-free. Further down the spectrum 'Humanisers' and 'Greeners' would like to see wider use of LETS, but are at the same time concerned that in its attempts to win wider support it might be losing its radical edge. At the other extreme are the anarchist 'Heterotopians' who do not wish to engage the mainstream in any way, preferring to work within and fill out civil society in opposition to the mainstream. Between greeners and hetero-topians we find the fault line between those who feel that LETS is a reform, and those who believe it is a fundamental attack on capitalism.

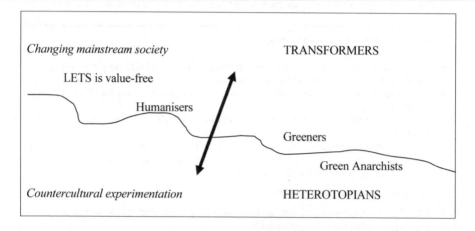

These are 'observer-generated' categories uncovered during fieldwork and ascribed by the researcher (Hammersley and Atkinson 1992:178). They were accepted as valid by informants but should not be regarded as exclusionary or exclusive categories, rather as points on a spectrum from 'strong Transformer' to 'strong Heterotopian'. The next task is to examine these four conceptions to illu-minate the differences between them and the extent to which, as hypothesised, LETS is a contested space in which two broadly opposing strands argue their positions: advocates of *transforming* the economy (working on political society and seeing LETS as a new policy), and advocates of building countercultural alternatives (working within civil society and seeing LETS as resistant politics), the *Heterotopians*.

'LETS is value-free'

The official policy of the Manchester LETS Core Group, and of LETSGo, is that LETS has no values or politics in and of itself. It is an accounts package, nothing more, and use of or membership of LETS is perfectly in tune with mainstream values if that is how participants wish to use it. Should members choose, there is nothing in the LETS design to prevent a trading relationship governed by the values of the rational, utility-maximising economic individualist of conventional economic analysis, under the logic and control of the mainstream economy, but using local rather than national currency as the means of exchange. Business should therefore see it as an unproblematic and beneficial financial innovation that it is in their interests to use; and LETSGo specifically aimed to persuade business of the value of LETS (Linton 1995). Consequently, those who regard

LETS as value-free have an ethos of professionalism, an emphasis on quality of product and of publicity materials, and of a businesslike approach that is likely to make LETS look credible to a business audience. Linton summed up this position:

> This is completely neutral – a bank account ... like store budget vouchers or air miles. Why piss about with all that if we can go to this market? If we can say to people – 'have a card that saves you cash', do we have to educate them, morally? No. Do they have to understand the system? No. They have to understand that it's saving them cash, and if they understand that, they're happy, and I'm happy.

The claim that LETS is value-free could be regarded as an understandable, and quite typical, attempt at frame extension by a social movement aiming, quite properly, to make propaganda in order to widen its membership. However, it is also a claim that does not stand up to detailed analysis which shows that the claims about made about money by those that hold that they are value free are social movement claims. Firstly, the call for more money and a claim that 'we' can issue it represents a challenge to neo-liberal concerns for financial orthodoxy and 'sound money'. Neo-liberals have no problem with money coming from 'them' – they are 'them'! 'They' do not want there to be 'enough' money – but scarcity, with Sir Keith Joseph famously arguing in the context of the UK in the 1970s that 'our inflation has been the result of the creation of new money out of proportion to the goods and services available. When the money supply grows too quickly, inflation results. This has been known for centuries' (Smith 1987:73). Neo-liberals therefore want to prevent irresponsible (social democratic) governments inflating the currency (Hayek 1990). Consequently, Hayek called for the abolition of the state monopoly on currency, and for a free market of currencies, whereby competition would lead to use of only the most sound and hard currency, issued by men of a 'conservative temperament'. He therefore called monetary reformers – like our LETS activists in this excerpt – 'cranks':

> in the past such demands have been raised over and over again by a long series of cranks with strong inflationist inclinations ... they all agitated for free issue because they wanted *more* money. Often a suspicion that the government monopoly was inconsistent with the general principle of the freedom of enterprise underlay their argument, but without exception they all believed that monopoly had led to an undue restriction rather than an excessive supply of money
>
> (Hayek 1990:12)

Secondly, the claim that money should not leak out of communities, valorisation of local economies, and advocacy of the substitution of imports for locally produced goods again is fundamentally at odds with the neo-liberal project of free trade. If strongly held it is an argument for autarchy, against Smithian conceptions of comparative advantage which advocate that communities, regions and countries should do what they do best and trade with everyone else rather than try to do everything within one country. If not full autarchy, it is a claim for what is in effect a local version of the import substitution strategies attempted in the 1950s and 1960s in Latin America that again represent an alternative to current economic orthodoxy as represented by the Washington Consensus against local tariff barriers. Neoliberals want money to flow where it can work 'best', most efficiently, most profitably not impeded by local regulation such as a currency whose geographical circulation is proscribed. Thirdly, the claim that money is just a social construction can, of course, also be challenged. Economists would claim that it does, in some way, represent the 'real economy' – the volume of goods and services produced – to enable these goods and services to be exchanged. It makes the 'real economy' fungible (Ingram 2004). Those who hold LETS to be value-free reveal their own value base in the frames they produce, a value base that is more in tune with their more overtly radical colleagues than with mainstream or business values than they like to admit.

Advocates of the position that LETS is value-free argue that although they do hold radical views, the key issue is that these views they are their own, personal political perspectives, not official views of LETS. Others need not sign up to these views to participate. However, they then argue that in order to ensure effective trading participants will be transformed in attitude, 'greened' and 'humanised', without these values being overtly proselytised by activists. The point is, advocates of the value free approach say, that LETS should be framed in apolitical ways to ensure mass participation, and to frame it as a green initiative is counter productive. It will put people off. But LETS is political. It does operate in ways that cut against globalisation, free trade and unbridled capitalism. As we explore in more detail below, advocates of LETS as value free argue that apolitical participants will be 'humanised' as they find the need to pay attention to the quality of the relationship with those with whom they trade. They will be 'greened' as they find the need to identify products which can be produced locally, and therefore are accessible for local money; or chains break down and participants find that they end up with a large store of unspendable credits. As these effects are designed in, LETS is a powerful tool for transforming the quality of relationships between economic actors (what LETS members call 'relationship trading') and building local economies. Those who publicly advanced the frame that LETS is value-free were privately also either Greeners or Humanisers (but not anarchists).

Secondly, advocates of LETS as a value free tool see LETS as a 'free association' of individuals with no formal organising committee or management. A Core Group is not empowered to manage relationships between individual traders, and participants should be left to do what they will with LETS. They say this as they rightly argue that to get widespread use of LETS, while individual members will bring their own political perspectives with them, none should be allowed to dominate to the exclusion of all the rest. Believing LETS is value-free is compatible with using it to carry out single political programme (greening, humanising), while allowing others similarly to carry out their programme – which may be an anarchist rejection of using LETS for conventional economic reasons. But this libertarian perspective is obviously a social movement claim – if anything, an anarchist value. Refusing to impose one value is as much a value as any other! Consequently, LETS produces a plurality of possible social change programmes, all knocking up against each other – Heterotopia – which can be contrasted with the role of conventional, state-issued money in enforcing labour discipline and the functioning of capitalist markets.

Thirdly, Libertarianism contrasts strongly with Manchester LETS' simultaneous ethos of running a professional organisation in which (as Landry et al. 1985 point out) the professional image requirement needs members to act with a certain amount of discipline and produce materials of a high quality. When they didn't act in a professionally impeccable way members of Manchester LETS received criticism which contradicted the professed libertarian stance. Anarchists felt alienated from the professional image, while a truly professional, business oriented, organisation would not have tolerated the quirkiness of Manchester LETS – which the anarchists introduced. LETSGo were similarly exercised by their simultaneous claim that LETS is applicable to business and their wish to develop on ethical principles – as will be discussed in chapter 8.

Finally, as they see no role for a Core Group in managing relations between individual members, including those with business members of LETS, they come up against the charge that their stance promotes the continuation of a destructive economy, and of 'polluting' Heterotopia by introducing exploitation into the system (Wall 1990:94, Coleman 1994:133–134). Introduction of exploitation might militate against their professed aims of building community and empowering participants. To resolve this it is necessary again to investigate whether the change in power relations, which the transformers claim makes traders act in a less selfish way, is real.

These considerations suggest that members of LETS are attempting to extend their frames through the claim that LETS is value-free (which may be appropriate strategically if allies who accept this can be identified within the Political Opportunity Structure). Alternatively, by making this claim members of LETS are not recognising that their claims are challengeable and represent social movement claims (Gledhill 1994:90). This may be as these participants have not yet had enough interaction with others to uncover these challenges or identified the stakes over which there will be conflict. Consequently, premature ascription of false consciousness to advocates of LETS as being value-free must wait analysis of how their frames were received by other actors. It should also be recognised that it is perfectly logical to argue that while LETS is value-free, individual advocate's views are not; and the reasons why individuals propagate LETS (which are political) can be separated from use of LETS (a tool for anyone). Again, these considerations will have to wait analysis of how LETS was perceived by other actors within the local Political Opportunity Structure.

Humanising the economy

'Humanising' summarises the individual worldview of many of those who publicly claim that LETS as a value-free tool. If there is a second key stake advanced by LETS beyond that of a struggle over money, it is a struggle over the nature of work. LETS participants often say that they joined because they 'want to get away from the money economy'. By this they mean that they want an economy that values people more than profit, need before efficiency, and quality before cheapness. The Humanisers therefore seek to 'humanise' or transform the economy by connecting spiritual values and economic values primarily by redefining and revaluing work, especially that often attributed to women, the young and the old, by refusing to define its value in narrowly instrumental cost/benefit terms. Secondly, as we saw above, they see LETS as subtly and subversively humanising those who join for purely economic reasons by providing valued alternatives to full time employment, and by educating participants about alternative livelihoods. Humanist economic thought traditionally categorised conceptions of the economy into the mainstream HE (High Tech, Exploitative) and those of a human or SHE economy which is Sane, Humane and Ecological (Schumacher 1973). LETS, consequently is claimed to be a more balanced economy that values the affective, emotional and co-operative as well as efficiency, organisation and the achievement of goals:

> I see it as a balanced economy – a balance between men and women, between the masculine and feminine in each of us … An economy that calls on each of us to practice in that kind of way is more likely to soften people than this horrendous situation that frightens so many people – men as much as women.

LETS is claimed to be a more SHE economy as Humanisers claim that, by design, LETS encourages or channels participants into acting co-operatively by changing the relationship under which economic activity takes place:

> The LETS community does look at a transaction as a relationship whereas the commercial world looks upon a transaction as a transaction. You need some respect for the person you are dealing with as you know they don't have to do it. It's got to be mutually beneficial, whereas a transaction in the real world does not have to be … there's an imbalance of power.
> I think that this thing about relationships … I always look at it as favours that happen anyway between people, regardless of the philosophy or the politics. Yes, I think LETS is developing that idea, by developing relationships you develop interactions … and the LETScheme is a system, an interaction on a human level rather than on a financial level.

The relations under which economic transactions take place are changed as Humanisers argue that there are not the power relations in LETS that there are in the mainstream economy:

> I don't think that LETS can actually be exploitative as my view of the currency is that it isn't actually currency and it's not actually worth anything. There's no actual legal enforcement – it's all voluntary and it hasn't got the capacity for a power relationship that the money economy has got. So I don't think that LETS can actually hurt anybody.

As LETS currency is unlimited, there are no credit limits, and no debt charges, there are no disciplinary methods of enforcing people to trade using local currency in contrast with Sterling which, as it is limited, forces people without independent means of support to get a job to earn it. I earn sterling as I have to, to live. I do not have to like the person I work with. I just need money, and am therefore structured into having to work, as is everyone else who lacks a private income. I therefore have to do little to persuade others to accept my money – they have to, as do I. Of course, for Simmel, the fact that money regularises economic transactions such that they are no longer governed by whimsical affect is one of its benefits (Simmel 1978/1908). Advocates that LETS is value-free would agree in principle, but they would also argue that Simmellian rationality is a limited conception of human relationships, that of cost-benefit analysis. They would prefer a more human relationship – "I want to be friends with people I trade with." Consequently, they argue that LETS has the educative function in that people who do not embed their trading relationships within affective, caring relationships will soon find that, as no one needs to earn local money, they will find no-one willing to trade with them. Chastened by the experience, the argument goes, they will in future pay more attention to how they interact with their fellow traders.

Humanisers look to redefine work away from the nine-to-five and away from a world of full-time employment to a blur of work and leisure. They look less for a return to conventional full-time employment to a freer, more informal economy with opportunities for a portfolio of varied work opportunities as a real alternative to conventional employment patterns. They seek to achieve this through breaking the division of labour down into a more flexible process of what one humaniser called 'energy transfer':

> swapping energies ... when you just don't like doing something, or ... it's a job that I can do – but, I can't be bothered! But I can do certain things for people that they would take four times as long to do! So why do all the shitty jobs that you find shitty, if someone else enjoys doing? It's wonderful that. Apart from ... that, which I call energy transfer, was in my own case was having time on my hands as I deliberately under-employ myself in the mainstream if you like. I refuse to involve myself in a lot of mainstream activity, therefore I do have time and I do believe in it ... you are empowering yourself and empowering others."

> (work is) creativity! ... leisure can be work. You can have leisure that you create through working for some people.

Humanisers emphasise the contribution and value of those who are not valued in the conventional economy (young people, older people, people with special needs, people recovering from mental illness). They look to redefine work away from the concept of a 'job' to 'valued activity', as a Humaniser explained:

> I became more and more interested in how people can actually participate in valued activities without actually calling it employment. Because, for a lot of people the opportunity to be involved in valued activity in the community is as important as a job. Capitalists call a job a way of earning a living but it's not actually about money, it's about being a valued part of a valued community.

> I believe that there are a lot of dormant skills in the community which people don't use, people don't value. People value experience in terms of putting a suit on or going to a job, or calling themselves 'a teacher' or calling themselves 'a road sweeper'. It ignores, people ignore the fact that they, we've all got huge quantities of shareable talents and skills which can be used to swap! You know, people could use it. And I think that's, that's a terrible waste of a resource. We need to have our community continually enlivened by creativity. It's dead and stagnant.

This process, they claim, promotes social inclusion rather than exclusion of those not valued by the mainstream. Lack of hope, breakdown of community and feelings of being abandoned by mainstream society are seen as the prime problems facing society, which can be addressed by a revaluation of work through LETS. Another Humaniser said:

> the fragmentation that we now feel on the outer edges of this crumbling economy or political set-up is what's causing most of our problems in society. No hope for children and young people, which is the cruellest thing. When we don't respect our young, 'cos then we don't respect the future. When we fail to do that it's the saddest thing. It's the whole problem right across the spectrum – the systematic abuse of women. And I call it abuse: the systematic political abuse of women in this society is not really understood. I mean I see it and it causes me an immense amount of pain … (and) I think we are crazy not to use the expertise of our old people. I think we're crazy.

In claims for the humanising of the economy, again LETS raises social movement claims for alternative livelihoods – for Schumacher's humanistic SHE economy. Consequently, members of other networks who make similar claims participate in LETS as a way of actualising and spreading these values. The Society of Friends (the Quakers) saw in LETS an economic extension of their principle of non-violence in action and their desire to 'let your life speak'. The Humanist Movement (and one of Manchester LETS' most thoughtful and active organisers was an active Humanist) describes itself as a loose network of people who wish to reinforce people's understanding of their capacity to change the world, that progress is possible, and that this is best done through people taking control of their lives locally rather than waiting for others to do things for them. Humanists work by inspiring local action and local democracy to give a sense of the power to act with what they call historicity (they use the same term as Touraine). A major barrier to historicity, they say, is that money is limited, controlled by banking cartels, and subject to usury (Silo 1994:69–75). As a consequence, the local action they inspire includes LETS, which they see as a tool for educating people about the effects of money and interest on the economy. Like Green Party members, they do not see LETS as a Humanist initiative in which participants are surrogate Humanists, but seek to build broad action fronts including LETS. Apart from one leading member, who does not proselytise in any way, any overt influence of organisational Humanism on LETS is hard to observe.

Thus, members claim that LETS is a more peaceful, humanised, ecological economy – achievable in the day to day. The extent that these claims hold water is fundamental to an understanding of LETS as a social movement, and this is a task for analysis in chapter 10.

Greening

The conviction that LETS is 'a very good piece of green politics in action' was raised by many participants in Manchester LETS, many of whom were active greens, either Green Party supporters or sympathisers. Greening values formed a spectrum connecting the Transformer and Heterotopian positions. Some greeners saw LETS as a way of greening the mainstream – a view similar to that of human-isers – while others were closer to the green anarchist position seeing LETS as a green space, counterpoised to the mainstream. The task here is to show how greeners felt LETS was a 'good piece of green politics in action'.

Greeners stressed firstly that green values include those of social justice, and they saw LETS as a major way of ensuring social justice through empowering the excluded, as a Greener commented:

> In terms of why it is green, I'm one of those greens who sees the social justice aspect as being totally intertwined with ecological sustainability, and that its vital to change the 'social' aspects of society as well as the 'environmental' aspects.

> the Green Party ... were concerned about what they saw as an impending ecological crisis, and people started to think about ways of avoiding environmental disaster and evolving sustainable ways of living. Then it got on to deeper and broader issues that were concerned with politics in a wider sense, and the relationship was drawn between protecting and sustaining the environment, and social justice and the satisfaction of people's lives and relationships between people, and ways communities and societies could be organised in a sustainable and sort of fulfilling way, which was in harmony with one another, and also the environment.

Secondly, as the quote above goes on to mention, Greeners felt LETS was green as it built community feeling, in terms of building trust, conviviality and friendliness without exploitation. A greener said:

> it's about creating friendly communities, a way of getting people in touch with other people who they might not otherwise have met by doing something friendly with them that's mutually useful without the possibility of either of them exploiting each other in the process of trading.

> And it's also, there has to be a large element of trust in it, in that yesterday I handed my £260 tent and sleeping bag and many other things to someone who gave me an acknowledgement of 30 Bobbins and that is not the sort of thing that normally happens in society, that you trust somebody else with a piece of property or whatever.

Thirdly, others organisationally linked with the wider green movement argued LETS was green as it encouraged recycling of resources used by the community. It was a slower economy. It takes time to get someone to do a task for you with the result that they believed participants would question whether the task needed to be done or not in the first place. Was that consumption necessary? Was it useful work or useless toil? Work for work's sake, or genuinely useful work or consumption?

> People need to share things more. I've got this expensive tent, I think we should manufacture less because of the environmental damage that manufacture does. So it's logical for me with expensive rucksacks and tents to want people to use them when I'm not, rather than buy them themselves, so I can similarly get use of someone's van rather than having a van myself.

Others commented, on the benefit of LETS in making available to all members resources that might be privately owned or controlled. As a result there would be communal access to everyday items such as washing machines, garden equipment, tools, computer and printing facilities, leisure equipment, and little need for private ownership of such items. On these lines, a recycling company commented:

> Our company joined LETS as we thought it was the sort of thing we wanted to support, which is basically, co-operation

LETS was felt to be green in that it built a local economy which reduced transport costs, and thus fossil fuel-burning, pollution, and the need for roadbuilding should be reduced. Multinational corporations, it was argued, have no attachment to place or to benefiting local producers or the local economy, and will move as soon as is necessary to maintain profit levels. Multinationals were seen as 'vacuum cleaners', sucking wealth out of the community as profits are repatriated to head offices abroad. Multinationals were seen as destructive of local economies where supermarkets are introduced encouraging the use of cars and leading to wider environmental damage.

More thoughtful greens said that LETS is designed using certain attributes which greens identify from the natural world (Dobson 1990:24). In particular, they cited nature's *diversity* by valuing a multiplicity of local currencies – even of different and competing values of local currency within one LETS system – and a multiplicity of developmental strategies. They mentioned *interdependence* through seeing a community as a whole and interconnected. Each act connects with all other actions, resulting in the greening of society through connection. Finally, they pointed to the natural world's *resilience*. LETS, they argued, is designed on the Permaculture principle of using resources at hand to build a stable and self-adjusting system with limited inputs. Each member trading with each member has responsibility for regulating the ethics of each trade; both ensuring the quality of product, and that they can meet any commitment that they may enter into. Thus as all the trades in a LETS system collectively add up to zero (the balance between all trades being made), the system is resilient with little human intervention. This valorisation of LETS as balanced and self-sustaining reinforced feelings against the need for government support for the running of LETS systems.

Finally, moving closer to green anarchist positions, greeners felt that LETS enabled participants to make more of an effort to live sustainably now. LETS reduces reliance on the conventional economy, which is subject as they saw it to international pressures and restructuring; thus providing a liveable, viable alternative in the here and now. A green anarchist said:

> (LETS is) a way of putting principles about how you feel you relate to one another and how you should go about actively working in a more sustainable way, putting more value on human characteristics and values and environmental stuff as well: It's a way of bringing that about. And it's not the only thing: things like co-ops and credit unions, co-operative things and recycling are part of a green way of life.

In particular, LETS was seen as a way of providing organic and ethically-produced local food at affordable prices. It enabled them to avoid supermarket-sold food that they saw as mass-produced and therefore tasteless, sugar, fat and preservative-ridden food often imported from southern countries thus incurring fuel costs, pollution, and involving the exploitation of cheap labour in the South. In contrast, LETS was about making links with suppliers of locally produced healthy food, but in a way that is affordable for ordinary people. In this LETS prefigured the later development of Farmer's Markets (Bentley, Hallsworth et al. 2003).

However, beyond the fact that Manchester LETS attracted greens, the extent that LETS was green in and of itself was less clear, as was the extent that LETS participants actively conceptualised LETS as green rather than an initiative that they supported. Those members who mentioned that they were active greens were concerned to emphasise the independence of LETS from the green movement. A Greener close to the Heterotopian perspective said:

> I kind of, would quibble a bit, about ... labelling the LETSystem as being an environmental thing. And also I don't think that LETS systems are only going to be set up by people who have membership of the Green Party ... Green Party members or green organisations don't have a monopoly on LETS schemes and I think it's just a difference between people who are in the Green Party and green politics and more mainstream types of politics are that they want to put into action in their daily lives principles that guide their political thinking, and LETS systems are one way of doing that. ... So I wouldn't like people to think that because they are in a LETSystem, all of a sudden they are in some way co-opted into the Green Party! (Laughter) because I don't think that there's that kind of a link with it.

This strategy of 'unconscious greening' through LETS mimics the 'unconscious humanising' of the humanisers. Here, LETS is best conceptualised as an example of frame extension on the part of the Green Party whereby, following electoral failure, they recruited non-greens to their cause in another, more supportive, political opportunity structure. They have done this by connecting with wider frames of building community and empowering (which we will examine in more detail below). In particular LETS connects to the frame of social justice, promoting sustainability through reuse and recycling, and strengthening local economies. In this conception LETS is a social movement organisation mobilising the green social movement sector more effectively than the Green Party – as a competing SMO.

LETS is therefore a process of soft rather than deep greening (Dobson 1992), a humanistic economy that blurs very much with the views of the humanisers rather than with distinctly green conceptions such as deep ecology. Greeners connect Transformers and Heterotopians. LETS was seen as part of a wider social movement *action repertoire* that included electoral activity and direct action. Greeners wished a fair wind to those who believed that wider transformation through mainstream uses of LETS is realistic and achievable. More radical greens expressed views that put less emphasis on top-down action, arguing for more of a reliance on bottom up action, which allied them with green anarchist positions. To import concepts of green politics, advocates of greening therefore fall into the category of "realistic" or *'realo'* greens while the anarchists are fundamentalist or *'fundi'* greens (Capra and Spretnak 1984:3–29).

Greeners introduced two more claims building on those that LETS is a social movement around money and work. They added that for them LETS is also a social movement around building community, and for a sustainable society. They disagreed with anarchists that LETS enabled participants to live a sustainable lifestyle now, and agreed with Transformers that LETS was in danger of being a cosy club of the like minded if it became too politically explicit. However, they sought to extend LETS through allying it with other struggles for a green society, rather than with attempts to humanise the mainstream.

Green anarchist politics

The third network that led to the formation of Manchester LETS was a group of people organised around community, permaculture, organic methods, food co-ops, and conflict resolution circles – all concerned with building oppositional or alternative institutions. Their political positions on LETS can be called anarchist in view of their antipathy to the state and to capitalism which resonates with that of Anarchist writers such as Colin Ward (1988), Murray Bookchin (1986) or Rudolf Bahro (1994). However, a small 'a' is used in recognition of the fact that many large-'A' Anarchists (discussed in chapter 5) did not join Manchester LETS as a reaction to what they saw as further commodification of the mutual sphere, and as a reaction to Manchester LETS' professional image.

However, small 'a' anarchist does describe their views. The Manchester LETS anarchists fall into the non-violent, Ghandian brand of Anarchism rather than the violent, Bakuninite class struggle Anarchism associated with newspapers such as '*Green Anarchist*' or '*Class War*'. They introduced the fifth claim, that LETS increasingly enables members to live outside the mainstream economy in the here and now. They were not interested in attempting to transform mainstream institutions, as they didn't think LETS would be capable of the task, or they felt that the mainstream would be unresponsive. They were concerned that in attempting to make LETS more responsive to the mainstream LETS was losing its value base. They were sceptical about attempts to create a hard form of alternative currency as would be acceptable to business, preferring to use the currency as a way of recognising the work someone has done, as a gesture of thanks, rather than a form of money that would accurately calculate the monetary worth of any transaction. They therefore preferred a currency linked to time, or resisted calculation entirely seeing this as unwelcome commodification. As soon as they had built up a relationship, they stopped exchanging bobbins as: 'you don't pay your friends, do you, for God's sake!'

They believed that social change comes from alternative institution building:

> I suppose also people taking things into their own hands in a way, if that's not too political like! I've always liked the idea of ... what do I mean? ... I suppose personally I've always liked the idea of making something out of nothing, you know? I'm a bit of a, I like making something out of nothing ... I like to do something creative from nothing. So I suppose that when I heard that you could actually do some work for people and not get paid cash but with a different currency, an alternative currency, it caught my imagination and I could think of loads of things that I could do.

They therefore sought to deepen LETS rather than widen it, and to withdraw from the mainstream rather than humanise it. They had no problem with local small businesses participating in LETS, but saw little likelihood of LETS being attractive to large business (if it was, they argue, LETS would be of little counter-cultural value). They felt it was more important to get food and other basic goods and services available through LETS, so those who wished to could live without recourse to what were seen as unsustainable and exploitative capitalist markets. They saw LETS as a scaffold around which a wider counter-cultural alternative to the mainstream can be built which would include credit unions as an alternative to banks; community businesses and co-operatives as an alternative to capitalist busi-nesses; farmers' markets and food box schemes as an alternative to supermarkets; public transport, carshares and bicycles as opposed to car culture and housing co-ops as opposed to mortgages. Heterotopians said:

> LETS schemes ... seemed like a way of living without having recourse to the mainstream economy, I don't really go along with that, and because I wanted to support community and relationships with people and get us back to a more ... aware that we can relate to each other in a happier and more comfortable way 'cos that fits in with how people are, people I think. Because I think basically are community creatures, and I think things like LETS schemes actually force us that way. A lot of stuff in our current culture, I find prevents the fostering of relationships between people and communities

Another commented:

> The great thing about LETS is that you can start to live life outside capitalism, outside mainstream work on the dole. Being unemployed is very soul-destroying and isolating, but LETS gives you a way to be part of a wider group and sell your skills so unemployment doesn't grind you down.

Thus LETS is a survival mechanism for those who wish to live outside the main-stream, or alternatively a heterotopian enclave of freedom within the mainstream:

> I think that it's one of the mechanisms that gets people in touch with other people in a way that they don't need the formal economy, they don't need the banks. They don't need the finance system. So the greater extent that you can meet your needs through the LETSystem, the less you depend on the formal economy.

The anarchists valued delinking by building larger LETS systems in smaller areas, strengthening community and resisting incorporation through accepting money from businesses or local authorities. They hoped that levels of communal support facilitated by LETS would, over time, grow and grow such that capi-talism would be superseded. Relations between people would slowly transform through participation in a growing alternative economy such that the use of local currency would become little more than point-keeping that would, in time, wither away. To kick off this change programme, they stressed valuing everyone's work equally, and were concerned that making LETS to attractive to business made this long term transformation in economic relations between people damaged by capitalism less likely.

The anarchists like the fact that skills which would be well remunerated in capitalist markets are not valued in the LETS economy. They like the alternative market signals:

> I'm going to grow some food on the system: that's my contribution and we need more of it. Then we can think about delinking. I also like selling my computer skills, that in the mainstream economy they pay a stupid amount for, of 6b an hour. OK no-one has used them, but its good that skills in the mainstream economy are worth little in LETS and vice versa. I don't actually know much that is useful in terms of survival, living, feeding yourself. LETS helps us rediscover that knowledge.

In the latter part of this quote we see part of the dystopian vision that inspires LETS enthusiasts – worries about the 'loss of the commons' (The Ecologist 1993). LETS aims to recover the self-reliance that it is felt communities had before expropriation from the land under enclosure in the 18th century. During enclosure, the peasantry was excluded from the land – where they were self-sufficient – and forced into wage slavery where they could not meet their own needs themselves. The anarchists are keen to reconnect in some way to the land they live in and be able to live comfortably within a self supporting framework. The growth of supermarkets, which limits options for buying from local producers, and people's increasing inability to cook basic, healthy foods are problems to be addressed if social breakdown is to be avoided. Anarchists see the 'lore of aeons' – local knowledges about local plants and foods as being lost. They argue that if trends towards the development of out-of-town supermarkets continue to erode local shopkeepers, then opportunities for self-reliant livelihoods decline.

LETS is an attempt to develop sustainable self-reliance whilst avoiding both a retreat into communes as advocated by Rudolf Bahro (what Spiro 1970 called the 'non-withdrawing commune') or social breakdown – but they do see LETS as being 'like a commune'. The diversity of currencies in LETS is felt to be more sustainable in the advent of the economic breakdown the anarchists feared, and which they felt was very likely as a result of the year 2000 Millennium Bug. Instead of a monoculture of currency, which may become worthless in the event of catastrophic breakdown, LETS means that there will be alternatives available, and the possibility of the re-establishment of a culture of self-reliance and independence. Thus the anarchists believe that LETS may mean the survival of humanity.

At the other end of the scale of survival from eco-collapse is the concept of LETS as an Anarchist Heterotopia, rather than a utopia. LETS also attracted romantics (the author included) who liked to see LETS as a part-time, post-modern utopia, separate from the mainstream and not contaminated by it, but also an alternative with a fairly easy entry and exit point. LETS is an temporary, evening and weekend utopia – what Bey (1995) called a Temporary Autonomous Zone (TAZ) alongside the mainstream in which the romantic can reinvigorate themselves and live for a couple of hours in the world as they would like it rather than as it is. Consequently, because it does not see itself as the one, final, end-state utopia, but as an alternative yet impossible space, it fits Foucault's label of the '*heterotopia*'. Melucci, it will be recalled, saw political change as not emanating from the full-time disciplined party man who lives to protest, but from the part-timer who lives and sometimes protests. Again, the extent to which this part time strategy in an impossible space becomes real will be the subject of chapter 10.

CONCLUSION: THE STAKES DEFINED

Pulling together the perspectives of the four positions outlined above, Extract 6.3 (below) summarises the stakes they identified. They suggest that LETS raises

---

Extract 6.3 The stakes raised by LETS members

Strongly transforming
- Articulation on political society.
- LETS as a policy innovation.
- Currency at parity with national currency.

1 *Value-free*
- LETS has the potential to create large numbers of jobs and regenerate economies, not necessarily just local economies.
- It's a value free tool that you can do what you will with.
- LETS is not political.
- It's not political in itself: it's something greens like to see happen.
- It's getting back to how we used to live.

2 *Humanising the economy*
- Connecting spiritual values and economic values.
- Subtly and subversively humanising those who join for economic reasons.
- Redefining and revaluing work.
- Revaluing work attributed to women.
- Including the young and the old.
- Educating participants about alternative livelihoods.
- Providing valued alternatives to full-time employment for money.

3 *Greening*
- Sustainability. Recycling, re-using, conserving.
- Strengthening the local economy.
- Democratic control over local economies.
- Ensuring social justice.
- The need for good, wholesome uncontaminated food.

4 *Green Anarchist politics*
- Living outside the mainstream economy.
- LETS is a commune.
- Showing an alternative to market forces is possible.
- LETS is better than capitalism, but can extend monetisation.
- Caring, sharing and co-operation.

Strongly heterotopian
- Articulation on civil society.
- LETS as political challenge.
- Currency at hourly rate, to wither away at first possibility.

claims about how society should be organised around four areas: money, livelihood and work, community, demonstrate that, as Cohen and Arato pointed out, social movements contain many widely contrasting values of social change. The four positions should be seen as points on a spectrum rather than as wholly exclusive categories, but serve well to illuminate the debates.

How should we react to these claims? At one level, as challenge to neoliberal orthodoxy LETS, could act as what Levitas (1990) called a 'mobilising utopia'. The extent that they are right or wrong is less important than the extent that they are a stimulus to action. A more local analysis would look to explore these claims in more detail. If members of LETS *are* able to recreate money and ascribe it the value they desire without it becoming fetishised (taking on a value of its own), LETS could be a micro-political illumination of the particular system of domi-nation in money. It could be a nomadic break-out from that system through the creation of new money, attacking power relations on a particular front within the particular systems of domination which LETS illuminates. Heterotopians argued that through LETS participants are able to actualise these statements, Transformers that LETS needs to be extended into the mainstream. LETS would then be one of Deleuze and Negri's 'thousand machines of art, life and solidarity' (quoted in Best and Kelner 1990:93). However as yet all that is provided aat this stage is an under-theorised understanding of money, a story about money without a detailed analysis of how money works at the site of domination (as Foucault would put it), on individual bodies. Analysis needs to uncover whether individuals and collectivities *can* break from real power relations and create their own money as work of art, or whether systems of financial domination continue into the LETS economy as actors continue to be disciplined by neo-liberal 'common sense' ideas that 'you can't spend money you don't have without indulging in 'Micawberism'' (financial irresponsibility leading to unhappiness).

This debate is one of many which are key to an analysis of LETS as a social movement. The metanarrative explanations are that ownership of the means of production matters (even defines in the last instance) over ownership of money (Lapavitsas 2003), and unless LETS breaks that system it is doomed. A Foucaultian analysis counters that power descends up from bodies rather than down from structures, so bodies can create their own means of exchange. The extent to which it can illuminate this particular facet of power and combat it by recreating value, will resolve the question as to the effectiveness of such micro-politics in chapter 10.

Social movement theory suggests that in these claims, we see a call for what Touraine says is the key battleground of programmed, post-industrial society (Touraine 1981:5). LETS is not a call for control of the means of production, the rallying cry of industrial society (it is not raised), but a call for control of life – in other words for *self management*. Self management, it will be recalled, is the core stake that Touraine identified as the prime claim of the green movement for being regarded as the potential premier social movement of programmed society. Although these epistemological claims were not found to hold water, Touraine helps identify that in this claim for revaluing work, the economy and payment, in this call for self-management, the social movement nature of LETS is primarily illuminated. Self-management here is also made explicit and a tool introduced to enable participants to put it into action without getting involved in a conflict over the means of production. The extent to which self-management may be achievable through participation in LETS will be examined in chapter 10. First though we need to explore in more detail the extant that members of LETS themselves perceive that they have an opponent.

CHAPTER 7

Self-Analysis: Do Members see LETS as a Social Movement?

Having identified the claims made, it is time to identify possible objections to those claims that might form stakes over which LETS as a social movement struggles. This will be done through an analysis of how members engaged in a debate over their strategy, and the implications of it – what Touraine called *self-analysis*. This section will discuss firstly, the extent that those members of LETS who see what they are doing as social movement activity, see it as being capable what Melucci called 'breaking the limits if the system'. This will show the extent that members have a consciousness of their historicity. Secondly, the principle of opposition needs to be employed to examine whether LETS members identified any opponents, who these opponents might be, and what they might do to challenge LETS or prevent it developing.

TRANSFORMATION, OR 'BREAKING THE LIMITS'?

Some members did not see LETS as a social movement, as part of the green movement at all. They joined purely for instrumental reasons – to use the services available in LETS. The following is a prime example of such a view.

> I joined at the beginning I think of LETS in Manchester, and a friend suggested that she thought, you know, I was me, and I do a lot of soft-furnishing type things, I've got someone to do all my ironing, cleaning my windows, I give piano lessons, so my main interest is the contact with other people. You do make good friends, you know, meet lots of interesting people. I think she knew that I wasn't working, we knew that I had time to do things and she knew I needed to meet people. She knew what, she knew what I could offer, and she knew what perhaps I needed, I suspect, as well – like I said ironing, that's just one example, that I could think of.

For those who do see LETS as in some way transformatory, a way of building an economic system that fitted their value system in a way that capitalist markets do not, the debate was between those who felt that an articulation on transforming the mainstream was what was required if LETS is to break out of being what they called a 'cosy club'; and those who felt that LETS should remain an alternative, separate from the mainstream and who said, for example, 'Because I'm a romantic I want it to stay as a subversive experiment.' Within this debate, though, there were Transformers who felt strongly that LETS *is* a vision of an alternative society that can transform the mainstream in a sustainable direction, and there were anarchists who were unconvinced of the likelihood of success. They would rather build an alternative system that will, eventually, be able to take over many of the state's functions in a peaceable transformation.

At the other extreme from the peaceable transformation model, and driving the transformers, was the catastrophist vision of LETSGo. Fast action is necessary to 'save the world' from imminent eco-catastrophe. Consequently, attempts to build slowly will not be quick enough, and a 'big bang' is necessary:

> there is little hope that the social and ecological context can hold together that long. The very pattern of conventional money-trading is destroying our world, and far faster than all the efforts of all those dedicated to arresting or modifying the process. LETSystems must become mainstream very soon if we are to have any hope of leaving to future generations a world in which they can even survive, much less thrive.
>
> So what do we have to do? Basically, we have to get our acts together; we have to start behaving as though this were a matter of life or death, which it very probably is.
>
> (Linton and Soutar 1994)

As the year 2000 loomed, many members of LETS, including the leadership of the national LETS body LETSLink UK believed the catastrophist visions then circulating of immanent technological collapse. This meant that efforts to build resilient local food systems through LETS became more and more important. But in 1995, outside the extreme transformatory views of LETSGo, few members of Manchester LETS saw LETS as being capable of overcoming the money system in its entirety, or of 'breaking the limits of the system' on its own. The differences came between Transformers who did see LETS as capable of changing mainstream institutions if they adopted the use of LETS, and Heterotopians who had less faith in the likelihood of LETS being adopted by the mainstream. They saw LETS as an observable alternative or a declaration of: 'other ideas in circulation. They don't necessarily mean that things are going to change, dramatically, and for me that doesn't matter too much. There has to be ... that struggle and new ideas.' They saw LETS as being what Melucci called a message back to society of the existence of an alternative:

> I think that to turn this culture in this space and time on this planet from something negative into something positive ... then we need a broader vision which includes visions of communities where intercommunal nurturing is seen as good for the whole and good for individuals within the whole ... I believe that the LETS economy is an advanced economy – an advanced economy, years ahead of its time. It's an economy for the new world really.

A similar comment is:

> to me LETS is mainly about the ... educative thing. I mean, the kind of capitalist cynicism that goes around, about market forces and about the laws of supply and demand and about people being basically greedy gits that rip people off all the time, I think LETS is a good way of demonstrating, *'No – that's not actually true'*. People are capable of being like that but they are also capable of being different. LETS is a good way of demonstrating to people even if they are not actually involved in it. They can see, well *there's* a community, a community that's scattered around Manchester.

Another member commented on the message LETS sent to non-members:

> When I was working, I told a lot of the guys at work that I was working with about it ...
> some thought it was a great idea, some thought it was crazy, but one of the drivers (said)
> "I saw that Bobbins thing in't paper last night – so it's really taking off in't it eh?". So ...
> I think that people didn't really believe it would happen and they are pleased that it has!

LETS members were attracted to the idea of people becoming actors, taking an initiative and just doing something about their situation, no matter how effective or well thought-out. They liked the inherent challenge and imagination of LETS. They liked doing something that sceptics would scoff at:

> I think we are also interested in *challenging*, challenging the order of the day. We came to
> Manchester against a background of people telling us it wasn't possible. Like we didn't move
> here for my job, we came here (for ...) to become a student and study for a degree and it's
> arse about face. We tend to do things in an arse-about-face way no matter how hard we try.
> And I, at the risk of being hopelessly inarticulate I like the arse about face-ness of the LETS
> system. ... I like the fact that it isn't a mainstream institution. I'm someone that's never been
> particularly happy in the mainstream and quite happy on the fringes. Anything with a hint of
> weirdness attracts me like a magnet! It also has imagination, the whole idea of trading in
> Bobbins and the whole way that it's set up: the fact of people imagining that they can set up
> a whole economic system. I personally find that attractive as it's based on imagination. The
> fact that people start to identify their own resources and what they have to trade in, the kind
> of weird economic exchanges that take place. I think that's great as it forces people to think
> for themselves rather than accept the shit that's fed to them. And I like that.

Greeners agreed with Transformers that, on its own, a countercultural LETS was an insufficient tool to build a green society. They saw it as one part of a strategy of building alternative structures, to be run in parallel with political action, by which they meant electing Green Party MPs or green-minded members from other parties, and political protest:

> I think it's one of the mechanisms by which capitalism can be subverted, because
> capitalism rests on a system of power relations. I don't think LETS has the same capacity
> for those power relations. And that is what's wrong with capitalism for me: there are two
> things wrong with capitalism: One is the power relations inherent in it. It's not that, you
> know, capitalism is a bad thing, it's that it inevitably has these power relations, and
> capitalism inevitably causes ecological destruction unnecessarily because it has to grow.
> And LETS is more geared to what people needs, far more so than the formal economy is.
> ... (But) I wouldn't think that LETS would be capable of it on its own. I think that its one
> of the mechanisms that gets people in touch with other people in a way that they don't
> need the formal economy, they don't need the banks. They don't need the finance
> system. So the greater extent that you can meet your needs through the LETSystem, the
> less you depend on the formal economy. So, yes, I think it's one of the important
> mechanisms. So I think the analogy I used before about taking the wind out of
> capitalism, is how I would best sum it up.

Others saw LETS as much more 'self-limiting' as Touraine puts it (Touraine 1981), feeling that LETS would not be powerful enough to survive a direct challenge to the mainstream economy. They felt that the money markets and international capitalism were far too strong to be overcome by LETS, and to aim at transforming society was to aim too high:

> I didn't get involved in LETS as I believed in it for a political reason. I don't have a strong feeling that we need to develop an alternative to the money system – I don't think it's possible to be honest. I just don't, I think that the power of the money system is just phenomenal. LETS systems will just jolt people into thinking a little more alternatively, a bit differently.

They felt that their life experience consisted of their inability to change life at the macro-level:

> I am a politically with a small 'p'-motivated person. I believe in the micro rather than the macro. Because in macro terms, living in a society which in my terms, in my life experience of living, the problems of the larger society are so massive that I can't be arsed with getting my head round them, using my energy, on changing something which in reality, in my experience of life, I've not been able to change at all. For most of my working and adult life I've lived under Margaret Thatcher's Conservative government. … So the big issues are totally beyond my control and I got fed up with thumping tables and with Politics with a big 'P'! But I do feel that what influence I have on the small scale, er … is putting my energy into organisations that I give a try to. So my initial thing was to, LETS, this feels good, this is an organisation where there is an attempt to swap skills with respect and equal value, which are things I hold dear to my heart.
>
> So I'd still … put an enormous amount of energy into anything that calls itself a community, because in that commitment I see that as one of the ways in which the world can change, as, you know, in my life experience it's almost impossible to try and change the world in a meaningful way for me by politics, or voting or standing on street corners and shouting. Even my Feminism, has come down to not the Feminism that shrieks the principles from the hilltops but it comes down to how I on a day-to-day basis empower women to gain a sense of personal power and to take control over their own lives. I've gone back to, you know, I'll concentrate on something I can actually do something about! And a community like LETS, which does things, shares doing things, is one of the most hopeful signs that this society might actually be making a (few steps in the right direction).

LETS therefore seems to be a self-limiting movement intent on building an alternative within society. These LETS members saw what they were doing as a response to their powerlessness to make wider changes, after years of Conservative government, and were acting where they felt they could make a difference. However, others were self- limiting as they felt that LETS would have strong opponents who would crack down, although equally they were unclear about exactly how this would happen.

DO THEY DEFINE AN OPPONENT?

Touraine's method suggests that the next question, after identifying the stakes and the extent to which they felt that their programme was a political challenge to the mainstream, is to identify 'the principle of opposition'. The question here is whether or not LETS members felt LETS had an enemy or enemies, and if so, what sort of threat the enemy holds to LETS. Extract 7.1 reproduces an extract from a focus group in which a 'humaniser' and a 'greener' debate who the opposition might be:

Extract 7.1 'Waiting for the clampdown?'

'greener': if there's a critical mass of economic activity of a LETS type in one big area, it's a bit of a public affront to Conservative-type politicians and it gets a lot of publicity across the country, then it's entirely possible that ... Inland Revenue will start saying that transactions which are not social favours have now got to be assessed for taxable value. Small businesses would be targeted as the easiest ones to get at: "Let's look at your books", make things difficult rather than make things easy for them ... Drawing a comparison with the Criminal Justice Act, direct action, hunt saboteurs, anti-road protesters, anti-nuclear protesters. They've all, the more successful they became, it got to a critical mass in the eyes of the Government ... they came to that stage when the Government has got to bring it into line so you've got the Criminal Justice Act. I see one possibility for the future of LETS is that if it is challenging the system ... and cocking a snoop and saying look we've done all this and you can't tax us or whatever, then it is entirely possible that it would be brought in line by legislation etc, to stamp down on a subcultural threat outside the mainstream economy ... If that is our aim in setting up local systems, to develop more and more in the system members who can meet their needs, people who can meet our needs like small businesses etc, outside money, then that can create a bit of a backlash. Initially from Government but equally from sectors of society.

'humaniser': I just think that LETS is craftier, more subtle than that. It's an education programme, sort of thing ... yes? People are actually doing it without realising it, that they are actually building an economy and empowering themselves and taking decisions about their community all the time. The people are doing it don't realise it, and I'm not sure if people up there in power realise it. When it does become, that thing about when it does become big, tax problems and all that does not worry me in the slightest. I find it absolutely *desirable.* ...

Desirable? ... yes! Let's not use the word tax, let's use "community resource-ing" for hospitals, roads, schools, social services ... the community pot. That's in London, and the person who used to be called the Chancellor is called the Resource Keeper ... right? Get away from all these conditioned ideas that we have about tax and that, yes? Throw that out of the window – that's an outdated concept, right? Do we want roads, do we want them upkeeping, do we want a transport infrastructure? Yes? I suspect we do, and I don't understand if the LETS economy, we have an economy at the moment and all we are doing is changing the means by which it is transacted, and a lot more besides, the means of control and the means of choices that, the way that they go about the, the aims that they have, whether they are more sort of green aims. Changing the world economy for the creativity.

We don't talk about economic growth, we talk about happiness growth, creativity growth. yes? The fact that there is all this creativity going on, it won't be anyway undermining anyone, it's just that one changing shape slowly ... It's still the same, and we have the same sort of things, but we've got a lot more good things like public transport instead of armies. Exactly the same thing is going on except that we are all wealthier. We have to get rid of ideas like 'Taxman'. 'Treasurer', 'balancing books', 'profit' etc. To me, it's a huge leap to a different type of concept.

'greener': My worry is that the Income Tax do see a problem with it as they don't see things the same way as you and me, and while the amount of transactions is so small ... they are turning a blind eye to it.

This extract indicates that LETS members here identified as enemies 'Them' – the Government, and in particular the Inland Revenue and Department of Social Security. There is also a reference to the 'middle classes', inspired by a question about LETS leading to a situation of ungovernability, and leading to a backlash from respectable members of society. The Humaniser saw LETS as being quite subtle in not offering any opportunity for a backlash of any sort, and felt that what was happening was an uncontroversial change in consciousness – as what Touraine called a 'self-limiting movement'. Interestingly this Humaniser, a sometimes Core Group member, here is attempting to speak 'on behalf of the movement' (Touraine 1981:152), and has many personal views which are closer to the anarchist perspective.

He thought that worries about enemies were 'unhelpful' 'old thought'. Here, if enemy is too strong a word, a problem in thinking is identified. 'Old thought' is a catch-all for attitudes of mind which in essence are 'hegemonic', 'sensible' ways of thinking (as identified by Gramsci) which fuel the mainstream economy, and which LETS participants are trying to move away from. Old world values, being main-stream, are in all our minds and as part of a personal battle we should be aware of this internal colonisation and fight it. Old world values are those of management, cost-benefit, rationalisation, control, of *'seeing everything in terms of pounds, shillings and pence'*. Ideas Touraine would characterise as those of 'managerial society'. Commenting on the perspective that LETS is value-free, a Humaniser responded:

> I think that's old world politics ... not new world politics. That's the old way of the world, that everything is seen as a currency and as an exchange, simply as, and that LETS is simply another form of capitalist currency ... I think that it is that view, of everything viewed simply in terms of, of another form of currency, is why, why our world is in such a bloody mess! Because actually that is separatist. It promotes separatism. It promotes buying from rather than involving in. It's my life experience that that is what the world is all about. That's what I'd like to change.

Thus for the Humanisers change will come about only if participants constantly monitor their own humanisation, and examine whether they were 'acting with love', with respect and out of 'true community' – in other words, truly building the Heterotopia using processes to be examined in chapter 10. Here Transformers and Heterotopians unite in a Foucaultian or nomadic micro-struggle – a struggle Transformers want to make more widely available.

Other members generalised and identified clearer, more macro-level opponents and the need for metanarratives to explain them – Humanist metanarratives of inter-national finance and anarchist rejections of power/authority. The Humanists saw international finance capital as the opposition. LETS members with more anarchist views took fear of the DSS and Inland Revenue further, to a rejection of institutional authority per se. They admired the self-organisation of LETS. A Heterotopian summed up this position: Commenting on the view of the Humaniser above that LETS earnings should be taxable and affect benefit, she forcefully disagreed:

> One of the things that attracted me to the LETS scheme was that it is not actually connected to the Inland Revenue, or the tax system. That it doesn't have the credibility of institutions. What is important is that people have their own credibility and are dependent on one another in the system. ... If I could I wouldn't pay tax as I don't think

I owe this Government anything, and I think that tax taken off me is money that is stolen off me that I have no choice over. I'm not interested in paying tax in Bobbins or anything else for stuff that I've earned in the LETS scheme, and if I only want to charge one Bobbin for anything I do how are they going to decide what to tax me on? What is a Bobbin worth then, does that mean that a Bobbin is worth a Pound and that you are going to equate a Bobbin with whatever the national currency is? ... I would rather that there were no Bobbins at all in the system. If there's no actual tally – if people aren't keeping a tally of what are they working for and what they are getting, but they are still getting their needs fulfilled by the system – I think that's all to the good. I don't think the Government, or the Inland Revenue, or anyone else, have an automatic right to our time and our labour on pain of armed robbery ... So I'm not really interested at all in credibility with the LETS scheme as regards the Inland Revenue.

One member effectively distilled the question as to whether or not LETS opponents. He felt it was too soon to tell:

(LETS) could be a challenge to the system, or that people in LETS could feel that they are really changing the system, in which case it can either succeed or fail at challenging the system ... it could try to grow within the system as it does at the moment, in which case it either spreads or it dwindles ... The third option could be that it tries to grow within the system while attempting to challenge the system, and it will either change the system or the system will stay the same ... I tend to think that we will be partly trying to challenge the system but partly working within it, so it might have an impact on the system as time goes by, especially if you look in a fifty year period. After 50 years it (LETS) should be less threatening.

In other words members of LETS could think that they are challenging the mainstream to the level of 'breaking the limits of the system' (in which case LETS is a true social movement as defined by Touraine). Alternatively LETS could grow within the system while changing it – a process to be examined in chapter 9. Thirdly there is the option of growing within the system, in which case it grows or it dwindles: irrespective of whether the system is transformed or not. Thus there is no agreement on an enemy. Those who hold LETS to be value-free say LETS has no enemies. Humanisers saw the possibility of everyone going through a process of education when they join LETS, maybe for purely personal reasons. Greens see the DSS and the Inland Revenue clamping down. The anarchists reject outright the right of the state to tax them 'at pain of armed robbery'. All agree on the claim that LETS is effective micro-politics that does not give enemies a chance to clamp down.

CONCLUSION: IS LETS A SOCIAL MOVEMENT?

In rejecting any attempt to discover in LETS a 'premier' social movement, Melucci's less adventurous programme, that of seeing whether LETS was a social movement with system challenging or system breaking potential (Melucci 1989:38), was adopted. If the values LETS members expressed are summarised they represent an ideological or cognitive challenge to capitalist values. If the question of whether LETS members think they are challenging or breaking the mainstream is raised, it seems that the anarchists and the Greeners do. Greeners see LETS as part of a wider strategy for extending local control and empowering people, a programme that humanists subscribe to. More radical Greeners agree with anarchists in seeing LETS as a way of challenging capitalism by changing the power relations from ones of economic domination and control of work, to free choice. The Humanisers again see LETS as a challenge to a flawed money system and wish to humanise work, but softer conceptions of Humanising disagree with anarchists and Greeners on the existence of an enemy, holding with those who hold that LETS is value-free, that all can benefit from LETS. While there are differences of view in LETS, can social movement theory help illuminate whether these differences are problematical or likely to be expected?

Melucci identified three continua for the study of social movements (1989:60–69). Firstly, he asked if the movement is seeking to change structures or cultural codes, and if the structure limits the ability of cultural codes to be changed. In this case is LETS looking to get elites to accept and use LETS, changing the economy in the process, or are changes limited to cultural values that do not diffuse out of LETS (as a 'commune'). Secondly he asked whether the social movement should go for integration with the mainstream, or accept marginalisation as an interesting but overtly oppositional 'other'. Thirdly, he asked whether the social movement prefers to develop an orientation on mass society or on strengthening internal solidarity. Table 7.1 (overleaf) puts the characterisation of LETS into Humanisers, Greeners, anarchists and value-free advocates through Melucci's schema and shows the differences in analysis.

This shows that LETS has a spectrum of opinions, all making social movement claims about money, work, community and sustainability, but with differing conceptions as how to achieve their goals. The task now is to take analysis further into a discussion of the Transformers and Heterotopians differing strategy.

Discussion to date has rested with the claims which LETS members made and their self-analysis, while chapter 4 painted a picture of the Political Opportunity Structure in Manchester. The two have yet to be put together: to go beyond the dualism of structure and agent into an analysis of the agent in struggle, in what Melucci called 'the frontierland'. To take analysis forward, Gledhill's comment (1994:92) should be borne in mind, that: 'the real issue is not deciding what is or is not "real" resistance. It is context which determines the precise structural implications of particular counter hegemonic acts.' Rather than stopping at an analysis that labels LETS as a resistant social movement, analysis should enter the arena in which social movement actors deploy their frames and make their claims to other actors within their Political Opportunity Structure. Whether LETS is perceived to be resistant by elites that they meet, or whether LETS advocates conduct successful frame- transforming operations will be examined in chapters 8 and 9, to ground the discussion. It is to that terrain, into the frontierland, that this discussion now ventures.

Table 7.1 Contested conceptions of social change through LETS

Ideology	Change institutions or cultural codes?	For integration or accept marginalisation?	Resonate with mass society or strengthen internal solidarity?
Value-free	LETS is a value-free tool that has applications in the mainstream. There is nothing particularly radical about local currencies. Businesses can use LETS and it will make them more profitable.	It is important to develop effective development strategies for mainstream use of LETS or it will remain a cosy club of the like-minded.	It is important to separate running a LETS system from how people choose to use it. Publicity should be value-neutral. Community building is not the Core Group's responsibility.
Humanisers	LETS is a value-free tool but it inevitably builds strong communities and empowers people. People should be empowered to develop new ways of valuing themselves and work.	LETS is a great tool to transform the mainstream. It can save the world and create a community built on peace and love. It is important to make sure it does not become a middle-class ghetto.	It is important to make LETS accessible and people will see the benefit of it and join. Once they do LETS will work subtly on them and make them more community-minded, as unless attention is made to quality of relationships, LETS trades do not happen.
Greens	LETS is a tool for empowering communities and strengthening local institutions. The mainstream needs to be decentralised, and LETS does that from below.	LETS cannot achieve its goal on its own: political action must be carried out at the same time, or LETS will remain marginal.	Developing alternative institutions and greening individuals is LETS' main role. The message should not be diluted. If LETS does not 'green' it has no value.
Anarchists	Attempting integration is a waste of time. LETS is a countercultural alternative that takes the wind out of capitalism, or a message back to the mainstream.	LETS is self-management and self-government. It undermines the mainstream. Mainstream uses of LETS take power away from communities and are not welcome.	It is important to develop more opportunities to live outside the mainstream. Want to see the use of Bobbins for 'keeping score' withering away as soon as possible.

CHAPTER 8

Transformation:
LETS and Economic Development

LETS: the extraordinary solution to ordinary money.

(LETSolutions leaflet)

Where there is a need, there is a need to meet it.

(LETS create caring communities' leaflet)

This chapter and chapter 9 focus on the capacity of social movement organisations arising from LETS as a social movement sector to widen usage of LETS out of its primary constitutive social networks through persuading institutional actors, local elites, and businesses of the benefits of LETS, beyond those claimed as a social movement. This is the strategy of transformation. Transformation will be analysed firstly through the RMT approach which illuminates the capacity of the Transformers to achieve their goals by mobilising the resources that LETS members themselves have (time, knowledge, money, arguments) and new resources that they access by acquiring external 'conscience supporters' (McCarthy and Zald 1977). The second strand of an analysis of transformation is inspired by the Political Process Model (Tilly 1989), which suggests an examination of how LETS negotiates its way through the political opportunity structure it encounters (McCarthy and Zald 1977; Tilly 1977). This will be examined, thirdly, by attention to the frames that LETS activists develop orientated on elites and other groups not already involved with LETS in an effort to get them to participate.

LEDA: MOBILISING INTERNAL RESOURCES

Following the RMT approach, the first task is to examine the resources that the social movement organisations (SMOs) aiming to proactively widen participation in LETS in Manchester can call upon; firstly, the resources of time, money, cognitive skills and social standing, and secondly, the effectiveness of their organisational capabilities. Can they organise themselves effectively such that elites are impressed by their capabilities, regard them as serious actors on the local scene, and consequently are more likely to be persuaded by their arguments. In other words, we focus on the internal characteristics, capabilities and organisational strengths of LETS schemes and their associated organisations in Manchester, not the environment external to them.

As one of the world largest LETS systems Manchester LETS should have had a wealth of resources to call upon to develop use of LETS more widely in the form of member's offers accessible through the directory and mobilised through payment for Bobbins. They had social status and organisational skills: in his survey of Manchester LETS Williams (1995f) found that approximately 20% of the 109 Manchester LETS members who responded to his survey had post-graduate qualifications and 46% were graduates. Members had long experience of working with political parties, churches and voluntary organisations, while others were community development workers. Williams found that 21% of members lived in a household with a gross income of over £20,000 a year (providing, it could be expected, money). He found that 43% of his respondents were unemployed, and a further 13% self-employed – both, it would be expected, could provide time. This was a fairly resource-rich network. Consequently, they were able, quite quickly, to secure new resources in the form of £10,000 from Manchester City Council.

However, having or acquiring resources is one thing: having the capability to deploy them effectively is another. LEDA was set up as a separate development arm for Manchester LETS as Core Group members were interested primarily in ensuring that Manchester LETS was professionally and smoothly managed rather than in looking outwards or in building links with elites. LEDA only had five members, one of which did work pretty much full time on LETS development, while another two put in a significant commitment. But LEDA was formed because while most members of Manchester LETS were, from their own resources, willing and able to create a vibrant LETS system with a quite profes-sional and well-oiled administration; it was neither willing *nor* able to create a development arm. So while extra resources were made available by outsiders, they were not utilised by the 550-odd ordinary LETS members who turned out to have more Heterotopian sympathies.

LEDA's directors were at a loss to say why they failed to mobilise more of the commitment of their fellow members for development work. The explanation can in part be found through Focus Group discussions, which identified the Heterotopian perspective – which did not prioritise external development. However, while Heterotopians could have participated had they been inter-ested, the barriers to participation identified by Mansbridge (1980) were also present within Manchester LETS. While Williams found that many members of Manchester LETS were well educated, rather than facilitating participation, LEDA unwittingly set up organisational barriers to participation in development activities. For many months LEDA did not publicise the time of its meetings, or circulate or publish the minutes it produced. Consequently, barriers and boundary skirmishes were observable during the research period between the Core Group and LEDA as to what was Core Group responsibility, and what should be the responsibility of LEDA. LEDA suggested initiatives to Manchester LETS that the Core Group did not support. LEDA introduced items for discussion at Core Group meetings, and there was confusion as to why the discussion was taking place. All these actions, coupled with LEDA's control over the local authority grant and lack of clarity about what the grant was for, created what Mansbridge (1980:43–70) calls 'psychic costs' of participation, which manifested themselves in a feeling of (at best) genial confusion, and at worst outright mistrust of the relation between the core group and LEDA.

Consequently, one Heterotopian claimed that LEDA 'are the group of people that run Manchester LETS'.

However, while ordinary members were unclear as to how to get involved with LEDA, rank-and-file members did not stress institutional barriers to their participation, beyond a perception that LEDA was a 'clique' like the Core Group. In part as a process of encouraging participation both in Manchester LETS and in development initiatives, and in part to overcome psychic and institutional barriers, the Core Group ran a 'Members' Forum' to encourage participation. However, this did not result in further participation in LEDA, demonstrating rather that only four of the system's 550-odd members wished to devote time to development work – the extreme Transformers. Some did not think development work useful (the anarchists) whilst Humanisers and Greeners welcomed the activities of LEDA but did not wish to get involved themselves. Manchester LETS, then, did not prioritise transformation.

THROUGH THE POLITICAL OPPORTUNITY STRUCTURE

The next task is to move from the RMT paradigm to an analysis of LEDA and LETSGo's interaction with their political opportunity structure, using insights from the 'Political Process' model (Tilly 1989). Here, analysis will focus on the effectiveness with which LEDA and LETSGo negotiated their way through their POS, developed an *action repertoire* that took advantage of opportunities that presented themselves, and persuaded other organisations (in particular, the local state) that the objectives of LETS and the objectives of the organisations with which they interacted, coincided. The tables overleaf summarise the key features of these two action repertoires.

Resources did need to be mobilised for the further development of LETS. Most LETS members were uninterested in development work, and those who were could not do it on their own. For example, when Victoria Baths, a beautiful nineteenth-century bathhouse, closed, one LEDA member who was also a member of the protest group 'Friends of Victoria Baths' had the idea of getting Manchester LETS members to donate 50 Bobbins each to help to pay for renovation, but he did not have time to follow the idea up. Another LEDA member had the idea of developing a café, managed workspace and LETS office, and was offered a building by Moss Side and Hulme development Trust – but at a market rate. She held a meeting with interested parties whom she had met through the 'Common Purpose' programme, who were all supportive, but again no-one could be found to run with the project and draw up a feasibility plan. So to solve these internal resource constraints, new allies with resources needed to be acquired.

The similar Action Repertoires LETSGo and LEDA adopted can be summarised into two areas of interaction. LETSGo articulated primarily on *business development,* while LEDA focused on developing new LETS, mainly in areas where it could act as a policy for *local economic development.* These case studies can be examined in more detail for an analysis of how effective the action repertoires of LEDA and LETSGo turned out to be within this specific Political Opportunity Structure.

Table 8.1 LEDA initiatives in Manchester, 1995

LEDA Initiatives	Description
New systems Start-up talks	Helping set up new systems in Wigan, Trafford, Bury, Stockport, Leigh.
Supporting existing systems	Helping LETS systems experiencing difficulties solve their problems or to run their own development initiatives.
Local neighbourhood contacts	Developing a network of local contacts for Manchester LETS who will carry out developmental work in their localities, perhaps eventually becoming local core groups.
Small business network	Running initiatives designed to promote business uses of LETS, including a business seminar.
Local agenda 21	Participation in Manchester's Local Agenda 21 process.
Central office development	Discussing the development of a central office for Manchester LETS, perhaps including a café, meeting and exhibition space and managed workspace.
Recruiting community organisations	Encouraging community and voluntary organisations to use LETS, especially North West Mind, a black-led small business organisation, and Chorlton Church.
Forum	Running a Members' Forum to promote participation in Manchester LETS.
Software development	Developing new accounting software.
Membership recruitment	Producing display materials and success stories to encourage participation and for the press.

Table 8.2 LETSGo development initiatives in Manchester, 1995

LETSGo Initiative	Description
Business development	Developing materials to show that large scale use of LETS by businesses is possible.
'Contribution to community'	Development of demonstration project showing the viability of CtC.
Global forum '95	Meeting delegates at a global environmental conference and explaining the benefits of LETS.
Work for change	Developing managed workspace using LETS.
Ethnic minority business	Working with a black-led small business network.
Inner city	Helping set up Hattersley LETS.

In this chapter we investigate LEDA and LETSGo's work with businesses, and their engagement with environmental initiatives in Manchester such as Local Agenda 21 and Global Forum. In the next chapter we examine work in the inner city.

RECRUITING BUSINESSES TO LETS

It is LETSGo that provides the most evidence for the applicability of LETS within the business community. As we saw in chapter 5, LETSGo aimed to build on Manchester LETS' name recognition and the greater level of environmental awareness that it was hoped would have been generated from press coverage of Global Forum to recruit a few key businesses into LETS. These 'early adapters' subscriptions would then fund a promotional campaign that would kick off a 'Mexican wave' or pyramid of business membership, which would then pass resources through to the voluntary sector through 'Contribution to Community' process. The strategy is similar to that of organisations like Amway – essentially pyramid selling. Linton summed up the business strategy thus:

> We've got to get it moving. This involves drawing in the major corporate players – I have nothing against signing up organisations such as Safeways or Sainsburys. Its characteristic to identify corporations as evil – a corporation is necessarily committed to following the profit motive – which generally means selling schlock to people who don't seem to know better.
> But if you can make a supermarket chain realise that their very viability depends on their participation in the local currency, this will force them to spend the money locally. This means local products and support for local community agricultural services will flourish. If these supermarket chains do not use the local currency, eventually they won't be using any currency at all.

> We can't simply blame the corporations for being the way they are – we have to change the context, and that means embedding them in an economy that is sustainable. These corporations have no interest in an unsustainable economy.
>
> (Birch 1995)

However, organisational and resource limitations meant that large-scale effort into the recruitment of large numbers of businesses did not materialise. The LETSGo approach was to for a six-month campaign that would hand a functioning Greater Manchester LETS Registry and a multiplicity of affiliated LETS systems over to locals, with upwards of 20,000 accounts and over 100 businesses. However, little groundwork was done before the project kicked off, materials were not ready, there was (as yet) no LETS system or Registry to recruit businesses to. Manchester LETS, finding the strategy unconvincing, declined to become a member of the Greater Manchester Registry and preferred to run its own accounts. The team spent its first few weeks running design programmes to see if software could handle 20,000 accounts, and setting up links with the Internet. Thus by three months into the programme the hoped-for business accounts had not materialised, which would have provided a revenue stream to pay participants for their work and develop initiatives. Without the hoped for business membership, LETSGo was under-capitalised for continuing development.

Secondly, the strategy seemed over optimistic and, based on what looked like pyramid selling, ethically suspect. LETSGo took place at the beginning of the late 1990s 'dot-com' bubble where some entrepreneurs made and lost sums of money unconnected with their business plan as markets suffered from one of their periodic bouts of 'irrational exuberance'. Like their fellow dot-com entrepreneurs, LETSGo expected to make big money, fast, and this understandably alienated those who joined LETS as they saw an alternative to the money economy (although, admittedly, no one was forcing them to take part in anything they were uncomfortable with). As Linton put it:

> People thought it was a scam as scams exist. 95% of it was fear of failure. (Some people were) always ac/dc about it. (Others) thought it was great, then all of a sudden thought it was immoral. They got scared. They had theories about money, business, exploitation, multinationals, some of it was just trepidation, some fears were real and have got to be addressed – and some were just crock – narrow perceptions.

Thirdly, the environment was not as conducive as was thought. Manchester LETS did not get involved: rather, many members were actively hostile to something that they saw as unethical, and parachuted in. Global Forum was not as high profile as had been thought. Seen as the follow-on of the Rio Earth Summit, Global Forum '94 was billed as an major international festival that would attract 200,000 visitors and delegates from all over the world. However, with a lead in time of only nine months, it needed £7 million which was expected to be raised entirely from commercial sponsorship. There were initially no environmental groups on the board and little communication with environmental NGOs. Business participation failed to deliver the hoped-for sponsorship, and the event was hastily reconfigured to an international academic symposium (Randall 1995). It became known locally as 'Global Farce'.

LETSGo consequently had to fall back on its own recourses, which after a few months were about five or six hardcore activists – two of which spent most of their time developing their new dot-com businesses. Resource constraints then meant that their promotional materials were not of high enough quality. Of 200 businesses contacted by telephone, LETSGo sent details about LETS to 100, but had formally visited only two businesses before their finances ran out. One, a theatre poster design company, agreed to join to help develop the system even though they did not do much business in Manchester, and who therefore did not see how they could use LETS in practice. They wanted to help provide a critical mass of businesses with whom they then might be able to trade. They did attract some businesses, including some members of Manchester LETS. In November 1994 the Greater Manchester LETS registry had 150 members, including a cycle shop, a vegetarian café, a club, an advertising agency, an accountant, a computer training company and a telemarketing agency. But the hopes for large scale business usage of LETS had yet to be demonstrated, and that they failed to make such a demonstration real.

LEDA's involvement in recruiting businesses to LETS was less overt than LETSGo's, beyond a conference for businesses about LETS held in 1994 covering marketing and promotion, cash flow and business planning, and use of computers in LETS. However, the seminar attracted few businesses and did not lead to an influx of business participation in LETS. This seminar apart, Manchester LETS did not make any determined attempts to recruit businesses: rather Manchester LETS stressed the number of business services available in LETS rather than the number of business memberships, and attempted to get ordinary members to provide business services to other members. As Humanisers they wanted to create micro-businesses that promote alternative lifestyles, and blur the difference between businesses and communities.

Thus the evidence from Manchester was that businesses did not flock to join. Those that did used LETS for only a minor part of their business, or they joined for political rather than for business reasons. Of the eight businesses identifiable from their business names in Manchester LETS April 1995 Directory, three (a cafe, a junk shop and a beauty clinic) joined LETS as their business had been in trouble in an effort to get more customers, but LETS had not made the difference to their eventual business failure. Of the five businesses that survived, one, a car hire firm, left the scheme as, based on the other side of the metropolis in Rochdale, it had no trade. The proprietor joined as he wanted to get away from "this money system that means we cut each other up and cheat and rip each other off to get ahead." The proprietor also ran a small grocers, and offered a 10% discount for Bobbins, which he quickly stopped when he found members of LETS demanding 50% discounts, and when he found that he could not spend his credits. Worse, he argued that competition with supermarkets was so tight that the 10% discount ate into his already meagre drawings. He felt that members of LETS who asked him to join but were 'well meaning people who do not understand the reality of running a business.' He argued 'I feel bitter about the people who led me up the garden path and then let me get on with it. They didn't support me at all. They wanted be to join their system and then they dropped me. It's a good job I didn't listen to them. If I had, I'd be bankrupt.' He did not renew his membership.

Other businesses did have happier stories: a firm of solicitors, a cycle shop, a recycling company, and a print company formed to print a book. However, these businesses joined for political reasons, out of sympathy with the values of LETS. The firm of solicitors was run by one of the founder members of Manchester LETS who was also a Green Party member. The print company was formed to print a book written by a core group member, and the recycling company joined 'as it is something that we want to support which is basically, co-operation'. The cycle company joined for political reasons after reading about LETS in the press, but they also recognised that many of the members of Manchester LETS, as good greens, would be keen cyclists.

These four of the eight businesses in Manchester LETS traded fairly success-fully, but at such low levels that it is impossible to see LETS as forming anything other than a minor part of their business activities. Certainly the activist got his novel printed when he could not find a mainstream business to do it for him. However, the cycle shop reported that trade in Bobbins was so low key that it made no appreciable difference to their turnover. The shop's turnover was £2,000 a week, while its Bobbin turnover in three years was only 140 Bobbins, which was accounted for in a 10% discount for parts or bicycles, and 100% labour payable in Bobbins. While he felt that many of his customers in LETS would have come to him anyway, he did perceive LETS to be broadening his clientele to other areas of the city. He felt, however, that even a large system of 550 members was too small a client base to make much of a difference to his business.

The recycling company felt that their participation in LETS for the first couple of years was part of their commitment to the community that was actually costing them Sterling – they would collect recycled material, costing time, fuel, wear and tear payable in Sterling – for less spendable Bobbins. While the business bene-fited from paying people to deliver promotional leaflets for Bobbins, they felt they were subsidizing LETS for political reasons. However, when they needed to get a new van, but did not have the knowledge or time to shop around for the best deal, they employed a mechanically minded LETS member to act as a 'van buyer' on their behalf whose knowledge and time got them a serviceable second hand van at a fraction of the price they were thinking of having to pay. Saving money therefore made LETS serious for the business. LETS played a minor part in the business of the solicitors (10% reduction in fees for Bobbins). None of the busi-nesses in Manchester LETS used the system for anything but a minor part of their business

Analysis of the opportunity structure within which businesses must operate, the micro-politics of business, demonstrates that there are identifiable reasons why businesses did not rush to join and those that did not trade actively. Thus it seems that LETS is not appropriate for most businesses, and without major frame transformation, which would rob it of its social movement nature, never could be. If we examine the arguments that LETS activists framed towards business, we can see how the frames and the political opportunity structure collide, and how frames did not go through enough processes of transformation. If we analyse the discourse aimed at business (see Table 8.3 below) we see a very different framing when compared with that aimed at ordinary members. Arguments about the nature of money, work, community and sustainability are ignored in favour of a discourse of profitability, sales and cashflow. When we compare these discourses with those advanced by transformers, we see that what was attempted was at least frame alignment, if not outright transformation. However, it was not one that resonated.

Table 8.3 Strategies for business to maximise the benefits of using the gmLETSystem

---

- Use gm£ to aid the sale of slow moving stock.
- Sell stock that is "for sale" quicker with a price in gm£.
- Accept gm£'s only in your quiet periods for selected stock.
- Clinch your sale with uncertain customers by promoting the benefits of reduced sterling price and interest free credit.
- Take gm£'s during special promotional events.
- Accept gm£s only on selling larger quantities or obtaining bigger contracts.
- If looking for new suppliers, consider using those who accept gm£'s to ease your cash flow.
- Introduce your suppliers to the benefits of using gm£.
- Advertise cheaply in the *gmLETSystem* directory paying with gm£ to attract new customers.
- Place ads in other advertising channels that accept gm£.
- Take part of your personal drawings in gm£ to be spent by yourself and your family on everyday items.
- If you wish to make a charitable donation, consider giving gm£'s. When your donation is spent the gm£'s can only circulate within the systems and may well come back to you.
- Give your staff gm£'s as a sales incentive rather than giving restrictive gift vouchers.
- Limit your sales in gm£s to a certain amount of each day or month.
- Reduce the cost and risk of giving credit to your customers by accepting gm£ for a percentage of the price. Your customers can pay the gm£'s immediately.
- Reduce the risk of involved in giving credit to new customers with uncertain credit worthiness by asking them to pay part of the price immediately in gm£'s. You get paid the gm£'s, and by easing your potential customers cash flow you make full payment much more likely.
- If you have current credit with your suppliers, ask for a cash discount and offer immediate payment in gm£'s.
- If you have a debtor who you feel cannot get the cash mention the *gmLETSystem* and tell them they could pay part of the debt in gm£'s. This could help get you and them out of a potential sticky situation.
- Spend gm£'s on extras that are not in your current budget to improve your business without disrupting your cashflow.

Source: gmLETS promotional leaflet.

There are a number or reasons for this lack of resonance. First, LETS was framed as improving cash flow, assuming that a business was able to receive payment in credits for its goods. This would not be a problem. Obviously, if people can pay for groceries in unlimited LETS credits rather than limited Sterling, they will. The problem comes when a business attempts to spend them. It would need to buy new stock and pay wages or drawings in local money, which assumes that its suppliers are in the network and that the network is robust enough for wages to be spent. This is obviously not the case while LETS networks are so small. Consequently those businesses that do use LETS only make small discounts to the labour element of their pricing. If the LETS network was bigger, then small businesses trading significantly in Manchester might find the system useful, and these were the sort of businesses LETSGo planned to target before its resources ran out. But while local money could be used for business services and stock, for businesses trading almost entirely locally, Curran and Blackburn (1994) found that very few businesses did trade so locally. The answer would be to develop LETS covering wider areas, perhaps at the scale of a region or nationally, like the Swiss Wir system – but this might be a scale too large for those who, for environmental reasons value the local (North 2005). Even then, widespread payment of wages in local currency could come up against both the Truck Acts which outlawed the scurrilous nineteenth-century practice of employers paying their workers in credits only redeemable at the company store for inflated prices, and benefit regulations whereby part-time workers would lose Sterling (fully spendable everywhere) for credits of limited exchange value (see Barnes, North and Walker 1996; North 1996). Lang (1994:111) reports the Trades Union Congress's attitude to LETS as being 'concerned at paying credits which could not be spent anywhere in the country and they would look carefully if the systems discouraged opportunities to bargain collectively'. An unscrupulous employer paying those desperate for work in credits would have an unfair advantage over ethical employers providing full-time work with full pay and conditions: a point recognised by Exmouth Chamber of Trade and Commerce (Correspondence, 1992):

> The LETS proposal, on the face of it, appears to be encouraging the very type of trading that undermines the businesses of our members. Carried to its ultimate conclusion, non-commercial trading of this type can seriously damage (or even cause collapse of) a local economy and bring about the failure of legitimate businesses. Ad-hoc jobbing of the type envisaged is generally carried out by individuals who do not carry business overheads (such as provision of premises with appropriate insurances, rents and business rates), and very often the on-costs required of a bona-fide trader to comply with their requirements for health and safety, fire regulations, food hygiene laws, public liability insurances etc, are ignored. In consequence the consumer is put at risk, and the legitimate business is unable to compete economically which can result in the laying-off of employees and a general increase in unemployment.

Why then should business people involve themselves in something framed as a way of making their businesses more profitable – if that does not happen? LETS activists attempted only limited frame extension into the business community, maintaining their rhetoric about LETS as a new form of economy, about new relations of work, and about building community. They did not transform their frames but attempted to persuade business to support their vision of an alternative world, and their critique of business ethics. Consequently their frames underwent only limited extension, and were perceived as what one business person called unconvincing attempts by ecologists with MBAs to talk business. Linton agreed, on reflection, that it would have been more appropriate to remove the rhetoric of community from LETSGo's publicity material.

> I'd agree with that but the leaflet was at the stage that we'd got it to. But why did we call it originally the Green Dollar? We got a lot of flak about that. I think it's a good way to rehabilitate the green consciousness. And associations we attach to it (widen the appeal). I want to go with both but I don't want to impede – although I'd agree that it was probably an impediment. But the whole damn thing was an impediment. People who said they would did not deliver (in more situations than just this leaflet).

If LETS does not resonate with mainstream business values, could it resonate more with people seeking alternative livelihoods through self employment, those for whom paid work is not attractive? LETS could be used to develop networks of small or micro-businesses like California's 'Briarpatch', a network of people with alternative values who support each other in their businesses. LETS could be used to pilot a new small business, as members of Manchester LETS have done. LETS may appeal to small business people who value independence – to 'be your own boss' – but who then find that they are often the 'losers' in an increasingly competitive economy. Rather than finding themselves independent they are constrained by their bank manager's control over cash flow, floating close to their overdraft limit. Entrepreneurs in this situation might be attracted to claims LETS advocates make about money and interest, and resonate with their defacto feelings of serfdom or self exploitation (Scase and Goffee 1982:12). Other small businesses may be run by reluctant entrepreneurs denied access to full-time employment, working long hours for little reward. The reluctant entrepreneur, like the poor, might be unwilling to chance the unknown in LETS (Tilly 1978:133).

If Melucci is right then LETS will be able to self-produce cultural codes about how life should be organised. If these codes translate into demand for products that are economic using local currency (even if uneconomic using Sterling) then LETS could make certain livelihoods viable that the mainstream economy would occlude. Examples might be ethically produced craft items, locally produced food. Here LETS operates as a tool for particular types of business – as a social movement of ecological small entrepreneurs attempting to build alternative models of employment. Those businesses that did participate in Manchester LETS between 1995 and 2001 quite happily, if at low levels included a cycling shop situated in the heart of south Manchester, where LETS membership was concentrated. Membership of Manchester LETS was good PR, and by limiting participation to 50% of labour, the cycle shop made sure that it did not build up an unspendable credit balance. Most of the credits earned were used by the proprietor as personal drawings. Unicorn grocery was a food co-operative that was established by a number of LETS members, who used LETS to pay for the refurbishment of their premises, paying off the resulting debit over time by allowing people to buy food for 50% bobbins on certain days. In this sense they used LETS as deli-dollars did (see Chapter One). Another business frequented by LETS members was Misty's café, which again used LETS as PR and restricted its commitment to spendable limits. For some businesses, local currencies can work. Ithaca shows that this can be quite a significant number of post-materialist, lifestyle businesses located in places with a large countercultural clientele that are likely to look on participation in the network as a commitment to the cause, not as a way of saving money (then again, saving money is a bonus!).

But to frame LETS as a tool that enhances business profitability would be inappropriate. In Manchester, even some sympathetic businesses found it hard to participate and by 2001 had dropped out or limited their participation. For example, Limited Resourses supported LETS for conscience reasons, as 'something they wanted to support', but found:

> We were doing recycling for bobbins and I think we found that it was quite ... it wasn't particularly useful for us because we were having difficult spending the bobbins we were having, and it was an interruption, to what we did for a living, to collect the recycling, but also for the sort of issues ... that we were realising anyway, as we got busier with unwashed empty bottles with foodstuffs was becoming a problem. Initially it wasn't a problem because we had a lot more time and a lot less transactions, but as it got busier, it did become a problem. And then, obviously, the time spent doing the recycling afterwards, so, ultimately, we decided that its better to spend our time generating income than spend our time doing people's recycling for bobbins that we could not spend.
>
> (Limited Resources ex-director, 2001)

Other designs of local currency might also be more appropriate for businesses. While the LETS design is, on the evidence in Manchester inappropriate for business development, 'Ithaca Hours' – New York State – attracted over three hundred businesses. Obvious differences include the scarcity of Ithaca Hours, and that the ethos of 'hours' fits more smoothly with people's understanding of money (through use of a banknote; with a high quality design, watermarking, serial number to inspire confidence, to be put in and out of pockets and tills like any other without central accounting, and more easily spendable). Other local currency designs may resonate with more conservative strategies of promoting local town pride or with strategies that see the community as stakeholders. Some large firms run credit unions, and LEDA see the possibility of developing LETS as a community-building mechanism alongside this.

LOCAL AGENDA 21

If business seemed to be a local field whose local rules did not seem appropriate to LETS, other local fields of knowledge might produce frames that LETS resonates with: frames about 'stakeholding' and 'sustainability'. The field where these frames were deployed by other actors, who might well prove to be conscience supporters of LETS, was Manchester's Local Agenda 21 process.

After the 1992 Rio Earth Summit, governments signed up to the 'Local Agenda 21' process whereby they committed themselves to consult their citizens and to draw up a plan to implement sustainable development for their countries (United Nations 1992). Local Agenda 21 emphasised the role of community organisations like LETS in working with other stakeholders to develop an agreed vision of sustainability. It gave LETS a right of consultation enshrined in an international treaty.

Local Agenda 21, then, provides an outwardly favourable local Political Opportunity Structure. Manchester City Council convened a 'Local Agenda 21 Forum', chaired by Arnold Spencer (as a result of elections within the forum) and managed by a partnership including NGOs, councillors, the Green Party and the Chamber of Commerce. Manchester City Council's 'Sustainability Team' particularly wanted participation from LETS. They wished to explore the development of alternative lifestyles and community-organised economic projects to give alternatives to full-time employment, and they wished to develop a way of paying people to recycle with 'recycling credits'. While the Forum met bi-monthly, with an open attendance, only one LETS member participated as a Green Party member, another as a youth worker, and another as a member of the Ba'hai faith. They did not have an institutional connection with Manchester LETS. LETSGo were completely uninvolved. The Green Party LETS member wrote a leaflet calling on LETS members to participate in LA21, which he called 'Local Agenda 21: Power to the People':

> Many people will remember the 1992 Earth Summit – it was called 'the last chance to save the planet.' 178 countries and 116 presidents and prime ministers went to Rio. It was the ultimate *top-down* event. Yet it also agreed initiatives that work from the *bottom up*: like Local Agenda 21.
> Because the Earth Summit saw politicians at the top water everything down some green and community activists have little interest in, or oppose, anything it produced. But public participation in local decision-making has long been a fundamental goal of the green movement. I believe activists owe it to the community to ensure that Local Agenda 21 produces a truly inclusive, comprehensive vision of a sustainable Manchester.
> Local Agenda 21 needn't end in 1996. In Latin America they're building it into their reorganisation of local government. This shows us that Local Agenda 21 can become a permanent way of giving power to the people to shape the future of the community they live in.
>
> (Eckbury 1995)

Non-participation by the majority of members of LETS was in part a fear that Local Agenda 21 was what theorist of participation Arnstein called 'therapy' – not real participation, setting agendas, controlling resources, making decision, but a veneer of irrelevant participation while the real decisions when on elsewhere. Some Manchester LETS members claimed to have 'a sensible distrust of local authority-organised talking shops', while another said 'not talking sustainability but living sustainably – that's more important' – and by living sustainably he meant developing LETS. A Transformer said that LETS was more effective than the Local Agenda 21 process at greening business: 'Getting businesses involved (in LETS) widens the debate, and pulls them into sustainable lifestyles. I'm not against what others are doing (participating in Local Agenda 21) but we need to widen the movement'. Others wanted to make sure that LA 21 was not just a talking shop. A third was sceptical about going to LA21 meetings and 'playing the big chief, the hero, getting out the red carpet. It does things to you psychologically that I don't feel comfortable about and I don't want to get involved with that. I don't want to spend my time going to meetings that spend hours debating about what bank account do you use or what do you do about the revolutionary communist party when they do their thing.' He argued 'that the thing to do is develop LETS above its current stalling at 550 members. You don't need to go to those meetings to do that and you will be deflected from the job of building a robust LETS. Its also too far away from Manchester LETS' original ethos of self sufficiency'.

LEDA did participate in the Local Agenda 21 'Economy and Work' planning group which had the remit of examining what sustainable work and livelihood would look like within the overall plan. However, the 'Economy and Work' group met once during the research period, and only was attended four people (including myself!). There was no business representation initially, and the university representative did not have time to convene the group. Eventually, a representative of the Chamber of Commerce and Initiative agreed to take over the chair, but he again was unable to convene a meeting. By the spring of 1996, when the first draft of the agreed plan should have been ready for consultation, business had been entirely absent from the process, and as a result, little work on economic issues had been done – and LETS similarly was not on the agenda.

Here LETS had been excluded from actively influencing Local Agenda 21 by the lack of participation of business. While Manchester City Council wished LETS to participate, opportunities were limited as others were not at the table and the need for an inclusive process meant progress was not forthcoming. As a result, Manchester's Local Agenda 21 process did appear to be a talking shop, and the Political Opportunity Structure did not facilitate the development of LETS through these channels. This perhaps vindicates LETS members' initial scepticism of the process. However, Manchester LETS also benefited financially from the Local Agenda 21 process – through a grant for telephone and computer equipment to cope with the expected flood of interest in LETS from inclusion of an advert for LETS in *Manchester Planet* – the local authority newsletter about Local Agenda 21 – (a flood which never came).

Had business come on board, to the extent that the 'Economy and Work' group could have done its work, would allies identified through the Local Agenda 21 process have contributed to widening the use of LETS outside the heterotopian 'cosy club'? Here is not the place to evaluate Manchester's Local Agenda 21 process, but to comment that the Local Agenda 21 process did not influence Manchester's essentially boosterist economic development policy. For Heterotopians, interested in living as sustainably as possible in the here and now through participation in LETS; then Local Agenda 21 was a therapeutic sideshow. Manchester Green Party recognised this, and while they participated in Local Agenda 21 they commented '(t)he council is pursuing an outmoded concept of economic growth which guarantees ecological degradation, not least from transport; instead of adopting a more modern concept of economic development geared towards sustainability' (Greenwood 1995). Spencer was marginalised from his position as chair of planning, commenting: 'We have to make people aware, not only the public and business, but even within the council. Some environmental aims are perceived to be at odds with economic regeneration. We need to show that greening the city is not in conflict with creating jobs.' (Greenwood 1995.)

In such an environment, LETS was excluded from active participation in a process that itself was excluded from the main strategic thinking on economic development and the future of Manchester. Deputy chair Richard Leese (who eventually succeeded leader Graham Stringer) made this crystal clear: worried that Local Agenda 21 participants felt they might be making policy, he said 'Proposals are valuable but they don't determine policy in any way, shape or form' and that addressing issues of the 'quality of life for the unemployed is a waste of time – the issue is to get them into work'. Taking a traditional social-democratic position, Leese saw LETS as a critique, an alternative vision, a statement of how things should be that he didn't agree with. LETS seems inadequate to social democrats who have more faith in state level solutions, and to whom LETS seems an inadequate self help market solution. LETS seems to people like Leese to envisage a world of small-scale craftspeople doing jobs and providing work for each other for local currency. It is a world of market flexibility and individual work on an informal basis. LETS was therefore seen as a green social movement with a critique of the dominant script in Manchester, and not as a viable policy innovation – in the specific local Political Opportunity Structure of Manchester, at least.

Participation in Local Agenda 21 would be of value to Transformers if their aim was to help frame future debate and raise awareness of LETS, and this is what LEDA hoped participants in Local Agenda 21 who were also members of LETS would do. Here, the local Political Opportunity Structure allowed members of LETS to create and deploy frames and cultural codes, but non-participation from business in the specific forum, and lack of interest from Heterotopians in any level of participation limited the resonance of LETS.

Participation from businesses, then, was limited. While LETS was invited into the Local Agenda 21 process, it was wary of involvement in something seen as therapeutic. Was more success achieved when transformers began to work with those attempting to address questions of poverty and exclusion in the inner city?

CHAPTER 9

LETS and the Inner City

The left were seen as belittling voluntary activity, seeing it as a poor alternative to direct state provision, and my party at times forgot its own roots in self-help, friendly societies, co-operatives and voluntary organisations, and the insights of Robert Owen and William Morris.

(Tony Blair MP, speech to National Council for Voluntary Organisations (NCVO), January 1999)

Most people, well-to-do or not, believe that, even when a man is doing work which appears to be useless, he is earning his livelihood from it – he is 'employed', as the phrase goes, and most of the well-to-do cheer on the happy worker with congratulations and praises, if he is 'industrious' enough …. in the sacred cause of labour. In short, it has become an article of creed and modern morality that all labour is good of itself – a convenient belief to those who live on the labour of others. But as to those on whom they live, I recommend them not to take it on trust, but to look at the matter a little deeper.

(William Morris, *Useful work verses useless toil*, 1884 (1993))

LETSGo and LEDA attempted unsuccessfully to proselytise LETS amongst businesses. In the field of inner city regeneration, other groups and organisations did want to explore LETS and liked what they heard – in other words frames resonated. Specifically, people on Hattersley set up their own short-lived LETS System. In Bury, Old Trafford and Leigh (all districts within Greater Manchester), LEDA was asked to give a presentation about LETS. LETS was also seen as a possible part of particular projects: in particular LEDA wanted to develop a LETS Office/cafe/managed workspace, looked at using local money for the renovation of a leisure centre, and as part of Hulme's City Challenge. Finally, an African Caribbean-led business support agency, The High Place Syndicate, sought to develop a LETS-like system of 'syndicate dollars'. These were all discussions, the implementation of which were, for the reasons discussed in the previous chapter, limited by resource constraints. We will use a case study of developing LETS in inner city areas to investigate the opportunities and constraints presented by the political opportunity structure in Manchester.

FIRST STEPS IN THE INNER CITY: HATTERSLEY

In Hattersley the extent to which LETS resonated as a policy for inner city regeneration could be observed. It will be recalled that Hattersley LETS was set up by members of Manchester LETS who wanted something more local, and involving people more like 'them'. They felt that Manchester LETS was a middle class, ecological network with which they had little in common, and, centred as it was in south Manchester, was too far away from their estate. Plans to set up a Hattersley LETS initially met with the approval of the estate's community development worker, who had learned about LETS from a television programme, and who had thought it appropriate for Hattersley. However, after some discussion it was decided that a LETS focussed on the estate alone might be too small a network, and, like Manchester LETS, a decision was taken to open membership to anyone in the local borough of Tameside: and especially to residents of the local town of Glossop. This had problems for resourse mobilisation. Plans for LETS to go borough-wide meant that the worker was no longer permitted to spend her time on a programme that 'does not benefit Hattersley directly' (as it was seen), and after the launch her organisational support was removed. At that time, the Community Centre was under pressure to do more to meet the needs of women and children, and the development worker's skills were seen as more appropriately used on other projects.

The result was that publicity material was of poor quality, the trading day with which it was hoped to launch the system was held off the estate and attendance was poor, with no attendees from the estate. The network did not grown above the mid 20s. From then on, support for Hattersley LETS was removed to the extent that LETS activists felt that the management at the Community Centre were actively against what they were doing. In discussion in a focus group members said:

> I think that one of the fundamental problems is that it was based in this community centre and that we've lacked a lot of workers' support. They've been against it from the outset, we've had difficulty getting room allocation, time on the computer ... virtually everything. We've had no workers input at all, virtually. We did have one worker who was assigned to help us ... that didn't work out, and we asked for another worker to be assigned to us and we were told that – 'Oh, we are all too busy'. Yet other projects have come up in the meantime and they've found workers for them. ...
>
> There were a lot of negative vibes off the workers. They had no idea of what a LETSystem was and gave out the wrong information, basically. When someone came into the building, the person they were most likely to see was a worker, and they asked about the LETS, and if there wasn't a LETS member available in the building, which there usually wasn't, they gave out information that was just incorrect. And that put a lot of people off. So I think that that was one of the big problems.

Then the management committee of the Community Centre changed and members had to deal with organisational in-fighting:

> Change in the management committee. That's a very important change. 'Cos the last one were supporting us, and this one isn't ... They started moaning about usage of the room, that we are occupying the room all the time, the office, even though no one wanted to use it. They said that we are putting people off as we are constantly there, that we had too much space, putting things on the computer that we shouldn't have done.

People whose initiatives fail often find it easy to blame someone else for failure, but the perception from members was that people with more power than they had were not supportive of their efforts. In contrast, the manager of the Community Centre felt that the Centre had been nothing but supportive:

In reality (the LETSystem) had been given a great (number) of resources. It had the near sole use of a room, the use of a computer, access to office resources and free use of a phone (the latter was really a substantial resource as the scheme involved making a very large number of telephone calls) ... The LETSystem continued to be resourced within the Centre for as long as it chose to remain here. Never were any resources denied to it as a project and it continued to have the moral support of staff and volunteers.

(Private correspondence, 29th June 1996)

More concrete barriers were identified. The micro-geographies of the estate were felt to impose barriers in that the north and south of the estate were split off from each other by roads, with the result that the two halves of the estate had contained and separate social networks. People in the south of the state did not feel secure in the north, and vice versa, contributing further to a feeling of isolation and atomisation. LETS activists found that their leaflets were mistaken for those from a finance company or loansharking operation. They also found that, as will discussed in more detail in chapter 10, prospective members skills were unused, dormant and forgotten. Consequently, they did not feel that they had much to offer to LETS, and could not see what they could get out of it. As a result of the observable failure to develop a functioning LETS system on the estate, Hattersley's Single Regeneration Budget bid claimed 'LETSystems had been tried on the estate and found to be inappropriate'. The manager did not feel LETS was appropriate as, echoing Richard Leese in the context of Local Agenda 21, he felt that the real need on the estate was for the well-paid jobs and hard currency that are normally taken for granted by those in work. He felt that Hattersley Credit Union was more appropriate to the needs of local residents. He felt that trading on LETS required more commitment from ordinary residents than they would be able to provide, whereas participation in a Credit Union requires little active input, beyond saving.

The attempt to set up LETS on Hattersley exposed the dissonance of Linton's frames in an English inner city environment – frames that LETS is value-free, running a system requires little participation, and 'money-is-just-information'. This was compounded by a reaction against the perceived middle-class nature of Manchester LETS and LETSGo (described as being *'like the moonies'* – not 'their type of people'). Both also contextualise paid workers' antipathy to LETS. Frames produced by LETSGo and Manchester LETS did not resonate on Hattersley as early frames reflected the way the LETS community was grappling with the production of social movement claims about work, money and livelihood, and with what the possibilities of LETS were in actualising them. They had yet to deploy them, and as they had not yet encountered allies and enemies, the frames they constructed were not yet submitted to 'Frame Alignment' processes. In the early days, when Michael Linton was raising peoples sights with challenging visions of MultiLETS and LETSystems with millions of subscribers, and the radical concept that 'money is just information', those attracted to LETS often came with a green tradition and with a theoretical interest in money, interest and local currencies. They wanted to wrestle with what the possibilities could be rather than limit their vision to a what they felt would then be just a small-scale support mechanism for the poor. They wanted to transform local economies. They became Transformers.

As the issues were debated, concepts appropriate to Canada and Australia (where they originated) were imported wholesale and unmediated from a culture that does not have the British experience of the welfare state, and where trading is an important and natural part of everyday life in rural, fairly isolated communities. Little (if any) publicity material had been written that reflected British cultural conditions, and Hattersley's leaflets 'cut and pasted' Landsman's[1] information which included a fairly lengthy theoretical piece on 'money and community'. Consequently, members of LETS on Hattersley were yet to find that their claims would not resonate with ordinary residents on Hattersley.

Within the RMT paradigm, Hattersley's failure is explicable by a lack of resources, in terms of commitment from members to set up the system – irrespective of the extent or otherwise of support from the local community centre. If there was energy and commitment members, could have set up LETS on their own, as others did. However, on Hattersley, there was no-one willing to make the commitment, to become 'project champions' like the members of Manchester LETS Core Group, or LETSGo. At the focus group, members discussed relaunching the system and one summed up the position: 'I'm disappointed that the system didn't seem to happen and I'd be really into relaunching it if possible, as I know that we've all got lots of skills and lots to offer, and I think that what we perhaps haven't got to offer is lots of time to get it started again but I hope we can.' The Community Centre Manager said that LETS's problems did not stem from lack of support from workers, but from no-one on Hattersley being prepared to put in the effort for LETS that local volunteers put into the local Credit Union:

> This credit union depends on the enormous, skilled input of over 30 volunteers. In one of the most disadvantaged communities in Tameside it has made over £1/4 million in loans, it pays a dividend on members savings and is now expanding its operation into the middle class neighbourhoods adjacent to the estate. The reasons for the credit unions success can be found in the dedication and hard work of the volunteers, their knowledge of and networks within the community, their good organisational and business sense, their skills in finance and accounting and their ability to market a good idea to a community that had never heard of credit unions and so on.
>
> (Private correspondence 29th June 1996)

However, as the Political Process model predicts, poor people faced additional problems in taking action not faced by the more resourced members of Manchester LETS: The Core Group members were otherwise engaged in setting up a co-operative cafe, or had got a job. They did not have much money so their introductory leaflet was of poor quality. They could not get many members to join, so their directory did not have many services on offer. They did not have the internal resources to set up LETS, and did not yet use frame alignment processes to win them. As Tilly's (1978) analysis, raised earlier, suggests, people in poverty find it harder to overcome the difficulties of everyday life, of getting by on a low income and budgeting from day to day, and without external support from conscience supporters they will find it hard to develop their own self-help projects

---

[1] 'Landsman Community Services' is Michael Linton's company.

unaided. The benefits of LETS, to ordinary people on Hattersley estate, were in the future – not real and available immediately as they would be to people from poor estates joining an existing system with middle-class members.

ALIGNING FRAMES: START UP TALKS

On occasions LEDA was invited to give presentations to inner city organisations on the lines of that discussed in chapter 6 (Extract 6.1 below, p. 77). In all cases, LETS was accepted onto the agenda by supportive local authorities. In an interchange in Bury the reason for the resonance of LETS within the specific local field of inner city regeneration was observable. The Chair (a Manchester City Councillor) said:

> Increasingly on council properties and on council estates there is alienation, isolation, marginalisation, fragmentation, atomisation ... whatever, whatever it is that is about incoherence in communities. There's a lot of it about. Now as a politician I don't feel that we have yet come up with, not myself, politicians have not come up with any solutions that can stop communities crumbling.

LETS here resonates with a feeling of powerlessness – a strong feeling that no-one has the solution to crumbling community on outer housing estates, together with a hope that LETS is appropriate to rebuilding what the Chair identified as 'that sense of enthusiasm for community that you both articulated this evening'. The frames LEDA produced resonated with preoccupations of the local state. Claims for community were accepted in the hope that LETS builds community, resonating with 'New Labour's call for 'strong individuals in healthy communities'. But did they mobilise more resources? Once through the door, did elites begin to work with LETS activists to develop more LETS schemes, with the result that they grew more quickly than had they been developed more slowly, from below, through the countercultural networks?

The answer is no. Despite an open hearing, frames had not been specifically aligned with this desire for a solution to problems of building community on outer housing estates, and the overall presentation left the audience members 'shell-shocked' and unsure of the value of LETS. The chair said:

> I think the scheme you have presented to us tonight looks radical, looks alternative, but barter has always been part of t'mainstream. So how do you then get it to become part of the mainstream so that people, ordinary people like those in the room tonight do not have any difficulties with it, because I think it's a matter of presentation in a lot of ways. I think a lot of the people in this room tonight, and this is no criticism of yourselves, a lot of the people here this evening can't get their mind around it. I think it's this kind of educational thing where people start to become more familiar with it and it becomes friendly, so how do you start to give it a friendly feel? ... I know that its been a culture shock this evening for some people, its been interesting and I do feel, like credit unions and other forms of organisations, this er, this kind of thing has got to, must take its time to settle down with er, with the mainstream.

LETS was seen as radical and resistant and needed to 'settle down'. To apply social movement theory the chair called for further frame transformation. Given the newness of LETS and, as an explanation for urban problems and a solution for them, its dissonance with the boosterist agenda of 'entrepreneurial Manchester' it is perhaps not surprising that LEDA were unable to persuade elites of the usefulness of LETS. Once LETS had become a more accepted element of the portfolio of projects that could be used to help solve urban problems, and especially after the election of New Labour in 1997, it might have become easier to gain urban funding. Indeed, the guidelines for the first set of Single Regeneration Budget (ie urban funding) written by the New Labour administration specifically named LETS as an initiative that should be funded. LETS was supported and developed by local authority, SRB and EU-funds in a number of cities, notably Greenwich (London), Leicester, and Liverpool. After 1997, LEDA in Manchester also found the door open to them. However, despite New Labour's rhetoric of wanting to engage with communities to solve urban problems, LEDA continued to have problems in getting LETS onto the policy agenda. LEDA met with a number of SRB co-ordinators in Manchester to explain LETS to them, and on the face of it received a sympathetic hearing: but action was slower.

> I did presentations to the City Council SRB social programme co-ordinators. And did lots of presentations around Manchester to different groups. And as a result of that LETS has started in Stockport and Stratford. That's helped to spread it to different areas. ... I went in and did this talk. And at the end the chairs said to me, what can we do to help? We had a very positive response from him. So I said, well, we could have a development post paid by the nine SRB areas and lets see where that gets us. Lets do the research, and find out if people know what LETS is about and whether it could help them and lets take it from there. I met a couple of the co-ordinators afterwards and had another sort of occasions, and one of them sent me an email. And his email was ... an encouraging email that said, thanks very much, unfortunately there are still a lot of sceptics around the table. And they contributed by allowing us to use their photocopier. But that's the kind of support that we were getting. It was not any greater support.
>
> (LEDA Director, July 2001)

Eventually the reasons for the scepticism, not articulated publicly, became clear:

> Well, there was a Councillor ... about 4 years ago (we) put in a proposal for developing LETS in one housing estate, Victoria Park. Her response was, 'Oh LETS is for middle class hippies' or something like that. I don't quite know, but it was something of that nature. She said, LETS only works for the middle class ... and you are not going to promote it in my area. ... So there were people with loud mouths and very little understanding of what they were talking about. Putting it down, to be honest. I tried to speak to her once about it and it was not possible to break through the prejudice. No openness at all. ... they might have had the view that it was not suitable of their area. But I don't know individually what they're reasons for not supporting it further.

The lack of support made him angry:

> To be honest, you get all this rhetoric from these agencies, saying what we want, what we need and what we get the funding for, is community led initiatives which will make a real difference. And then you go along with something which will do all this ... You explain how you do all this, you explain how it's already happening and you explain

quite comprehensively the kind of benefits that can be gained from it. And they somehow think they are more intelligent than you, and without any experience of it seem to be able to make a judgement about whether it will work or not. And to be honest, at that point you start saying, well, I think I'm gonna find another way to do this. And that's the point that I got to.

Look, I don't know who these people are really. They *completely* contradict both the words they speak themselves and everything that's written. Everything in their job-description is all about community involvement. You go there with what you see as a good solution, if not the perfect solution, [...] and you're putting in hundreds of hours of your free time to develop it and they don't support it. And you think, why should I bother. It's not put me off LETS, it's not put me off the concept, it's not put me off wanting to promote it, but now I'm looking at other ways to do it. I'm not gonna do it through those channels. You know, it's not my responsibility to ... No, I'll turn it the other way ... I think they have a responsibility to ... if they make comments and they turn things down, which are coming from the community, they have to be really sure to know what they're talking about. Because otherwise, you know, they're obviously in very dangerous water. So I think, I'd like to see a great deal more responsibility taken by these people that are supposed to be working for us and helping to develop our communities.

For a door to be open does not mean that the message will be heard, or that it would be in the interests of activists in social movements to engage with the local state in the new urban policy partnerships that, under New Labour, began to drive urban policy. There are a number of significant problems in engaging with part-nerships (Hastings, McArthur et al. 1996; Mayo 1997; Anastacio, Gidley et al. 2000). Community activists often don't understand the bureaucracy or the jargon, let alone speak the arcane language from which bids for funding are constructed with their 'outputs' and 'outcomes', 'delivery mechanisms' and 'appraisal processes.' Partnership is not a level playing field. The community side is often unsupported or poorly supported, does not have its own staff, premises and access to independent advice. Community activists often have to work through the day, then in the evening come to these long, unpaid (often boring) meetings. The other partners are consequently more powerful, while activists get burned out though the shear grind of work and/or family responsibilities on top of community involvement. Worse, if not ignored, community involvement can be taken advantage of. While communities are often consulted and their ideas listen to, there is no guarantee that these ideas will be translated into the agenda. Given the challenge process, the agenda is often heavily set by the lead bidders' (usually the local council) understanding of what the judges of the bid (central government) are looking for. As Diamond (2001:9) puts it, 'at crucial stages of the development of the bid decisions have usually been taken away from the neighbourhood in which the initiative will be based. A "nomadic" army of professionals has emerged who are directed from one area based initiative to the next.' These regeneration professionals – sometimes council employees, sometimes consultants, sometimes short term agency staff – are those who turn the ideas into 'SRB speak', making decisions about what will or will not be 'acceptable'. Space for community groups to put forward unconventional agendas is thus potentially limited as decisions about what is in and out of the bid is not ultimately theirs, or at the very least is subject to strong pressure to remove 'unacceptable' suggestions. Thirdly, the local knowledge of these 'nomads' might be limited, and there may be a tendency to substitute programmes seen as 'acceptable' to judges, but which local people might not regard as best for the area – for those which are genuinely rooted yet less 'glamorous' for a beauty contest. The short term nature of professional engagement makes it difficult for them to separate what is genuinely a well thought out if 'un-sexy' idea from the merely mundane.

The problems above, and LEDA's experiences, would suggest that engaging in urban policy was not a fruitful opportunity structure for community activists to engage. Partnership is a diversion involving little more than a therapeutic consultation to mask real decisions being made elsewhere. It carries a huge opportunity costs. Activists could be doing other things with their time. They could make more progress outside with demonstrations, petitions and pickets. They might make more progress developing their own forms of regeneration outside partnerships (North and Bruegel 2001).

LETS AND MENTAL HEALTH

LEDA had more success in working in the field of mental health due to its claims for empowerment through the promotion of alternatives to work. Here LEDA's claims were accepted by conscience supporters, and funds were allocated to development work – a job to which a LEDA member was appointed. Salford NHS Trust, in partnership with Mind North West, wanted to develop approaches to caring for people with mental health needs that were a preventative primary alternative to medical intervention. They saw LETS as a way of increasing feelings of self-worth experienced by mental health sufferers, and give them a say over their treatment ('self-referral'). Prestwich Mental Hospital had been closed as a result of the 'Care in the Community' initiative and was to be gifted by the NHS trust to a charitable group of mental health professionals who wanted to develop alternatives to medicine.

This group met monthly in their own time to draw up their vision of a client-run mental health centre that would make alternative therapies (massage, reiki, aromatherapy, dance and music therapy etc) available in one place to be accessed by members at their own pace. It was seen as a permeable organisation that would include members with variable needs who would drop in and out of use as they felt appropriate, and run in a way that would make it accessible to people who needed preventive support. With their emphasis of providing alternatives to conventional work at a level people would be able to support when they were not feeling well, they aimed to enable participants to earn LETS credits through working in the cafe and later perhaps use LETS for day-to-day maintenance (cleaning, decorating, office work, work in the gardens) of the centre. The new project, known as the Creative Living Centre, was launched in March 1996. The Trust manager was concerned that:

> only 7.5% of people with mental health problems access specialist mental health services. A much greater number of people will be seen by their GP. In Salford it is expected that around 15,000 people would visit their GP per anum with a diagnosed mental health problem and as many again would not have their mental health need

diagnosed or recognised. Together this represents a figure of 1 in 7 Salford people. Within the NHS as a whole, around 77% of its mental health budget is spent on hospital and medication and only 23% on community mental health services.

(Creative Living Centre, 1996)

These figures showed the need for alternatives to medication and hospital for those who do not access mental health services or get referred by their GP. An alternative was seen as one that users would control at their own rate. LETS was seen as a way of enabling participants to control their own access to alternatives, pay for them, and work at a pace that suited them. The challenge for the Creative Living Centre was to ensure both that a management openness to LETS was transformed into real user empowerment, and that top-down support was not a substitute for a lack of user project champions – with advocates of LETS becoming a new class of community development professional unintentionally substituting themselves for users of LETS. However, the experience was not generalised. Another LEDA Director, working this time in the health field, had similar experiences working to write up a bid for funding to develop a LETS system to enable people with mental health problems to engage in therapeutic work:

We got stitched up. We didn't fail, we got stitched up. ... he 'phoned me up one day and said, Basically, I'm just doing the final things for the Department of Health, it has to be in by 5 o'clock – it was about 3 o'clock in the afternoon – 'can you tell me by the way why this is good value for money?' You know... do me a favour! So ... when I finally got a copy of the bid ... the revised bid that they'd submitted to the Department of Health, which I had not been involved in, they'd not shown me, it was the biggest pile of crap I'd ever seen, it didn't reflect my project, our project AT ALL. So he'd stitched us up. And he later said to me in a phone call that he'd looked on his computer under LETS and what it had said was an evil subversive group. He used the word evil. Evil, subversive something or another. He actually used the words evil. I couldn't believe it. So we didn't get it. And then the Lottery bid failed after that and another bid failed after that and we were always near the post with them. I got the message in no uncertain terms that there was no political will for this in Manchester and that I was beating my head against a brick wall the whole time.

(LEDA Director, July 2001)

INAPPROPRIATE FRAMING, OR AN UNFRIENDLY POLITICAL OPPORTUNITY STRUCTURE?

While the critique of LETS as an 'evil cult' is extreme, it does suggest LEDA still struggled to align their frames to those of urban and health service professionals. In particular, the accusation that LETS worked best for the post-materialist green middle classes from leafy South Manchester stuck – probably because it was also true. The experience of LETS in inner city environments suggests that there were a number of problems (Barnes, North et al. 1996; North 1996). These included firstly benefit worries. Prospective members of LETS were worried that they would get in trouble with the benefit authorities. There was considerable confusion about what the attitude of the benefit authorities actually was, as while the formal position was that LETS earnings would be treated exactly the same as sterling, which would mean that benefit would be reduced pound for pound, the reality was that there was little evidence of benefit offices showing any interest at all in what were small amounts of 'money' that could only be spent in a very small network. Despite the gap between feared and experienced sanctions, the uncertainty at least was a barrier to the vulnerable joining LETS.

The second problem was that the vision of a co-operative economy characterised by reciprocal networks of mutual aid like LETS seemed a utopian vision for those living in environments characterised by mistrust, high levels of crime, the isolation often experienced by the vulnerable (be they lone parents, the unemployed, the sick and disabled), and unsettled circumstances. Life is hard for people on low incomes, and vulnerability lowers people's confidence, pure and simple. LETS schemes in inner city areas found it hard to recruit new members from populations that felt that they had little to offer, had few skills, or that those skills they had were rusty or unsellable. Being on low incomes, they had few resources to share. Used to the stress of getting by, they often had little energy for new, untested ideas that promised more than they delivered. The result was that recruitment was slow, the network remained small, and few services were available. Those that did join found that their needs could not be met either as no one was offering what they wanted, or they would make 20 calls (in itself, assuming you have a phone, your trading partner has a phone, and you can afford the calls and the time to phone round) and still not get what they wanted. The limits of economies based on 'taking in each others washing' were quickly reached. Finally, there was a perception that informal work for cash was a better alternative: Twenty pounds for fixing someone's car is untraceable – LETS records all these previously informal options. The result was that LETS did not take off in inner city areas to the levels hoped for. By 2001 none of the LETS schemes surveyed in 1996 (Barnes, North and Walter 1996), were still in operation. A final problem was that often the problems meant that the networks stayed small, and those that did join got little practical benefit from their membership. This was even a problem in a larger scheme like Manchester LETS. By 2001, two of the leading heterotopian members of Manchester LETS who had spoken movingly of LETS as prefiguring the sort of green economy they wanted had left when they became unemployed:

> Strangely, when I became unemployed, I ceased to renew my membership of LETS which is slightly contrary to peoples expectations ... that LETS can be practically helpful to people on the dole. Maybe that refers back to my motivation for being a founding member anyway, in that my motivation was not practical, more ideological, and when it came to being unemployed, I wasn't motivated to stay a member. ... The main thing was the lack of practical benefit. Another factor that demotivated me was ... there was a hundred Bobbins or so that was supposed to be credited to my account, and the people who were running the accounts ... did not put the paperwork through and I did not get credited for the work I was doing, or I did not get round to sending in the cheques, so it seemed like the accounting thing wasn't working and I was losing the motivation to pass through zero. ... So the two things together, the lack of practical benefit, and it seemed to get so successful that it almost didn't need me.

> (Former Heterotopian, July 2001)

ORGANISING AT A NATIONAL SCALE: REFORMING THE SYSTEM?

For many urban policy professionals, the key issue that kept the networks small was that poor people who joined LETS might have lost scarce, fully spendable pounds if they earned LETS credits, of limited spendability. This was an obvious structural barrier, and LETSLink UK, the national LETS development agency and a group of Labour and Co-operative Party MPs started a campaign to change benefit regulations. At the same time, the government began to show an interest in the problem. Guided by the work of Granovetter (1973) on the importance of wide networks and Putnam on social capital for enhancing job search for unemployed people (Putnam 1993; 2001), the Social Exclusion Unit's Action Team on 'Jobs' examined, amongst other issues;

> what benefit rule flexibilities it might be helpful to pilot; for example, whether changes to earning disregards, or an easier regime for Local Exchange Trading Schemes (LETs) (sic) would be cost effective in drawing people back into work.
>
> (SEU 1998:61)

LETSlink UK were invited to contribute to this process. Of course, they were here faced with a chicken and egg problem. They argued that the economic benefits of LETS were limited due to benefit worries, and as a result, struggled to provide the Government with evidence that LETS did help socially excluded groups into work. In November 1999, and after some considerable delay, the Policy Action Team on Jobs finally reported (DFEE 1999). The news was, superficially, good in that the PAT report effectively accepted LETSLink's arguments for a need for changes to benefits, and this despite a recognition that 'hard evidence that participation in such schemes could act as a bridge to the open labour market for jobless people in deprived neighbourhoods could be hard to come by' (1999:114). However, the report was also concerned at what is called the 'risk' that combined LETS credits and casual income was 'sufficiently high and predictable to make a combination of benefit and LETS credits more attractive than a job' and consequently argued for a disregard of LETS earnings up to £1000 if agreed with and policed by a personal advisor. The Government's work-centred and dependency-based welfare agenda, its reliance on work related outputs, and the delay in reporting combined with a failure to discuss its proposals informally with LETSLink made LETS suspicious of its intentions. The report rejected making changes in benefit regulations in their entirety, and in the event not even the PATs proposals for pilots were taken up.

Interestingly, another form of community currency was far more successful in an urban environment: Time Money (Seyfang 2003). Heavily promoted by the London-based New Economics Foundation which had the ear of New Labour policy makers, the Time Bank model began to attract considerable support from urban and health policy makers after 1997, with 69 Time Banks in place and another 39 in development by March 2005 (TimebanksUK 2005). Some aspects of Time Banks are undoubtedly better than LETS in meeting inner city needs: they were promoted more sensibly as a community building, social mechanism rather than a solution to the problems of the capitalist industrial system. Few claimed, as they did with LETS, the Time Banks will 'save the world'. The result is that they seemed more credible, and take up in policy communities is greater, and the Government agreed that currencies denominated in hours would not affect benefit. They seemed more credible as they made fewer claims, but they also achieved the more limited tasks they set out to meet. The innovation of providing a broker to who phones members to meet requests for help was an improvement on hit-and-miss LETS. Urban policy makers could have some confidence that the vulnerable will be not left dangling in a scheme that claims it can meet their needs, but in reality falls down on the job. Ideally, brokers could make an intelligent decision on the best way to meet need, through Time Banks or from mainstream provision.

Given the difficulties LETS encountered in developing in inner city areas, it is obvious that this is a job that is beyond the possibilities of volunteers. It was an advance that the state recognised that community building was something that could contribute to reducing social exclusion, but given short term grant culture funding is often time limited and a Time Bank will have to fall back on volunteer time after the grant ends. When funding for a pilot Time Bank in the Elephant and Castle, London ended while a full bid was written up, people were left dangling. LETS would have got on with the job!

CONCLUSION: HOW EFFECTIVELY WERE RESOURCES MOBILISED?

The RMT approach shows that LEDA and LETSGo were not adroit at navigating their way through their political opportunity structure. LETSGo spent innumerable amounts of time and resources chasing the chimera of transformation of business, which led them to adopt a private-sector entrepreneurial approach that alienated potential conscience-supporters. When LEDA were invited to participate in the development of other LETS systems, lack of interest on the ground meant that nothing came of development, and after 1997 they found themselves unable to work effectively in the new partnership culture. When people have few resources, LETS seems not to work well and the key structural barrier, losing spendable cash for LETS credits of a limited value was perhaps the issue that killed LETS in inner city areas. It developed in leafy Withington, Didsbury and Chorlton, not Hulme, Moss Side, East Manchester Hattersley. Time Banks seemed to have a more open hearing, due in part to the New Economic Foundation's ability to access support from national elites, better frame alignment to New Labour's concerns about social inclusion, fostering and volunteering, and, for the vulnerable, a better product.

The Transformers were limited in their success as they did operate, despite their rhetoric, as an immature social movement that did little frame transformation. They operated as a social movement around money, work, livelihood and community. LEDA failed to mobilise the resources of Manchester LETS as most of whose members were not prepared to put effort into transformation through LETS. LETS is self-help undertaken by members of these networks themselves, rather than something that requires elite facilitation. The reason for this is that LETS does not require many resources to be run independently of elites, beyond (at most) access to a PC and a photocopier. A LETS system can be established in the first place by a very small number of people – a group of friends, or a community group – and start trading with each other. While trading at that level will inevitably be small scale (if of incredible benefit to people with few cash resources), LETS is easy to run. It requires no registration with any statutory organisation or complex process of accreditation. Little cash is involved so no complex processes of accountability need to be developed. Software, while still quite inaccessible to the computer illiterate, is available at little cost, or systems can use manual bookkeeping. Provided there are enough committed individuals in an area with their time and commitment to run LETS, starting is easy. LEDA failed to mobilise the resources of Manchester LETS for wider transformation efforts as the values of doing it yourself, independent of the actions of elites, motivated them. They did not see their role as solving problems of social inclusion through, as Time Banks do, promoting volunteering and the co-delivery of services by professionals and clients. Their strategy was far more radical: developing sustainable local networks of co-operation and non-exploitative work from below, as an alternative to what they saw as an exploitative and unsustainable capitalist economy. Consequently they did not feel buy into the focus on developing LETS as part of inner city policy, and felt that LETS was beginning to feel 'quite corporate'. A former heterotopian, commenting in 2001 argued that he felt:

> uncertainty about what the organisation was doing and what its relationship was to these other LETS organisations (LEDA and LETSGo). It was almost like a corporate feeling, I suppose, which is not very pleasant ... Not very fun. ... (PN: Who were the other groups?) ... Well I tried to ask people about this, I believe there was one, and I got very unclear information when I talked to people about it. There was one, wasn't there one that was trying to, there were these weird groups in the newsletters, never much understanding of who they were and what they were doing! One that was trying to engage more with business, as I remember, and trying to get more of them on board, yes, and they were, weren't they, they had links, or some sort of friendly relationship with Manchester LETS? ... I remember Michael Linton coming over ... but it was like it was sort of underground to LETS, what was going on beyond the original LETS, I didn't seem to penetrate what was going on. ... A sense of a loss of ownership, and stories of infighting or disagreement. ... As I say, it got as bit corporate, like they didn't care that you didn't know what was going on? Or if they were in competition or not, you know...

New Labour saw liberation as coming from paid work. Members of LETS disagreed. To what extent, then, could they actualise this new form of economy?

CHAPTER 10

Explorations in Heterotopia: The Micro-politics of Money, Work and Community

What if we just went ahead as though the revolution were over and we had won?
(Rudy from Twin Oaks Commune 1970, quoted by Houriet 1973:266)

I participate, you participate, they profit!
(Slogan: Paris 1968)

This chapter examines the extent to which the benefits that activists claim spring from trading with Bobbins, an experience altogether different from trading governed by mainstream values, are realisable. Based on relationships, and building community as a by-product of 'relationship trading', the claim is that trading with local currencies operate under completely changed cultural codes when compared with those governed by economic relationships undertaken by the logic of capitalist markets. This chapter therefore aims to establish the extent to which anarchist Heterotopians can operationalise their aims of building a space that operates under the cultural codes they raised in chapter 6. After an analysis of the extent to which members of LETS are able to operate as knowledge producers creating new cultural codes and new forms of organisation, analysis moves to a consideration of the extent that the capturable and observable Political Opportunity Structure, observed through anthropological investigation, restricted what could be done. In conclusion, this chapter will consider whether, if the codes produced could be actualised, LETS can best be conceptualised as effective micro-political politics.

If LETS should turn out to be a representation that illuminated power relations associated with work and money, but was unable to devise effective micro-political struggles against them, then it may best be thought of as a method of self-producing an alternative form of knowledge. This knowledge can be thought of as a dramatur-gical demonstration of the problems of mainstream society; through what Melucci (1989:78) called prophesy (showing a possible future), paradox (showing by exagger-ation the illogicality of the system), and representation (showing society's contradic-tions to itself). A poststructuralist analysis might counter that this play of image is all that can be expected, and is central to change in a world in which information is key. However, recalling that I take, with Foucault, as my guide the language of battle rather than of signs; then my original prejudice about LETS – as a vision of the good life without a useful (perhaps nomadic rather than linear) route map of how to get there – might, unfortunately, be reinscribed.

To remedy this, Foucaultian analysis can be employed to identify whether effective micro-struggles against diffuse power grids are possible through nomadic un-hierarchical struggles. If these new codes are realisable to any great extent, then LETS is a heterotopia – a liberated space – and successful struggle against specific, local power relations. If they are realisable only fleetingly, then LETS is of value as a temporal heterotopia, as what Bey (1995) called a 'Temporary Autonomous Zone' like a pop concert or tribal gathering, a momentary effervescence structurally limited in its implementability and suggesting the need for meta-narrative solutions rather than micro-solutions. If life within LETS just doesn't add up to the claims made, it may still be of value at the level of information, a Baudrillardian sign, or a vision of an alternative, unrealisable yet inspiring 'mobilising utopia'. This analysis does not want to finish at the level of the sign: rather it looks to explore the frontierland between actor's capacity to self-produce knowledge, and of the extent that locally observable structures limit this self-production. Consequently, then the capacity of members to implement their codes, and achievable in the here and now rather than as goals put off for the future, will be central to this analysis.

'IT ONLY HAS THE VALUE WE CHOOSE TO GIVE IT!': CHANGED, CHANGING OR REINSCRIBED CULTURAL CODES?

In chapter 6 the cultural codes that members of LETS claimed were those by which they wished to live were raised. The task now is to examine these in turn, to see the extent that their claims about the benefits that would spring from the use of new forms of money hold water. Firstly, they raise claims about money, and this section looks at attitudes to the *currency* – the Bobbin. Can members create a new currency that is more liberating than Sterling as successful micro-politics? Alternatively, does the currency become 'fetishised', thereby either recreating an alternative power relation, just as restrictive as the operation of Sterling, re-inscribing capitalist power relations? Secondly, is *work* revalued through use of Bobbins? Are new, more ecological or more free livelihoods made possible that are impossible in the mainstream in a micro-politics of work? Thirdly, is *community* built? Does mutuality spread and does use of the Bobbin concomitantly fall off? Is a realm of freedom achieved as the Heterotopians wish – a micro-politics of community?

CHANGING CONCEPTIONS OF MONEY

Central to LETS is the core claim made by activists that money is a simulacrum, socially created and thereby socially creatable by members of LETS. If a new form of money is designed, a new form of society, co-operatively organised, will spring from this design which changes the premise on which economic life takes place within the capitalist system. In this reading, LETS is a micropolitical attack on the power relations of money, which, by being limited, enforces the labour discipline on which rests the capitalist system: labour discipline allowing the accumulation of capital and the extraction of surplus value, from which exploitation, alienation and inequality all follow.

To what extent did members feel that in their day-to-day life they were able to redefine money? Did they find that the Bobbin became, like sterling, a new fetish recreating the oppressions of the social system? If a fetish, the Bobbin would become a thing of value in-and- of itself, which people would work to acquire (as they do for sterling), rather than being merely a measure of the skills and resources of members? This would manifest itself by, for example, members 'forced' to earn to pay off 'commitment – thereby labour discipline being re-introduced. Did people care if they had 'Bobbins savings'? The Heterotopian perspective aimed to avoid this by regarding Bobbins as a temporary transitional mechanism into a non-money economy based on friendship, trust and mutual aid. To investigate whether cultural codes around money were transformed, it is necessary to consider whether, in practice, the currency becomes a fetish or dies out into a space of co-operation, in which Bobbins were seen as a temporary lubricant or crutch for those not ready for purely co-operative relations.

Certainly, experience varied. For some, use of the Bobbin was discontinued quickly after the establishment of a trading relationship:

> When I started it's hard to get away from the notion of money and that you've got to have some before you spend some, sort of thing, but the more I got into it the less that seemed important. Now I'm not really bothered by Bobbins, and there are a few people that I know quite well and we don't bother with Bobbins, they do things for me and we just 'do it'. Like the woman that uses my dark room, she made a shawl for my little baby niece who's just been born, so I said use the dark room free for a few times and we left it at that really. I think the more relaxed you get about it, at least for me, the less important Bobbins become.

Another Heterotopian agreed that use dropped of but explained why he personally continued to use Bobbins:

> I'm very much the same. Of those wormeries that I built, it varied from zero, to a bob a job I used to do, and then (a humaniser) convinced me to charge a decent amount because of the added benefit of keeping the system going, but, yes, I see it as favours basically, you know – doing something for someone else and empowering both of you.

A Greener similarly found no difficulty in refining what he saw as the value of currency. He was more concerned at what other people considered a Bobbin to be worth than perceiving that it had a value in and of itself:

> I base it partly on what the other person thinks a Bobbin is worth, (b) whether they've got lots of them that they want to get rid of, or they haven't got many and they don't want to spend very many, and (c) other people might think that my negative balance, I ought to do something, get my act together and make it a positive balance for a while. So I take into account a sort of mish-mash of things. I'm fulfilling that particular objective by hiring out my tent for Bobbins, erm, so whether I take 10 Bobbins or 50 Bobbins is rather irrelevant to it. And to be honest the only reason why I think I ought to get my account into credit sooner or later is what, what some other people might think.

Another member felt well able to redefine what she thought about money in the early days, but found that in time she became concerned at the level of her 'commitment'. She had received many services and had her life significantly improved, but was now stuck with a heavy commitment for which she felt responsible:

> I used it a lot at the beginning because it had a lot of things I wanted, quite essential things rather than luxuries, things that others would not see as essential. And I really wanted those things and I was quite creative about getting them. Sometimes people, I managed to coax people to do things that they weren't necessarily offering in the directory. I knew someone that was quite handy, and they'd done a bit of plumbing and I suggested that they would be able to remove some gas piping. I had this big gas thing in my front room and I wanted a fire there. I coaxed them into removing that, which was really good. Someone changed my toilet for me who wasn't ... who needed a little encouragement a bit but it was a brilliant job. A guy got my car through the MOT ... So I felt like I really needed these things, so I went out to get them. And then I sort of panicked as I owed so many Bobbins! I was earning a few but it was really out of balance with what I was spending so I sort of reigned myself in, and I started working, stuffing envelopes and delivering to pay some of it back, but I was finding it difficult. I don't know whether I was offering something people didn't want, or ... I tried to be very inventive with the offers but that's difficult. I went through what people wanted and would ring people up and would say "you want this" and earn some Bobbins that way. I found that if I just sat back, it didn't tend to happen that much. I haven't done much trading at all, recently, in fact for quite a time. I've been consciously not spending Bobbins as I've been aware of being in commitment and I feel quite responsible.

Old ideas of debt from the mainstream money system continued to colonise her mind and the micro-politics of creating a new money system did not break through. Responding to this, in the Focus Group the following interaction took place. A Heterotopian commented:

> I think people do still think of it as money because why would they have problems ... (others: "yes, yes") ... about getting into debt? I know someone who has a balance of minus 300 Bobbins, and she's having a great time ... (others: "yes, yes") ... because she's just going out and spending *more* Bobbins and that's great because it generates trade within the network, and it means that someone else says suddenly "oh, I've got Bobbins: what shall I spend it on?". The Bobbins are no good just lying under the counter. I think it is a different attitude ..." (Other focus group member): We have all this indoctrination ... (Third focus group member): We think of it like a Credit Card ... (Heterotopian): No! Its not like a Credit Card! You are not paying interest or anything. It's completely different. As long as sooner or later you are putting back into the system, in fact even if they don't, people paying for or obtaining goods and services from the network are actually generating Bobbins, because every time you make a trade you generate Bobbins. You just write out a cheque, and suddenly there is five Bobbins that did not exist before. That comes out of your account, and if you want to get those Bobbins back you do something for someone else: so it's worth just generating Bobbins. Because there isn't any interest or anything being paid in, it doesn't really matter if you are in debt, provided you still want to participate in the scheme it's not actually debt. But it's very hard to get away from the idea of being in the black or in the red, and that whole attitude is conditioned by our experience of using money. It's not the same thing when you are in a LETS scheme.

Similarly another Heterotopian said that the Bobbin was starting to take on the life of a real currency, which she bemoaned:

> I thought at first that it wouldn't be and it shouldn't be, but it's turning out to be a bit! I have a reasonable feeling that I have a few in hand, I don't know – about 500, and I'm quite happy, if anyone hasn't got enough, to ship them off! … whether it should is another matter. But I'd be far happier to see it all as a commune.

In contrast, a Transformer felt use of the currency was dropping off too quickly into a realm of co-operation, which she felt would end up as the 'cosy club' Transformers wished to avoid. This made her angry. As a lone parent, she felt that a benefit of LETS was being able to pay her way like any other member of society rather than live a life of favours, beholden to friends. She was angry when people did not cash her cheques and saw it as 'charity' – 'Isn't my money good enough for them?' Her day-to-day existence was improved by being able to participate in the mainstream as a result of the childcare she purchased.

However, the above evidence for the existence of cultural change comes from the active traders. Only 142 of the 550 members had a turnover of over 160 Bobbins, so had a limited amount of trading experience. While turnover is an inappropriate measure of economic activity precisely as use of the Bobbin drops off in time, cultural innovation was restricted by the small scale of trading, even in one of the world's biggest LETS systems. The small scale of trades that takes place, when contrasted with the magnitude of economic and social interactions governed by mainstream logic, severely limits the amount of cultural innovation possible. As a result, many members have little experience in redefining cultural codes.

Consequently, not everyone entered this space operating with these redefined codes:

> I think the thing that attracted me was … at the time was I was unemployed at the time, and very very skint and it was like, it was amazing for me to be part of this scheme which meant that things would be accepted that weren't acceptable for Sterling. I thought it was wild that all these things I'd needed doing for a long time that I hadn't got done as I didn't have enough Sterling, all of a sudden I could get them done. … I've found it a good way of meeting people as well … But I thought that I quite quickly found that, I got frustrated that one or two people would, that my experience was that things weren't moving very quickly, and that often the people I got to do things for me, often that was the first time that anyone had called them and asked them to do anything. … So I was quite shocked that we've got this amazing new scheme … I got quite a few people to join, … and I couldn't understand why people weren't using it in the same way.

While the active members in the Focus Groups found it possible to change the way they operated within LETS, the low traders found it much more difficult to participate in this cultural innovation, and there were specific barriers to trading. Some were limited in what they could do by a lack of time, being without a telephone (even in some cases those without an answerphone found that people did not call back). Other low traders were those living some distance away who found people were unwilling to travel (incurring Sterling costs). Others lacked confidence to make the first move, and pick up the telephone to commission work from strangers. They were wary of going into commitment. Others did not have skills members wanted.

As result of low levels of participation, people found it hard to innovate and often fell back on governing their trades by familiar values associated with Sterling. Members found negotiation difficult: how much to ask people to do, how much to pay them, what they could or could not be legitimately asked to do. Consequently four norms that governed use of the currency emerged. Firstly, one based on parity with the mainstream economy – a Bobbin is equivalent to a pound, the skills of members should be valued in terms appropriate to the mainstream. Resisting what they called a 'poverty mentality', they felt that as there are always enough Bobbins available to pay whatever rate the person they traded with chose, it was appropriate to 'act from abundance' and pay themselves a 'good' wage – often 10 or 20 Bobbins an hour. Secondly, other members developed a norm of equality – set at 6 Bobbins an hour. Only the extreme Heterotopians resisted use of Bobbins and operated thirdly a 'Bobbin-free zone' (no Bobbins) or fourthly, Bob-a-job (one Bobbin).

The ability of members to socially create their own value systems was secondly limited by the intrusion of the mainstream economy. Members complained that others were not accepting Bobbins, and were trying to charge what they regarded as unreasonable levels of Sterling. One member wrote to the Core Group:

> I feel that LETS is becoming rather too money-orientated. More members are asking for Sterling and Bobbins for their labour as well as for their products/services. We could do with a general meeting to discuss our ethos. LETS is, in certain senses, beginning to mirror the money economy and the capitalist class system. Given when Bobbins only are charged there is a tendency for those middle class members whose talents and skills are highly valued in the money economy to charge pro rata for Bobbins. I believe this is wrong and devalues the original LETS ideal which was to subvert the money economy. Unless we can get back to the notion that an hour of my time is worth an hour of anyone else's, then I fear many whose skills are poorly used/not valued at all in the £ economy will feel disillusioned and will leave.
>
> (Unnamed member's letter, January 1995)

This is evidence for Offe and Heinz's (1992) charge that LETS commodifies the previously uncommodified. In regard to a similar case, a Greener commented:

> (Someone) was going to give all those services for free, and who (then) thought he was devaluing himself by doing that and that he was going to charge 15 Bobbins an hour – I think this is capitalism coming in. And I think that's, to me, against the spirit of the thing because he's now decided that he's worth more than someone who only charges 6 Bobbins.

The ability of Heterotopians to operate though changed cultural codes around money was therefore limited by the Transformers, who professed themselves to be 'quite intolerant of this attitude' – one which they felt was against their ethos of personal responsibility. For Transformers, LETS is a trading tool for people to do what they want with, and it is for people to take control of their trading decisions without asking someone else to decide how trading should or should not take place. LETS, they argue, is supposed to make people be responsible for their own lives, and they felt that this person was not taking responsibility for themselves without seeking protection from the Core Group. The official ethos was that it was not the Core Group's responsibility to set prices; it was for people to negotiate, and if they thought the sterling price too high, then not to trade. Transformers wanted Heterotopians to understand that LETS operated *alongside* the mainstream economy, and did not (yet) transform the real world:

> I want to say to people "get real". People still have to live and make their way and pay their bills so they would have to charge Sterling to pay their bills, and people needed to understand that the self-employed person had a right to a good income as well and to respect that. I'm more and more telling people not to be backward about putting up the Sterling component of their charges and not exploit themselves.

Consequently, Transformers were more tolerant of mainstream values impinging on LETS and regarded it as the individual right of every member to set their own values. They therefore set the limits of how much cultural codes could be transformed. While Heterotopians could say that money is 'just information' and could make the jump and revalue fairly easily, Transformers ensured that the system was open to all comers and therefore those with 'old' ideas about money were able to join. Transformers insisted that it was for individuals alone to decide what they would use as their definition of value, and for individuals to wage individual wars against those who had values different to their own. The most active members with Heterotopian perspectives were able to create networks that traded using their changed value system. For most members, however, the small volume of transactions through which these individual wars could be fought ensured that attempts to trade often ended with a refusal to trade with those who did not accept the acceptable hourly rate, rather than a collective process of redefining cultural concepts around money. Alternatively, members found that cultural codes were not changed and the influence of structural forces in terms of commonsense values about money – that 'debt is wrong', 'it's good to have savings', 'you can't spend what you haven't got' – remained to govern the system. Cultural change around money, then, was limited for many, but possible for the active.

CHANGING CONCEPTIONS OF WORK

The second claim members made was that LETS revalues work, employment and livelihood. They said they participated in LETS for the chance to use their skills and for the feeling that LETS was an organisation that valued their skills. Members spoke movingly about what they called the spirituality and the psychic benefits of participation in an economy that valued and included them and their potential contribution; as much as about the chance to use pre-existing skills and cost-benefit calculations about tangible benefits. As a result, members were more concerned to stress the intangible value of the feelings that they got from participation in LETS, even when evidence of tangible participation (in terms of the number of Bobbins traded) was low.

What I really got was the value of people coming together with something that they all supported and with a commitment that they all shared. It's something that's difficult to put into words, difficult to categorise, there's something almost political about it, if certainly not party-political, that had never happened before. The catalysing of all the potential energy which I'd never seen before, and I couldn't believe that all these people who'd been kept apart before had come together and I got most out of actually mixing with them and meeting with them through the excuse of the trading events and questions and answers and that, and of course the trading all fitted in perfectly, but this seems like to cap that, the value of sharing.

However, while much of the attraction of LETS is in the aspiration toward alternative forms of livelihood, others were successful at actualising these alternative forms of work, beyond aspirations. They were those who had recognised that LETS valued work differently from the mainstream economy and acted accordingly, that 'there are all sorts of things that you can get done in LETS that aren't that easy to get in the money economy, in fact you can't'. Members found that Bobbins could be earned for services that most people would be unwilling or unable to purchase for Sterling, so market signals provided the possibility of alternative livelihoods. An example is a member who found a market for his abilities as a 'psychic healer':

For me, what really interested me was the tremendous amount of energy, drive, skills and publicity that the Manchester LETS scheme got to start with and the great perk for me being in the first directory, I was one of the first people to offer healing in the directory, and when the BBC Breakfast News did a piece on Manchester LETS, my entry appeared on TV, you know, a page saying ... "Psychic healing", "Chakras" ... so that I could say, you know, "as seen on TV!" (laughter). My experience of the LETS scheme is that I haven't had the time to go for everything, but I appreciated how wonderful it was ... and it's always given me a great feel good factor to be part of it ... I haven't really gone for the "daily routine" services or jobs. I offered healing, and preferred to offer it for Bobbins not cash because I think that people have expectations of someone offering a service for Sterling, and I thought that I'd have to become a Russell Grant-type before I could offer healing, but I was quite confident offering it to people as I done it for friends and relatives, offering it for Bobbins ... So it's been me actually buying things or doing things I couldn't do or I wouldn't normally do, or doing things for people that I wouldn't normally do. It's not really been the ordinary things: it's been things that wouldn't normally happen.

Another member found a new outlet for his skills as a 'wormery' builder (a composting device using large numbers of worms):

I think that it is a new area where people are on the one hand asked to try things that they wouldn't do as a job or in a professional role as that role, say wormery builder for me, isn't there. LETS enabled me to do it and it just happened that I believed I had a professional attitude to it. Turn up on time, with what I need, get it done – and it worked. So in one way it enables you to do things that aren't "professional", but obviously it's the attitude with which you do things. But I think that some people do see it as a hobby which, you know ... They are getting into it for the right reasons perhaps, valuing more people's input.

Thinking innovatively, jobs can be created that would not occur to the participant in the mainstream economy – jobs that would not be viable or that would be unattractive. A recycling company was able to create a new job of 'van-buying consultant'. They needed a new van, but did not have the knowledge or time to shop around for the best deal. They employed a mechanically-minded LETS member to act as a 'van-buyer' on their behalf. This members knowledge and time got them a serviceable second-hand van at a fraction of the price they were thinking of, compared with a credit package on a new van. Saving money made LETS serious for the business:

> We probably saved four thousand pounds in Sterling because of his input into our decision, and he didn't actually tell us what to do. He gave us all the information so we were able to make an educated decision and, you know, it turned out to be the right decision as it went very well for us. That money, although we haven't saved it directly, we've not got to spend it, if that makes sense. … So for us that was probably the most important transaction that we have made, its one that I can't see how we would have bought that for Sterling. It's because of the fact that he cared enough about our business to want to suggest that we do something, and for … his only gain was to see us do better plus he gained some Bobbins. So I can't see how we would have ever got that help outside LETS. He did treat it as a job: he spent four evenings with us going over it, did quite a bit of background research with us, but it was a trade that switched it over into us taking it more seriously.

If the business made hard savings from LETS, another member saw LETS as a way of experimenting and trying alternatives safely:

> A lot of things that crop up all over the place, not only in LETS: Aromatherapy and the other things we associate with the spiritual side, in LETS less so than in the commercial world, it's very much less than in the commercial world that you risk the charlatan who makes use of people's gullibility with it. I think that's happening a hell of a lot in industry and in the commercial world. Even people who call themselves Buddhists and get themselves into groups. Some of them are fine, but you get an awful lot of sort of hocus-pocus … you get an awful lot of that, but less so in LETS. I would say that the people who look at LETS and who don't say "Oh that's a lot of nonsense" and who really realise the value in it are less likely to be the charlatans!

Others thought it was a way to value skills which were possessed by social excluded people, but which were undervalued by the mainstream. They felt that participation in LETS was a way of valuing the contribution of people the mainstream did not appreciate:

> I can't even remember how I first heard about it – I think it was from a friend; and I thought "It sounds like a good idea, a way to meet some new people and do different things, sell some of my drawings …" I work for an organisation for people with drug and alcohol problems, and thought it would be really good if the members who come to me could recognise the skills that they have got but haven't been used for a long time.

High traders then did manage, often, to redefine work. The LETS economy gave out different price signals and made work – as a healer, a wormery builder, a batik workshop facilitator – viable. Another was brave enough to offer to trade 'perished rubber gloves'! Members could surf the New Age safely without fear of the financial abuse of possibly vulnerable people. LETS is a desire-driven economy operating under different rules, with different market signals.

However, again there were limits to the ability of members to revalue work. Again, with the volume of trades being so low, many traders found it hard to break through into an understanding that the LETS economy operated under different market signals. They continued to think in terms governed by their life experience within the mainstream economy (as they had with revaluing money). Firstly, they found it hard to decide what skills they had, and what was or was not a sellable skill. They found it hard to say what was or was not an acceptable skill level for which they would feel comfortable receiving Bobbins without being thought of as a 'cowboy' trader:

> I feel that on occasions people do not take responsibility for their product when they advertise it, you know they advertise it as, you know, being a gardener or being a graphic designer, er, and I know it's up to the individual to negotiate about their skills base when you are forming a contract ... It's about honesty and integrity. I wouldn't dream of telling you I could mend a bicycle. Unless I was sure I could mend a bicycle satisfactorily, safely, and that you would be pleased with the product ... Because that's one of the rules in which interaction works, you know we don't have relationships which are open-ended, ... we have carefully negotiated relationships. It just seems to me that LETS is begging that issue. ... One of the things that we learn in co-counselling is, very very clear contract setting. We learn how to make clear contracts with people with whom we swap, people who we exchange with (as) obviously the contract needs to be very clearly defined for safety. But it works! People say, begin to learn how to say very clearly this is what I need, and it enables the person who's the co-negotiator to say "yes I can deliver that service" or 'no I can't'. And that's something that, for me, needs to be more clearly defined, perhaps, in LETS.

Others felt that some traders felt 'anything goes' in LETS and they wanted the quality that they associate with the mainstream economy:

> I had a person who wanted the Bobbins as they were a student and all the rest of it, and she wanted cash as well so I was paying partly in Bobbins and partly in cash, and her performance was not a valued performance. She treated it like it didn't matter! And therefore I in good faith was paying her money and Bobbins, and in good faith there was for me a contract around a quality of performance, and that is not my experience sometimes with LETS. That people who want to, erm the benefit of earning things or having things done for them that they themselves can't do, sometimes I find, I feel, don't give the same commitment with their giving as they do with their receiving! And that's not a judgement but a sadness because I think well, LETS will only survive and grow if the ... if the Bobbins are earned with respect. And the tasks are performed with respect.

Some members found that when the trade was based on mainstream, narrowly economic instrumental values rather on relationships they felt cheated and abused:

> I remember trading with someone and I got some very strange kind of feelings about it, you know, some real uncertainties. ... I wanted to check this person out so I went to the directory, look in the directory to see what else they do to build up a profile, and the

person wasn't in there! So I'm sort of, ... wow! And so somebody's rung me up out of the blue, I don't know them from Adam, they've told me they are from LETS but they are not in there, and I got all these bad sensations from them. I believe this person used LETS as a market place basically, to go and acquire goods that people wanted and then, ... Hey – it's a good marketing technique. ... I think that made us realise how vulnerable it was, and how vulnerable you were making yourself with your name appearing in lots of people's houses that you didn't know and, and that you could be being run up by people that you assumed had been, kind of vetted, not in a horrible way, but in a personal way that is important if you are in a big city. You know? You don't know everybody. You can be done all the time. And it feels like a dangerous process there. ... I think that that shows our naiveté."

Members showed a lack of commitment to trading. Too many members mentioned making many calls for someone to provide a service, which meant that for the committed member earning Bobbins was not a difficulty, but the loop too easily closed off and the member with a high credit balance found himself unable to spend. One member felt that he was fooling himself by trading and accepting Bobbins he could not spend:

I've accumulated a great pile of Bobbins in my Bobbin account – which I haven't as yet spent! I don't know where to spend my Bobbins! I must say that I'm feeling a smidgen frustrated at this as I think I'd prefer at the moment to be paid Sterling as I could spent that and I'm finding it very difficult to spend Bobbins as when I look through the list ... It's all a bit frustrating ... So I let it ride, so in fact what I've been doing is cheating myself in a sense, as in letting it ride I haven't participated in the practice of the LETS scheme as I've played only a peripheral part. I've used it as a vehicle to in effect provide this person with (a service) and this miffs me a bit as I've been cheating myself at the end of it, and I need to make some sense of that. I'm still trying to work it out! ... I don't buy very much anyway – I suppose I'm not a very good consumer! ... of the sort of things LETS offers. I think that what I would like to have done would be to employ a LETS cleaner but we have a cleaning lady who's been coming for *x* number of years and its impossible to change that relationship. It wouldn't have worked at all. It would have been impossible to keep her.

One member felt that LETS was a rather empty political gesture rather than a genuine way of revaluing work. She found that since many members did not operate under the changed cultural rules about work, they did not actively trade with and interact with those the mainstream did not appreciate. They were intolerant and critical of those that operated by their own cultural norms, and whose understanding of a quality product, of timekeeping, and of acceptable personal behaviour, was different. This saddened her:

I really got interested in LETS, because I felt that it might be an opportunity for people to have recognition for their activities in terms of Bobbins while it would have been impossible for them to go out to work as such. Although unfortunately, I don't think LETS ... that's what it's about. I think it's actually quite privileged! I think it's quite a middle class thing! Er. I think it's ... as always, you know, incredibly PC, that is, probably a lot of gestures about, you know, middle class people who can afford to have these grand gestures! They've got nothing to lose, they have got a job. Or if they haven't got jobs they are developing themselves, on a personal development path, you know!

Others did not take up offers to learn new skills that were available:

> The main things that I offer are like art and craft, whether it's teaching someone how to do it or a commission or use of the workshop to do their own thing, 'cos I've got a dark room cum workshop myself and when I was part time I had plenty of time to do that sort of thing so I did quite a few batik workshops, and one worked very well (but) I had another really BAD experience ... when I felt quite annoyed about the whole thing as it takes a full day of my time to do it and like four hours to set up the workshop on top of that, and I'd asked people to book a place before so I know how many are coming as there's not room for more than five, and I'd confirmed people coming and then on the day only one person turned up on time, one turned up three hours late, two people cancelled but not until one pm, half way through the day, and ... what happened to the other one? I think they came in later or didn't come at all. I don't think they even rung.
>
> I felt really annoyed about that as I felt, you know, I've given up my day to be here and planned it and put quite a lot of effort into it and they couldn't be bothered to ring me or just turned up really late and that meant the whole thing was really rushed for them and the workshop ran on beyond time and I felt really hassled. I felt a bit like the workshop was being devalued and people weren't taking it seriously ... or taking me seriously ... and I felt really annoyed about it. I think as it is Bobbins sometimes people don't value it in quite the same way, think it is only Bobbins or that you aren't really good at doing what you are offering.

The same problems observed with the micro-politics of money became observable with work. Work was either successfully redefined – or not – individually; rather than collectively and with support. The ethos of keeping administration light left members alone to sink or swim, to decide what to offer alone with little support in teasing out hidden skills.

Consequently the libertarian ethos was abandoned slightly and one Core Group member decided to offer monthly trading surgeries in order to support members in trading. The network of neighbourhood contacts was expanded to form local support networks for trading. However, those who had skills that they were unlikely to be able to make a living from – tarot readers and the like – found a genuine outlet for their skills, and those with skills the mainstream valued found that as LETS operates by alternative rules there was little market for their skills. Active traders did find that cultural codes around work and livelihood operated under different rules in LETS and they were able to live the alternative lives they wanted, to some extent.

CHANGING CONCEPTIONS OF COMMUNITY

The third claim is that LETS changes cultural codes about relationships from atomised individualism to caring, sharing community-mindedness and support. The following extract from field notes shows one of the community-building mechanisms members of Manchester LETS used:

> Core Group meeting, at Lynn's house in Levenshulme. In the room she uses as the office, cushions on the floor. Siobhan, back from Australia, walks in and is given a hug by David who hasn't seen her for a few months. I sit next to Peter, who facilitates the meetings, and next to Barry (Computer Group co-ordinator). Everyone brings biscuits

to share. Suddenly Peter says "Shall we start?" and without warning everyone (all 8 of us) sits on the floor and holds hands to form a circle. Everyone closes their eyes, I don't know what to do so do as I'm told! I don't know what I'm supposed to be thinking but keep quiet and wait to be told what to do next. I don't know how long we will sit like this. I want to see if everyone's got their eyes shut but dare not look, like a fifteen-year-old's kiss (are her eyes shut?). After a minute, Helen exhales deeply, and stretches. Barry gives my hand a friendly squeeze. I open my eyes and Stephen winks at me – he knows what I was thinking! Mike looks embarrassed. Peter starts the meeting by asking everyone to say one good think they like about the English weather.

When we get home I asked Peter what all the hand-holding was about. He said it was called 'attunement' and was meant to get everyone to clear their mind of what had gone before, think about what they wanted to say, and to feel part of the Core Group and dedicated to the well-being of LETS. 'Commitment-Building mechanisms' – I thought.

(Field notes, 1st March 1995)

Heterotopians and Transformers alike claimed that LETS builds community. LETS should be an economy built on friendship, connections, trust, and co-operation. Community would be built through linking economic and social life into what members call 'relationship trading' – the opposite of the ethos 'nothing personal – it's just business'. Members looked to build friendship with those with whom they trade, as a Heterotopian commented:

I suppose I kind of expected to trade with people and like have a *relationship* with them ... and also particularly some of the people that I have met through the LETSystem, like, it has occurred. It's like ... let's forget all the institutional structures around things, we are talking about being alive on the earth and the experience of being a human being and how we all connect with each other ... and what do we fundamentally have in common outside all the social and cultural structures. It has that sort of rootedness about it. And sometimes I've met people where I've felt like, you know, I've ... I've really, struck, struck a chord there. There's a kind of resonance.

Another Heterotopian commented:

When I'm talking about community I'm talking about connection on a human level, on a personal level. You know, when you meet people ... it's like you've got to, you know everyone in LETS says "I know your name", "I've read your name" and, like you go through the Directory there are all these names and people who are offering things, Like (someone's) offering, offered perished rubber gloves and I'm dying to meet (that person)! You know, there's something very fascinating about it, like its a lonely heart's column!

Community should develop through trading. The following experiences, of an active trader, are typical of LETS at its most effective in building community:

I've had quite a few good trades but one that stands out is a woman who I rang up who I'd never met before who is offering massage, and she lived very locally and it's something I wanted to look after myself a bit more and relax, I thought that would do very well, so I rang her up and had a massage and it was absolutely wonderful. She's a very talented woman and knows a lot about different types of massage, but there were loads of spin-offs from that first meeting that have continued regularly. She's really into gardening, I've got a lot of herb plants off her and advice on herb gardens, we've got to know each other quite well and we are friends. When I went to the (craft) workshop (where this informant works), she was interested in becoming a volunteer there as she also has a background in fine art. She's gone on to become a volunteer where I work and she's given a lot to the organisation as a volunteer…

So that's gone really well. She lives round the corner and we didn't know each other at all and now we are friends and I really value that. It turns out she knows lots of people I know so the networks moved a bit further, I've told lots of people about her when they've been joining LETS and want massage so it's nice to get some more clients for her. So its grown and evolved and is really nice. That's my happy story … because I think it's great meeting people who live round the corner who you'd never have met otherwise. I've met a lot of people that I'd never have met on a daily basis which is crazy as we are really near to each other. And just the fact that you do things for each other, like she was looking to do some kind of work-type thing and volunteering really seems to work well for her so it's really nice for her and I benefited a lot which is one of the things that she can give me. I like that: giving and taking, giving and receiving.

From friendship, trust emerged:

there has to be a large element of trust in it, in that yesterday I handed my £260 tent and sleeping bag and many other things to someone who gave me an acknowledgement of 30 Bobbins and that is not the sort of thing that normally happens in society, that you trust somebody else with a piece of property or whatever. One of my motivations for joining LETS that I haven't mentioned yet is that people need to share things more. I've got this expensive tent, I think we should manufacture less because of the environmental damage that manufacture does. So it's logical for me with expensive rucksacks and tents to want people to use them when I'm not rather than buy them themselves, so I can similarly get use of someone's van rather than having a van myself.

From trust grew a softness towards others, and understanding and caring for others who might not see the world the way the participant might, and which made those critical of the quality of work done for LETS feel that they were being mealy-mouthed:

I do decorating, and I heard of one bloke that did decorating and the person had to ask them politely to stop working as he just was not good. In that instance the person said that they didn't mind because, is all a part of, that's what LETS is all about, it was a learning experience for them as to whether they were going to say anything, and they got something positive out of it.

Softness developed through practising co-operation, sharing and support for others:

My initial thing was to, LETS, this feels good, this is an organisation where there is an attempt to swap skills with respect and equal value, which are things I hold dear to my heart. There is perhaps an opportunity for people who don't work in mainstream employment to still have a way of earning some sort of currency which they can use to purchase things for themselves.

A community that shares:

I looked at this directory and I saw loads of people sharing resources, time, skills, energy … and *love*. Incredible!

And sharing supports difference, 'Community is about inclusions of difference and ability and all the rest of it':

> Community (is) important to me but also important to think about … for families rather than for single people in a way. Because we haven't replaced the extended family at all, we do need community, community for … for people with young children as it's much too intensive in a small family. Far too much for them. And for old people …

Care was found by a member who found support for his disabled partner and who gave him a break:

> In some ways I'm a bit trapped as I can't even go out for a pint unless I arrange for someone to sit here, so in that respect of being in control … I'm not in charge of my life. Although, on the other hand … I've just done a deal with a girl that we know that will do baby-sitting and we couldn't afford pound notes so we've just got her to join LETS. So I get baby-sitting for Bobbins now which gives me more time to do what I want to do … Yes, (LETS) gives me a break from my situation. It makes me happy to work at something I enjoy, getting out of this environment and doing some real work as it were, even though people say it's only for Bobbins. It's just as good: it gives me a break from the everyday things in my life, and gives me Bobbins to pay for baby-sitters etc. I enjoy doing that.

Another member found that LETS gave her the support structure she needed to be able to choose to live life alone without feeling that support was not available:

> As I live alone, because I choose to spend my life without a partner's support, what is really important to me is that I need all sorts of different sorts of support from different sources. So for example, you know in a crisis where I am sitting on the floor disempowered and thinking "Oh my God, how am I going to deal with this!" The, for me, the back stop, that there's that little book, that I could actually, because I have made a commitment to be part of this community, I can actually not have to go to the yellow pages but go to that book and know that in principle there are like-minded people who wouldn't be, and who would accept my confusion and my "Oh my god!!" and not be patronising or judgmental about it. I find that quite comforting.

Community then did develop for active members. Heterotopians explicitly wanted LETS to build community and act as a community, whereas the Transformers' position was that LETS should be just a trading network, not restricted to those who wanted close, communal relations with their fellow traders:

> unless it's like an alternative to ordinary money a lot of businesses can't equate the value of it and can't get involved. Therefore, the community will not have a wide range of services within LETS. If they don't have that, it will stay very marginal. It stays very marginal and it doesn't have a great effect on poverty alleviation. It doesn't have a great effect on anything. So I think I start from the point of view that it has to be effective. … I suppose the question then is, effective in doing what? I think it should be effective as a money system. It should be an effective currency that people could use. With all the benefits of the LETS currency as opposed to cash. And I think the consequence of it is that it does build community. I think that community is a very important part of everything we do. Whether it is in the cash economy or in LETS. And every time you

have a transaction with someone, whatever it is, there's an opportunity there for building a relationship. And I think, because of the nature of LETS, it makes that probably easier. But only as a condition of its effectiveness as a money system. I've never been of the view that you should do 10 hours work and charge one Bobbin.

Transformers argue that LETS builds community through the process of trading as members organically and automatically build networks. They argue that the key to successful economic activity is also the building of relationships – relationship trading. The most active traders, we have seen, were able to build community this way, while Heterotopians wished to spend more time on building community and saw trading as secondary to that.

However, literature on similar attempts to create community through trade alone – from the co-operative movement – explains why the Transformers' strategy falls down for all but the highest traders. Essentially, there is not enough contact through simple trading to develop relationships unless the trader is very active and proactive in meeting new traders. As with the co-operative movement, communication and community-building in LETS is based on trading, through either purchasing from the co-op store, or through providing services in LETS. Neither brings people in contact enough for relationships to develop unless participants make a conscious effort to build such community, since individual trading lays few demands on the individual and the bond between them is therefore so fragile that communality does not develop (Buber 1949:77). Community based solely on economic trading is 'least suited in itself as a cell of social reconstruction. It brings people together with only a minimal and highly impersonal part of their total being' (1949:74).

The Heterotopians recognised that community needs to be built because connections through trading are too tenuous for community to evolve sponta-neously. However, as they did with the revaluation of money, the Transformers set the limits on transformation into a community rather than a network. In widening LETS out of a green single-issue group, the Transformers brought in people who wanted instrumental economic connections rather than transformed relations based on community trading. Secondly, interviews with low traders revealed that they did not have time, inclination or ability to spend time individually building up relationships, or didn't feel confident enough to phone strangers and build community with them. Others were geographically remote. Thirdly, the Heterotopians in Manchester were also involved with the other environmental networks discussed in chapter 5, or were active within the Green Party. Consequently, they were happy to let the Transformers set the limits of how community would be built, and the Transformers' conception of LETS as a value-free network based on trading was ascendant. Why the Heterotopian current did not do more to make its perceptions central is the next question, a discussion of attempts to strengthen internal solidarity within LETS.

STRENGTHENING INTERNAL SOLIDARITY

Melucci's second question for a constructivist analysis of a social movement is to examine how members of LETS debated whether to concentrate on strengthening the internal life of LETS – deepening heterotopia – as opposed to widening participation by other groups through frame transformation as discussed in Chapter Seven. The debate was between the Transformers' perception that LETS was just a bank account, available to all; and that as a result no attempts at collective self-government were appropriate, and Heterotopian conceptions of LETS as a community in which it was appropriate to deepen processes of self-government. The development of internal self-government can be analysed firstly through a discussion of a Member's Forum called at the initiative of Heterotopians, which sought to strengthen the internal operation and community life of Manchester LETS. Secondly, by examining what happened when Heterotopians sought to inspire collective self-government through a discussion of who should – or should not – be a member of Manchester LETS.

In July 1995, a Heterotopian member of the Core Group ran a 'Member's Forum', which was an attempt to get members together to collectively debate how LETS was developing and to involve them in future activities, (rather than leaving them to individually regulate LETS through their individual trading decisions). Consequently, it was an attempt to deepen internal solidarity rather than widen participation from the mainstream. The Forum would form an opportunity to illuminate strong debates and conflicts between Transformers and Heterotopians. Heterotopians would have been able to change the dominant libertarian ethos of the system if they wanted to. Certainly, Transformers believed that the Forum was 'not our day'!

In the event there was no observable conflict at the Forum. Noticeably absent was any suggestion that the work of the Transformers, through LEDA, should cease or be controlled by members (given disputes about use of the government grant). A strongly live-and-let-live, or unstructured position was maintained by both sides and LEDA felt that their work was legitimated by the Forum. However, the Transformers did not get allies for the transformation project, and Heterotopian sentiments for future actions prevailed. The extract below shows what was discussed at the Forum, arising from members suggestions as to what initiatives they would like to see Manchester LETS undertake:

Extract 10.1 Developing collective government in Manchester

- *Community and social group*: A social committee formed that organised social events.
- *Ethics and exploitation*: A group of members discussed charging for services.
- *A LETS centre*: Members wanted a drop-in centre, perhaps including a LETS office, cafe and workspace.
- *Decentralisation*: Members felt that Manchester LETS was too geographically disparate and discussed developing local LETSystems, including Neighbourhood Contacts.
- *Food:* The perennial burning issue. Some members wanted to be able to live exclusively within LETS, and sought to develop access to organic food.

Notable from the above is that the planned initiatives all aimed to deepen rather than widen LETS, with the exception of the planned Drop-in Centre (which was suggested by Core Group members). Secondly, the strongest emphasis was for community in the shape of social contacts, and for discussions about ethics. These cut against the 'official ethos' of Manchester LETS that such matters were for individuals to sort out for themselves, and that community would arise spontaneously from trading. Members therefore put more of an emphasis on building community.

This may be a result of the Forum being identified with the Heterotopian wing of Manchester LETS, and many members who were uninterested in building community did not attend. Consequently claims that the Forum was in some way representative cannot be sustained, but discussion at the Forum, all initiated directly by members, shows the Heterotopian position effectively.

If the Forum was an exercise in toleration, what happens when Transformers aim to go a step too far and do something that the Heterotopians object to – and the limits of this toleration become observable? What happens when members of LETS have to negotiate about the results of Transformers' success in making LETS conducive to businesses and, as a result, the Transformers recruited a business that Heterotopians did not feel was appropriately ethical – a sinner! Here, Heterotopians claimed that LETS should make collective decisions about what should or should not happen in LETS, whereas Transformers wished to have LETS open to all comers – and if members objected to anyone, they should not trade with them.

A beauty salon placed the following advertisement in the directory offering non-invasive cosmetic surgery (see below). In response, a member wrote to the core group complaining that 'It's hard enough fighting the propaganda around women's issues and the right for women to be happy with their bodies as they are, without finding such stuff in the LETS Directory. What next? Ads for clinics to prevent male baldness, porn magazines, or trips to Sellafield?' (*Loose Threads*, June 1995). More letters followed, demanding that the community should decide where the fine line between acceptable and unacceptable lay.

> Yes, it is a fine line. So where do we draw it? The important thing is to understand WHY we draw lines like that. I'd like to suggest a reason for LETS refusing to include certain things in the directory: because they are *exploitative, manipulative or oppressive*. It is fairly well established that such adverts play on people's fears – and are thus manipulative. Specifically, they play on *women's fear*, and are thus discriminatory, and thus oppressive. And if an advertiser seeks material gain out of manipulation or oppression, I think it's fair to call it exploitative.
>
> Could we write something in the Constitution to say we won't accept Directory entries or adverts which are felt to be either manipulative, exploitative or oppressive.
>
> (*Loose Threads*, August/September 1995 – emphasis original)

This member described why he had written in:

> Basically we were up against the question of what do we censor, as if you don't have elements of censorship some things that are oppressive creep in there, and my attitude was that we allow anything in the system unless it was suppressive, exploitative, or manipulative ... I think that's a way of keeping Multinationals out, and people extracting lots of surplus value could be regarded as oppressive, manipulative and exploitative.

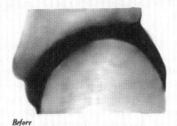
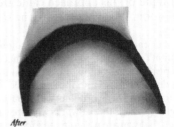

Another commented:

> No one should be allowed to sell drugs through LETS for a start, and cosmetic surgery I should say is … a questionable thing … and 90 and one other services that are completely unethical such as selling videos that should be nowhere near young people … Yes, I think the community should do this … A meeting should be offered and they have their say, and someone arbitrates then they have to accept.

The critique of this approach came from one of those who hold LETS as value-free – Linton. When interviewed, he said:

> It's that (attitude that) people shouldn't, this should be, people should equal this or shouldn't equal that. My attitude is that we've got to get this thing done fast or we will all be up shit creek without a paddle. So if businesses are in barter clubs and loyalty cards why don't we move into the same field and find a more ethical way of doing it and get it out there. I have no problem with a business, which is just an organisation, a collection of people, perhaps three owners who are shareholders, or a co-op. Form whatever you like! Given that you are not going to exclude people, if you don't like that system join another in a MultiLETS Registry … I don't think it's realistic to say LETSystems are only for good people and that doesn't include businesses.

So on practical grounds no one should be excluded – but also on ethical grounds:

> I can't see any problem of capital accumulation from people using a currency that you can't hoard, so it's never been an issue for me. That's why we bring in the multinationals, to educate them out of their irresponsibility. So that's a non discussion for me, both at the practical level and the ethical. And whether the ethical one has any weight or not is secondary to the practical one. Given that there are 300,000 businesses in the States *doing* this, are we going to say they shouldn't, they wouldn't? Come on – let's go and do it! I've got work to do!

Defending the lack of opportunities for collective decision-making and a welter of individual trades, the LETSGo position was that trading is the responsibility of members and they decide for themselves who they wish to trade with. The LETS System has no other responsibility:

> A LETSystem is like a club, but to think of it as a formal Association can be misleading. It's more like a community that comes together to hold parties or meets regularly on Sundays to play football. A core group is useful in getting the system up and running. But for the day-to-day running, a committee approach brings unnecessary bureaucracy and can be contrary to the spirit of the LETSystem.
>
> In a LETSystem there is always enough information to allow participants to regulate the system themselves. There is no need for a separate group to 'govern' the system. But organisers are needed to make the system work. Like all other participants in the system, they are accountable to everyone involved.
>
> Once it becomes clear who does what, there is no need for regular meetings, constitutions and other legal paraphernalia. All that is required is that responsibilities are clearly laid out and consent to those arrangements is freely given.
>
> (Internal document)

The LETSGo position was that structure is not required beyond the provision of accounts, and within LETS all are equal. A similar misconception with regard to women's movement prompted Freeman's seminal 1970 article 'The tyranny of structurelessness', which suggested that as in any relationship there are always power relations, organisations should make these relations explicit before they make themselves explicit. Declaring themselves to be a network with no power relations, different levels of power held by different members manifested themselves in an uncontrolled manner.

These debates made visible the limits of how far LETS could evolve away from a community of like-minded people (with similar perceptions and levels of power), into a diverse network of disparate traders with different power relations between them. The Heterotopians limited the Transformers' room for manoeuvre in widening LETS. Similarly, the Transformers limited the room for manoeuvre of the Heterotopians through their official ethos that LETS is value-free and through their involvement of members who do not want to build community – seeing it purely as a skills exchange, as a network. Their position needed to be protected. Consequently, the extent of self-government was on the Transformers terms, at the individual level. This individual ethos was reinforced by the Core Group's decision to no longer organise members' social events centrally. As a result, members organised events themselves locally, which were much smaller, chaotic affairs that did not give the same feeling of community as the larger events.

Consequently the extent that LETS could develop into a self-governing entity was limited. The individual ethos meant that in LETS there were few of what Kantor (1972) called 'commitment building mechanisms'. In her study comparing 19th and 20th century intentional communities, she identified that longer-lasting 19th century communities in the United States acted positively to build community through a series of mechanisms. These she identified as *Sacrifice* and *Investment* (giving something up to join the community and making some investment, financially or spiritually, in order to stay in it), *Renunciation* and *Communion* (turning your back on your old life, family and ways of thinking, and embracing a new life which is reinforced by communal acts of co-worship or study such as ritual, group discussions, shared meals, which reinforce community and connection), and finally *Mortification* and *Transcendence* (leaving your old self spiritually and psychologically and joining a new whole in which the individual is transcended by the group or by subservience to a charismatic leader). Examples of successful communities who adopt all of these are the Bruderhoff or Hutterites who have hundreds of years of experience in living in community through complex rituals, group events and connections from adopting similar language and dress, and living all parts of their life in common. These 19th century communities have lasted into the present day by building the role of the group *at the expense* of the individual, who gives up considerable autonomy in return for benefits of transcendence. In contrast, Kantor found that the sixties communes she examined had fewer of these commitment-building mechanisms.

LETS was not seen by anyone, Transformer or Heterotopian, as an intentional community completely apart from society (hence the Heterotopian label rather than utopian). Therefore, no one argued for strong boundaries and commitment building mechanisms. Transformers recognized that modern life is more diverse, technologically and economically interconnected, and offers more personal freedom than the 19th century and therefore needs to enable members to join and trade in LETS at whatever level suits them, building community through trading. By contrast, Heterotopians sought to cross the boundary from the mainstream into heterotopia and back out again with each trade – a postmodern intentional community. Whilst LETS was effective in enabling participation at a rate set by the individual – at the same time, without large trading levels and more chances of personal contact, commitment-building mechanisms will be absent so that, as with communes in the 1960s, 'jobs remain undone, conflicts never get ironed out, and 'family feeling' develops only with difficulty'. (Kantor 1972:184).

In Manchester LETS there was little attempt to build a collective identity. Rather, the ethos was of considerable tolerance and mutual agreement to knock along against each other. A Greener summed up the attitude most people had about differences of opinion:

> I've a very flexible attitude towards what people want to do to save the world because obviously people have got different conceptions of what constitutes 'radical' anyway, and who am I to tell them, 'No, don't do that, do this ... probably from my own perspective would have criticised some people for their attitude to LETS, because they've got an un-radical attitude to LETS, if you see what I mean, without prejudice to what I've just said about not having the right to tell other people how to think about it. I think that what I mean is that I have a bigger, more utopian ideal about what LETS can achieve than some people do.

Heterotopians also were often very active in other ecological activities. Consequently they did by and large join the Core Group and therefore did not engage in constant warfare with Transformers but were happy to be participants in LETS. Few group-building mechanisms were therefore employed outside the Core Group attunement process. In the early days, the Core Group included a 'maintenance person' with responsibility for ensuring that the group worked effectively at an interpersonal level. Social and Trading events were centrally organised which did include group discussions, but this practice was discontinued and responsibility put back on members to organise them. The Core Group position that LETS is a trading network rather than a community or tool for participatory democracy remained dominant and no further fora were called. The Core Group member who initiated the Forum was also ejected from his position as Core Group facilitator later in the year. Heterotopians did not organise another Forum.

DID MEMBERS FEEL THAT THE POLITICAL OPPORTUNITY STRUCTURE RESTRICTED OPPORTUNITIES FOR PARTICIPATION IN LETS?

The final question is to consider whether members felt that the political opportunity structure that LETS operated in restricted the movement's ability to self-produce cultural codes and condemned them either to adjustment of the codes or to margin-alisation. Chapter 7 examined the extent to which members felt that what they might be doing will provoke a response, with some members feeling that the tax and benefit authorities might limit the extent that LETS could spread. This section will therefore concentrate on the extent that the POS restricts life in Heterotopia, in non-engagement with institutions. In starting to draw discussion of LETS as a social movement to a close, it is necessary to consider at a strategic level the extent that, taken as a whole, members of LETS can live the sort of lifestyle they aim to – as part of a collective struggle for a new way of living. One member of the focus group discuss felt that he was not restricted at all in living the sort of life he wanted:

> many of these things are about how people live their lives and I do think we have choices about that. ... we presumably have these ideas as we believe they are right and hope it will make us happy. ... so what I'm saying is that this thing with growth is a good example. I don't do the things I do because ... I do them as I think they are good for me but other people might not find them so enthusing ... So, I hope that I *am* doing a lot of these things! Obviously I can't dictate what will happen around me but I do think that most people are the same. That it is a way forward.

It is claimed here that LETS enables a Heterotopian to live entirely as a Nomad of the Present, as the 1970s communards hoped 'as if the revolution had happened and we won'. The choice to act in a certain way is with us all and we can choose to live freely if we so desire – and LETS enables us to link up with other like-minded people and speed the process along. While this is the politics of lifestyle, LETS builds a collectivity out of those individual lifestyle choices. These are the most extreme claims for LETS from the Heterotopian perspective.

A Greener felt that LETS is more of a step towards a future green society rather than a way of living it now – but a vital component within a process of social change that included, along with building alternative institutions, political protest and electoral action:

> I would never say that you could change society from the top down, so if someone was trying to create a green society from the top down then I think that they would probably fail because it would be hierarchical and people would rebel against it, erm, but if you've got things like LETS and any other, sort of socially empowering ideas, then people are getting the hang of social empowerment, and if you've got political changes that are actually in tune with that, then that should I think be the way to achieve it.

Greens have the same objectives as the Heterotopians but feel individual action is not enough. Everyone needs to be able to live sustainably, and has different views of sustainability, and that takes political action. A greener said:

> When I think of building a sustainable society and what can happen now I think not just in terms of can I do it but can everybody else do it as well ... It would take a massive growth in the number of LETSystems and in the capacity of LETSystems to allow everyone even in, in this city to live off LETS, and then there is the question of, you know if people are going to carry on wanting televisions, erm, there is going to have to be a television factory somewhere that operates on Bobbins ... And this is something that I don't think LETS in itself can solve. This is something that needs political action of a more formal nature.
>
> I don't think LETS on its own can create localised economies ... If you don't want a telly, and you are prepared to live on an allotment in a bender, that sort of thing, then

LETS, no doubt, could do that now. Erm provided you were the one growing the food because I don't think anyone else in Manchester is doing it ... on the LETSystem! But if you want a public transport network, if you want to be able to manufacture a bicycle, that sort of thing, then we really need local economies and that will take political action.

I don't think we can completely build an alternative ... as long as they've got that power because you know we are then abdicating that power ... I think all Greens who are being sort of logical, have got to see everything that they do in a holistic way, so there is no one panacea for sorting everything out.

Another Greener felt it would take time for a more developed local economy to emerge and LETS at present is no more than a small step along the way:

I think that there's a certain loyalty from me to the LETSystem, although it's not at a state where you can meet all your needs, where you can swap from a Sterling economy into a complete Bobbins economy, so there is a certain loyalty to trade to ensure that there is a progression to where it might be nearer that point where you can meet all your needs ... We have to be a future thing where you only get the occasional flash ... as only occasionally can you break through LETS to get what you want normally out of life as it's not a full alternative economy ... I think that you will get more of that when you can meet basic needs and you've got a more complete local currency.

Transformers agreed. They argued that LETS is still at a very early stage of development and does not allow participants to meet their basic needs outside LETS and focus on the need to get businesses involved, along with the local authority, utilities, community and voluntary organisations. They responded to the comments above 'you choose to do that but most people don't'. Another commented that LETS is just a subculture of the moment. The Heterotopian statement above was then modified to a need for partnership: while you can live green now, tomorrow wider resources are needed: for a more fulfilling existence provided by a local economy

We are working against the system that's already in place outside ... I consider it's a way of doing something constructive in an environment that's not conducive to doing that. People getting together to do something constructive. But they might not get the full potential.

So again, conclusions are mixed. Transformers and Heterotopians differed in the extent to which they perceived that what they wanted to do was limited by the political environment in which they operated – if they wished to live without a car, without hi-fi systems or washing machines, they could. It was little more than personal choice. But LETS cannot provide the opportunities of the mainstream economy, and as we saw in discussions of businesses the whole private sector of the capitalist economy is an area outside the control of LETS. Heterotopians cannot pay rent, taxes or yet get basic needs in LETS. Consequently they agree with Transformers that the local economy is still infantile. They see the need for a more complete local economy, but feel that this will be achieved by slow, organic growth of an alternative sector in opposition to the mainstream.

CONCLUSION: THE LIMITS OF HETEROTOPIA

So what of Heterotopia? Is it a message back to society, an ephemeral space that gives a vision of an alternative, entered only spasmodically my members through their limited trading experiences? While members can decide to change the way they value money, work, and community relationships between themselves, they are constrained in their ability to maintain this ephemeral utopia by their limited resources. Does this mean that the Marxist critique of Utopianism as a 'dwarfish' form of co-operation limited by the resources of those excluded from control of the means of production, or is it more than that – the autonomous zone of Buber and created by effective Foucaultian micro-political struggle? Alternatively, is it limited to the signification of an alternative, a form of postmodern information war in which its value is of a message rather than of a reality?

Of course, as Melucci said, Heterotopia is of value in that it provides an alternative lifestyle for those who choose to live outside the mainstream. The benefits of LETS *must* be in the day-to-day experience of participation and the new codes – about the way money works, about work, and about community and connectedness – self-created my members of LETS as knowledge producers. LETS *does* enable life to be carried out under different rules in those micro-realms, where members are active enough to make the transition to trading under transformed codes, and where their resource needs are access to occasional organic food to supplement their own allotment, or they live in a housing co-operative. But LETS is limited by the resources that members do not control.

LETS is micropolitics and effective micropolitics at that. As a challenge to commodification, a challenge to labour discipline, and impersonal market forces; which are challenges all tied up in the concept of 'relationship trading' – LETS is both educational for members *and* a practical example of the effectiveness of a real, observable alternative under particular local rules around money, work and community. LETS changes the rules within which this market operates, by internally changing the material basis on which trading takes place: and all this under the guise of an un-threatening alternative bank account rather than by the socialist programme of externally organising against capitalism. It is building the fabric of an alternative *within* capitalism.

However, its effectiveness in widening Heterotopia through accessing the outside resources of the mainstream economy – the means of production – is limited for the reasons discussed in chapter 8. LETS as heterotopia does not talk the language of business. Consequently, political action is needed alongside the building of such an alternative – those intense periods of offensive movement mobilisation against other power relations (the state and its armed power, private property) if it is going to break the limits of the system. As a micro rather than macro challenge, the Heterotopian challenge is effective in terms of its own local rules about money, work and community, but similarly ineffective outside its own local rules for which it has no answers. Outside Heterotopia the Transformers provided the strategy – but as chapter 8 showed, outside its local terrain – on local rules of business development – the Transformers' strategy was locally ineffective.

PART III
CONCLUSIONS

CHAPTER 11

Conclusion:
The Long Term Trajectory of LETS

THE LONG TERM TRAJECTORY OF MANCHESTER LETS

Much of the discussion above was undertaken in 1994–97 when LETS were on the ascendancy. The task then was to use social movement theory to uncover what this new movement meant – why did people join these alternative currency networks? Did they have a meaning beyond a group of people wanting to share and exchange goods and services? Too much of a criticism of the overall performance seemed inappropriate – it could be that LETS as an immature movement had not yet achieved its full potential, and too much critique of the performance of a small network might be premature.

Taking a longer view, LETS was certainly not the sort of phenomenon that do not last very long (Lapavitsas 2003). Recall, Manchester was founded in November 1992 with 120 members and grew at its height in April 1995 to a membership of 463 members. The chart below shows how membership on Manchester LETS changed over time from data gathered from directories.

August 1993	120
April 1994	163
October 1994	395
April 1994	463
April 1996	352
August 1998	325
August 1999	199
August 2000	184
August 2001	151

In 2001, 40 of the 151 members had been members when the scheme was at its height in 1995. The highest trader's turnover was B8347, with a balance of B1006. The balance of people who had left the scheme was B77558, with a positive balance of B722, which suggests that there had not a problem of people leaving the scheme with high negative balances. The total system turnover was B270,305.19, which is equivalent of 135,152.60's worth of work, or 45,050 hours of work. Of the 40 members who were members in 1995 who were still members in 2001, 5 had turnovers above B5000, 15 had turnovers above B2000, and 20 between 0 and B2000. There were four net debtors (balance below B200 with the lowest at –B736, 18 trading 'in balance' (+ or – below B200), and 18 creditors (balance above

B200). The highest net creditor was also the highest trader, with a credit of B1000 on a turnover of B8347. This suggests that LETS did seem to work as a self managed system, with little serious defection, and that at least 40 of the members did seem to be able to develop networks that worked for them such that they had remained in the network for more than 6 years. For these forty at least, the scheme was more than just ephemeral.

As many of the depth interviewees and focus group members of Manchester LETS who could be contacted were interviewed in 2001. 12 members were interviewed, six still being members while six had left. Of the six who had left, two had been active transformers but had found engagement with local government and health managers a dispiriting experience. They remained connected with their LETS networks, but were not traders. Four were from the green/heterotopian current, and had left as they felt that the ideological feel of LETS had changed as the transformers had begun to take more of the lead in LETS once New Labour came to power. Of the six that stayed members, two more dropped out soon after or just before being interviewed.

If we deal first with the leavers, one had featured in the discussion as the wormery builder and as director of Limited Resources. We dealt with Limited Resources reasons for leaving in Chapter Eight, but his personal reasons for leaving were as a result of his uncomfortableness with what he regarded – as a heterotopian – as the inherent commodification in LETS. He preferred straight co-operation:

> I believe that I have a got quite a big network of people, and I do, these unpaid transactions are going on all the time, they are just not in any formalised scheme. They do not go on outside your network of friends. ... But those things go on for me now. I don't really need to get involved in a LETS scheme. I do believe in that, but I also question about the monitoring of it and the billing of it really, because ... you know, I see it more as a philosophical and a spiritual way, if I can do something for somebody then I'm in a rich position, if I'm able to give, and if it's a problem then its up to me to recognise that ... So I suppose the LETS scheme, I agree with it in principle, it gives great benefits that you can get outside your network of friends, but I don't need to do that. For me its not necessary.

Another felt that while LETS was important, on reflection he felt wider changes are needed. He left as when he became unemployed he could no longer afford the membership fees for what he used only sporadically:

> I think we do need both, we need to build, keep practical examples but personally I feel that the practical things for me are a bit like, you know, I used to be part of the hippy movement ... if we would have called it that then I don't know ... but looking back, a lot of what happened in those sorts of movements, sort of alternative lifestyle, it could be categorised as personal lifestyle rather than things that are actually changing the world around you. Other people looked at it in a different way and said that those movements had impacts that have changed the world, but I feel that things like LETS, in many ways, a lot of the experience for me as a member of it was as a lifestyle thing. And I think that the energy ... the energy needs to be put into more than just LETS as an example. Its good as an example to other people, (laughs) its good as an example to other people, but I don't want to be a member myself! ... I suppose that's what I'm saying ... sounds strange that, doesn't it?

I think that ... myself and quite a few people, anticapitalists included, would really like to see a complete restructuring of the global economy into a localised economy, and it ... very much fits that. I feel now the task is to change mainstream society more than to build projects up amongst small groups of people which is just a lifestyle thing in the end, so I do look at it more, it was lifestyle enhancing and I enjoyed it. But I think that the real challenge is to change the way mainstream society actually works. So that's more of a green goal for me than participating in a project that seemed green.

Another former heterotopian found that when he became unemployed and was living on £47 a week the £8 subscription was not viable. Again, he had only been a sporadic user. But he also felt that LETS was changing ideologically:

I saw LETS as a process for getting people into contact with each other who would be then be as co-operative and community minded as possible ... but there was this ideological change that made it seem more like the cash economy. One person who originally said he wanted to do everything for free, to encourage that sort of thing, eventually decided that he wasn't valuing himself enough then wanted to charge 15 bobbins an hour. And that reawakened the arguments: you know, there had always been discussions about is one person's time as valuable as everyone else's. ... Originally it was possible for people to have a lot of different attitudes and still inhabit the same LETS system, you could see it as like the cash economy and see it as more of a process, and one of the things I really liked was that those different attitudes could cohabit. But there was a time when we were encouraged to go out and earn more Bobbins, and someone I know thought that was not in the spirit of LETS ... and I was getting into Bobbins debt because of the service charges, and there was also a sterling charge, and as a sporadic user of LETS I could not justify it. ... Its not that I now think LETS was a bad idea. I still think that LETS as a process is a very important thing, its just that I could not justify it.

A second problem this member had was that as an activist he did not have time for LETS, and when he was chased up by activists wanting to get trading going, he felt that he was being policed as a reprobate, where he was fully engaged in co-operative engagements:

I was very active in the local community in a radical way through the Green Party, without using Bobbins. ... when Earth First started actions at the airport and wanted help with the press I got involved, so I was active but not for Bobbins, and I possibly began to feel a little *resentful*, even, that I was being chased to go and get Bobbins when I felt I was doing things that were socially and ecologically useful for free ... I suppose there are only two ways to resolve that. Either everyone in the activist community is in LETS and gets Bobbins for what they do, or we have a more flexible attitude towards what Bobbins are. When we remember that the original reason we chose Bobbins is because in the local vernacular that means its worthless, it has no intrinsic value, then I started to feel a little policing. ... I wouldn't necessarily object, because I know that if I had been one of the people driving it I would have thought what can we do to get this going again, and I would probably have come up with similar ideas, having contact with people is a good way of jogging, getting them to rejoin the system at that point. I would have been happy to stay on the books, but to stay on the books you had to pay a service charge.

Moving onto those that stayed as members, one, an active humaniser, debated his friend, the heterotopian wormery builder. He explained why he stayed a member, right up to just before the interview when he, too, left due to lack of time and lack of access to resources in what was by now quite a small network. He sympathised with his friend, but felt he was wrong:

> I still think that LETS is very important. I've got to say that I've got more out of LETS than (the wormery builder) has. You can see that from the turnover, I've thought more about it, I've interacted more with people in it, so I see it just as richer than yourself. Your spirit is a bit troubled by the monetary (side) ... In the end, actually, if we like it or not, that money thing actually enables (us) to win all round and I see it as a lot broader than that. We all know about the pound economy out there and all that, we all know about the friendship 'economy', even though it doesn't have the word economy in it ... I've also used a van in the last couple of days, I called in favours from a mate. No money changed hands or aut like that. (The wormery builder) was there, seemed to work alright. ...

He saw LETS as a middle ground between the cash and co-operative economies

> But beyond that, I do think that there is a middle ground when you need it, and the truth is that (the wormery builder) doesn't need it, right? I have needed it, I don't need it at the moment, right? The middle ground is that bit between the two. Is a great big bubble that you can put in between two roles. It can be a small one, or a bloody great one. It's not to the exclusion of the others, its complementary to the others. You can live all your life using your friends, or a bit of money, or doing a hell of a lot through the financial economy and occasionally calling in a friend to help, but people compartmentalise their lives in different ways and the fact that its there is better than it not being there. So, the idea of being able to pay someone that I don't know otherwise just through a network is just a fantastic concept. I just marvel about it to this day, that I can just tap in ... you know. Far out.

He felt that heterotopians saw LETS as a commodification of the co-operative economy, where he saw it as a way of humanising the cash economy. For the wormery builder, LETS was 'not good enough', where for him, it was better than capitalism, a step in the right direction:

> There were mental blocks for a lot of people. You can look at it two ways. The sterling economy working backwards, or your friendship economy working forwards into that middle ground. (To his friend) I think you've looked at it from the friendship economy. I don't pay my friends, I don't want to be paying this other person who I know anyway ... but I look at it through the Sterling economy backwards as hey, I haven't got much money anyway and this is really good way of getting something that I would have had to pay for otherwise, bear in mind. A lot of this stuff, if I didn't do it for you, you'd have to pay for it. Its not coming from friendship, its coming from Sterling backwards.

He saw it as a way of cleaning up the sterling economy, a step towards a more green and sustainable economy – not the commodification of co-operation. The alternatives were utopian:

> This bit of the sterling economy, I can launder it clean. The sterling economy, the capitalist economy, is one that I think is quite foul, actually, so, if you can replace any of that with something sweeter smelling, that's fucking brilliant. Yeah? You don't have to

exchange something that's favour and exchange. That's something that (another heterotopian who also left) feels to this day. She jumps right to, we shouldn't have to pay for it, you know, Bob a job? No, I thought, lets step down the staircase rather than trying one leap? Quite frankly.

Moving further way from the heterotopian position, the highest trader was firmly of the opinion that LETS was value free, an economic tool like any other, which she joined because she could use it. She valued community and treating people with respect, but she did that in the cash economy. LETS was a way of getting things done. It worked for her as she had skills in high demand, and, needing help around the house and garden due to illness, could spend her Bobbins.

> Oh yes, I've enjoyed it. I enjoy making things, and I've enjoyed giving piano lessons, and I've enjoyed having people in the house doing things, I've not made them feel oh they're really doing a chore. I've always given them … extra Bobbins. I've never stuck to the, you know, six Bobbins an hour. If they've really done a good job I'll give them extra. I've tried to be very fair. Because I know how many Bobbins I can earn in an hour, so, and I know how long it would take me to clean my windows. Painful! So to me it's worth it! And there are a lot of people in the same situation. …

She did not want to see use of Bobbins drop off into pure co-operation. Asked if she stopped using Bobbins as friendships developed, she replied:

> No, that hasn't actually happened. I know it could happen. I've got someone who pops by and does a bit of gardening, and she hasn't had any piano lessons for a while. She had a baby. Well she came round to see me, just popping by, and she said that while she is here she'll do half an hour's gardening. She likes gardening and she knows I struggle to do it, so that could work like that. But in a way … I don't know, it defeats the object of it. You might as well use Bobbins. It keeps it square, doesn't it? … I think its important to keep it square, because it keeps it more, sort of, official. … I don't think I treat people differently because it's Bobbins. I'm conscious of not doing that. Yes. Because I wouldn't expect people to treat me any different. … it is the same (as cash), its just a different means of paying someone, but it still is the same.

She felt she was an active trader as she knew how LETS 'works'. The tacit, unlearnable knowledge about how to get the best out of the network, what tricks work, and the confidence to call strangers worked:

> Yes, it certainly gets easier once you understand how LETS works, and also, I ring up people in the wants, as well as in the offers. The wants and the offers, they often overlap. And if people looked, at the wants, it would work. But I don't think people look in the wants. And also something else I've done recently, anyone I've known who was new, or that hasn't got many Bobbins, or that's in debt, I ring them up and ask, you know, what other things do they do beyond the things they are advertising, because not everybody advertises everything that they can do. So I do that as well which I think other people could do. That would make it wider wouldn't it?

Perhaps she was still a member, and still actively working the system, as she had been unable to spend one in every four Bobbins she earned. On a turnover of

8000 Bobbins, income would be half that – 4000 Bobbins. And she had a balance of 1000:

> I feel, to a certain extent, I feel at times why am I bothering? But I feel that to leave obviously with all those Bobbins! I've earned them, I mean I've worked hard to earn them over the years, haven't I. So maybe they've left because they can't find people to do the jobs they want doing. There's a shortage of some things. There are plenty of therapists but you can only have so much. I mean, I've had some aromatherapy and massage for my shoulder, but there's a lot of things, the ordinary, everyday things.

A key transformer, still a (fairly) active member in 2001 put the success down to trading. Pure co-operation was over rated:

> Reciprocity is a great theory, but as I found in lots of situations, that people quite often in situations of reciprocity, they take but they don't give. And so, people need to feel … to feel good about giving, you have to know that the other person is sticking to their end of the bargain. It's not to give in order to receive, but if you in a part of the system where the idea is, everybody gives or receives roughly the same to make it work, then you need a measure of that. … With all the work I've done on LETS around the country, in other places as well, I've always found that the ones that started off with the community, focusing on the community and not recording trades, they never grew. They never went through an exciting phase of really taking off and getting lots of skills and trades. … my experience was that they … they were talking a lot and enjoying it, but it was a small club.

This Transformer was a member of LETS until 2004, when directories were no longer printed. Manchester LETS experimented with a website,[1] to save the work of printing directories. By 2005 he no longer used bobbins, but said that he regularly traded with members of the LETS network. Perhaps it is not an accident that many of the heterotopians who, in 1994–7 spoke so movingly about building community and co-operation had left by 2001, leaving the active traders and humanisers who stressed the importance of trading, and building out of the cosy club. But neither did the transformers get their way, perhaps, as we saw in the discussion, as they were ground down by partnership working, but perhaps also because their project is a social movement critique of capitalist markets that governments and businesses will be uninterested in. As Bowring put it:

> Indeed, if we are really to applaud the ecological benefits of LETS – and especially the way they encourage an ethic of resourcefulness and self-reliance which, in reducing the perceived value of conventionally paid labour, *reduces the dependence of workers on the owners of capital* – then we cannot in the same breath promote LETS as a local economic development tool with politically neutral macro-economic merits. If LETS harbour the potential to weaken people's dependence on the existing social system and to foster the self-productive use of their time, then the same schemes cannot simultaneously be championed as the saviours of work-based society, as the means by which the unemployed can be reconnected – and re-subjected – to the dominant system of wage relations, private companies protected against the vagaries of the business cycle, and the market economy placed on a more stable and efficient footing.
>
> (Bowring 1998:103)

LETS was, and is, a social movement making valuable claims about what is wrong with money, with work, and for sustainable, convivial and co-operative livelihoods.

CONCLUSION

Chapter 6 identified LETS as social movement rather than a value-free policy development. Despite claims that LETS was as uncontroversial as a bank account, members simultaneously raised claims that money is a simulacrum and as such changeable at will, that work needs to be redefined and humanised, and that local economies need to be developed as part of a move towards sustainability. They also claimed that elements in the design of LETS eliminated the power relations associated with money and labour discipline, and that capital accumulation was meaningless in local currency (being unlimited and earning no interest). These claims I identified as social movement claims which were resistant to the logic of the capitalist system. In social movement theory they represent a claim for 'Self Management', which Touraine identifies as the key social movement struggle in programmed society; just as worker's control was the key struggle in industrial society. Although Touraine's epistemological claims for the centrality of information and self-management were not sustained by the evidence, his claim that in the struggle for self-management the green movement has the potential to make a major contribution to the struggle for a new society was sustained. Evidence shows that members of LETS see it as a struggle for self-management of their livelihood. They are making social movement claims, not uncontroversial ones.

In Touraine's terms LETS is, however, an immature social movement in that it has as yet failed to agree on an identification of who its opponents are. LETS poses a theoretical antagonism to growth agendas, free trade, neo-liberalism, profiteering and coercion in the capitalist economy. Opponents which were identified included 'big business', the Inland Revenue, and the Department of Social Security (ie, coercive state apparatus). It is interesting to note that the department of social security's unwillingness to change the rules in regard to LETS was seen as a major block on the development of LETS in poorer areas, while the decision to disregard Time Money also gave it a fair wind. However, members who did identify potential opponents were derided by some members as having inappropriate thoughts – engaging in 'old thinking'. Traditional political categories such as 'ally' and 'enemy' were regarded as out of date and inappropriate to the new world being born.

If analysis is restricted to modernist linear approaches to social movements, LETS must be rejected either as immature, or as a diversion. The American school would charge the Heterotopian majority in LETS with immaturity for not aiming to enter political society. Marxism would critique LETS as a re-inscription of utopianism, doomed by a failure to identify the working class as the only social force with the power to overthrow its exploitation. Only postmodern approaches to political change associated with the European school would validate LETS as a social change strategy, not focussed on the state. Foucaultian analyses would see LETS as a form of micro-mobilisation against the specific forms of power which LETS identifies. It does this by creating a discourse that shows (in activists own words) how money, being limited, created by 'others', and flowing from localities to where it can get its best return, restricts the choices available to 'us' who must work to gain this limited resource, controlled by 'them'. This discourse holds that money is a Baudrillardian simulacrum, socially created, and socially over-throwable. Similarly, LETS indicates that alternative lifestyles and work opportunities can become possible given this new economy, with social change possible without engaging with the state. Finally, LETS indicates the existence of a community operating through mutual aid rather than by competition and the division of labour. This community economy operates below the cash economy, but above pure, co-operative exchange. For some, LETS is a way for people to get to know each other, who then co-operate without using the alternative currency.

LETS has value as a form of micro-mobilisation against these specific, and local power relations. It is consistent in its own right, by its own Foucauldian 'local rules' – rather than against a metanarrative explanation such as the need to engage with pluralistic political society to gain resources and credibility, and therefore to align its frames accordingly; or to develop links with the organised working class. The success of LETS lies rather in the day-to-day activities of members as they illuminate previously-hidden power relations and develop, in LETS, a technology that overcame them, within the resource constraints imposed by their lack of access to the means of production, and the limited opportunities for the development of mutual aid imposed by the Transformers.

Its strategy aimed at building a sphere of co-operation below the level of the state, which, it is hoped, will eventually grow and overcome capitalism just as capitalism slowly overcame feudalism is, of course, a longstanding anarchist and co-operative strategy. More recently, it is one that has been adopted by the Zapatistas in Mexico or the Pickets in Argentina, as well as myriad autonomist projects for social change associated with what, after Seattle in 1999, became known as the counter globalisation movement (Brechter, Costello et al. 2000; Notes from Nowhere 2003). The theorisations of this strategy that caught the imagination were Hardt and Negri's concept of the 'multitude' (Hardt and Negri 2000; 2005), those millions of people working formally or informally, who are unemployed, who work the land who all have an interest in social change but who do not necessarily assume the identity of a worker. While it would be ludicrous to conflate a Zapatista fighter or an unemployed Argentine *Piquetero* with some of Manchester's globally still quite privileged green middle classes, they both share a rejection of what they see as an unethical and unsustainable global capitalism, and want to develop new ways of working within a market economy that are not capitalist – without 'waiting for the revolution.' The economies they work in are market based, but not capitalist either (Gibson-Graham 1996). Working below the level of the state, they do not seek solution in the state either – they want little from the state except to be left alone, do not seek state resources, and are cynical about any engagement with the state, not seeing it as their job to solve capitalism's inequalities on behalf of the government. Thus they want to 'change the word without taking power', as John Holloway would put it (Holloway 2002). As we saw, within limits, Active members of LETS with dense local social networks they could change their local world though work with non-capitalist oriented businesses, new contacts through LETS and a strong non-capitalist cooperative network to provide their needs. They avoided the supermarket, preferring their allotment and the local food box scheme – and though LETS they set up a food co-operative. Housing could be provided co-operatively.

But LETS is not a unitary social movement, but heterogeneous. It cannot effectively or appropriately be 'tamed' (Routledge 1994) into a false unity by relation to meta-narrative explanations of social change, as this taming would obscure the multiplicity of strategies produced by the diverse membership of LETS. This diversity I categorised into four strands which form a spectrum of options about the processes of social change advocated by members of LETS, which inform their decision to participate in the social movement, and which guide the initiatives they take to strengthen LETS:

Transformers	LETS is value-free
	Humanisers
	Greeners
Heterotopians	Green anarchists

Transformers see LETS as a value-free policy suitable for adoption by all, whereas Heterotopians see it as a counter-cultural alternative. These conceptions led to conflict over values; over whether the unit of currency should be linked to the pound or not, over whether everyone should be paid equally, and, over whether efforts to widen use of LETS by mainstream institutions – primarily businesses and local authorities – might limit the extent to which LETS can operate as a counter-cultural alternative. As a postmodern movement, however, members of LETS showed some tolerance over the diversity of tactics they would need to achieve their goals. No metanarrative was privileged within Manchester LETS. Less tolerance was displayed to LETSGo. Manchester LETS achieved some sort of equilibrium around a neutral public face, with an overwhelmingly Heterotopian membership that tried not to prevent Transformers carrying out development work – as long as they did not interfere with administration. Transformers similarly limited the extent to which commitment-building mechanisms were put into place.

Given these two alternative value-systems, the process whereby the two tendencies debated their strategies and operated to meet their needs – the Transformers through widening LETS and the Heterotopians through deepening it – shows both the extent to which LETS is perceived as a social movement or an uncontroversial policy innovation, and its effectiveness an dealing with its diversity. Chapters Eight and Nine examined attempts by Transformers to gain allies, and again LETS was found to be a relatively immature movement that did little to transform its frames to win allies. LETSGo concentrated on winning businesses to LETS but was unable to mobilise resources to achieve considerable business membership. Manchester's Local Agenda 21 process invited participation which was not forthcoming from Transformers. Manchester LETS did produce a social movement organisation, LEDA, that found allies who recognised that LETS might be an appropriate tool for economic development, community development, and empowerment. However, the extent that allies could be accessed was limited by the perceptions of the heterotopian wing which refused to get involved in widening use of LETS.

Chapter 10 discussed Heterotopia. It showed that members who were active were able to revalue cultural understandings of money, labour and community, and develop a concept of 'relationship trading'. On these fronts it did represent an effective micro-political struggle. However, Heterotopia was limited by the resources outside LETS. As Marxist analysis indicates, control of the means of production by others, who are not members of LETS (unlikely ever to join if the analysis of the usefulness of LETS for businesses is correct), means that full livelihoods cannot be lived within LETS. While the resources obtainable through LETS are greater than those obtainable by working people in the 19th Century, the level of co-operation achieved by too many Heterotopians still merits Marx's dismissive categorisation of individual, private attempts at co-operation as 'dwarfish' (Marx 1863, in Fernbach (ed.) 1974:90). The wishes of Transformers in making LETS attractive to businesses introduced members who did not share their values, and with whom Heterotopians clashed.

However, members of Manchester LETS debated these issues fairly amicably, although they were more forcefully contested within the Core Group. Heterotopians did not prevent Transformation work although they declined to become involved in it. Transformers insisted on a laissez-faire ethos that also enabled the Heterotopians to set their own currency values. The schism came in relation to LETSGo, whose more intolerant extreme transformation strategy alienated the vast majority of supporters of LETS. In these cases, LETS shows itself to be a self-regulating and self-limiting system.

THE APPROPRIATENESS OF SOCIAL MOVEMENT THEORY

Social Movement theory is a powerful tool for an analysis of LETS as a form of political action. The perspectives of Touraine and Melucci were used to deconstruct the movement and explain what claims it raised and why. They also allowed an examination of the extent that there were conflicts and differences in claims made. Social movement theory starts from the social movement and explains what it is, rather than imposing metanarrative explanations. Similarly, the American School's realist perceptions ground analysis within a Political Opportunity Structure, and suggest an analysis of resources that are available to the movement which underpin its capacity to achieve what it wants to. While members of LETS did find value in LETS as a message of the possibility of an alternative, they also wanted to achieve a livelihood, using this alternative form of money, within a vibrant economy. They could all point to reasons why it was not happening and saw the need to strengthen the community economy. Therefore they were not entirely nomads of the present. Participation was not enough if it did not bring benefits.

Touraine's model of Sociological Intervention was a useful place to start the analysis. Working through a process of identifying who the movement thought it was (the principle of identity); who it saw as its opponents and allies (the principle of opposition); and the extent to which it had developed a coherent and total set of claims about what they hoped to achieve – or ducked hard questions (the principle of totality) – helped flesh out the extent to which LETS was a social movement. Observation of and the analysis of the production of frames helped take the discussion out of the focus group room into the wider POS. However, the sort of questions this approach raised failed to give sufficient emphasis to those who joined for non-political reasons. They did not think there were problems with society as presently organised that needed to be rectified, but wanted a babysitter. Sociological intervention strengthened the voice of the more overtly political member.

The perspective of Transformers is that in its early days LETS attracts overtly green members who join because they want to build ecological institutions. These early joiners will be supplemented by members who join the system for its economic vibrancy and because they can obtain goods and services from LETS. Green members therefore benefit from this widened local economy. If those with strongly held political opinions do not actually trade, and later drop out of the system, and non-political members who do not find discussions about political strategy worthwhile replace them, then a misleading impression of the likely future trajectory of LETS – that overemphasises social movement claims made by members of LETS – will result from work with early, political members. During research, I met such members by interviewing a wider tranche of traders, and through ethnographic participation – but their voices do not speak in this discussion of political strategy. If not read with others that address issues other than those of the political views of members, this discussion will give a false impression. Other work should balance this thesis; and thankfully, Williams (1996 a, b) Lee (1996), Thorne (1996), Seyfang (1996) and others provide these insights. That said, research in 2001 and 2005 did not show that in the long term the political members dropped out and were replaced by apolitical traders. This reinforces arguments that LETS should be seen as a social movement.

The work of the American School, with its distinctive perspective on resource mobilisation was again a useful research tool, but its perspectives on inclusion within the polity and the need for the identification of allies does not fit a more countercultural phenomenon like LETS. Even the most extreme Transformers, like LETSGo were not seeking inclusion – but rather the adoption of LETS by mainstream institutions. Transformers held personal values that did not distinguish them from their Humanising or Greening collegues. The Transformers claim was that elite groups needed to adopt LETS if ecological catastrophe was to be avoided: LETS as Bahrovian 'Global Turnaround Movement'. The RMT school's emphasis on the production of SMOs showed that members themselves could establish a fairly complicated, well-resourced, and efficiently administered LETS system delivering real benefits to active members. It did not need to seek allies for this, if the aim was to produce a countercultural alternative space.

Seeing social movements as knowledge producers best fitted the analysis, philosophy and approach of members of LETS. Heterotopians did not wish to engage with this structure, and Transformers as idealists wished to remain open to all possibilities. They both took a constructivist approach that bordered on the obliteration of structure and reification of the actor as producer of their own reality. The question then arises itself that, if many members of LETS do not wish to engage with structures, are they a resistant social movement – or what Melucci called a therapeutic network? Given that for Touraine a social movement is the struggle of a class actor against their class adversary (1981:1), the low level of mobilisation in LETS of even some of the most active members and the absence of offensive social movement events like riots, strikes or demonstrations, raises a doubt as to whether LETS is engaged in combat. However, I believe that in the message LETS sends of the existence of an alternative, LETS is a cultural struggle. The existence of a different form of currency, the possibility of alternative forms of livelihood outside labour discipline, and the establishment of a community characterised by mutual co-operation is a political demonstration of an alternative economy, a struggle for historicity and for self- management. It is the politics of alternative institution-building within the rich anarchist and utopian tradition that goes back through the communards of the 1960s, the stamp scrip and co-op activists of the 1930s, and back to Owen, the Diggers, and communal movements like the Anabaptists. The practical demonstration of an alternative and micropolitical struggle against particular power relations is more than therapy. As Holloway (2003) would put it, it is also a shout of 'no!', a resistance to a capitalism that puts the need for financial stability above getting needs met. In the UK the quest for financial stability leads to unnecessary deprivation, lives not as rich as they could be, people struggling to get by – but in the global South it leads to hunger, death and disease. LETS is part of the global resistance to this.

Social movement theory therefore needs to pay more attention to movements that don't engage with their Political Opportunity Structure outside the realm of civil society. The assumption needs to be challenged that they are either immature and will soon come up against their limits (Touraine 1982), will eventually seek inclusion (the RMT approach), or are part of a post-1989, post socialist democratisation of western-style civil society founded on unprobematic rationality (Cohen and Arato 1992). Future research should therefore move further into the realm opened by Foucault's archaeological method and analyses of power, to uncover more micro-political power relations which social movements confront. Rather than the constructivist metaphor of language, a Foucauldian metaphor of battle should stay in the mind of students of social movements.

I found attempts to unify social movement theory less useful than a pluralist approach that recognises that the different approaches form a toolkit of approaches, each illuminating different regions within a whole analysis, and showing tensions between approaches. Rather than attempt to annihilate the tensions, the diversity of approaches should be retained and used by social movement theorists as appropriate. More work has recently been done on this, so that with a combination of insights from the two schools – that perhaps do not make such sense seen in isolation anymore – provide a rich toolkit for the analysis of social movements (McAdam, McCarthy et al. 1996).

NOTE

1   See www.manchesterlets.org: still not live at time of writing, June 2005.

Bibliography

Albery, D. (1979). 'Alternative Plans and Revolutionary Strategy.' *International Socialism* **2**(6): 85–97.

Aldridge, T., J. Tooke, et al. (2001). 'Recasting Work: the Example of Local Exchange Trading Schemes.' *Work, Employment & Society* **15**(3): 565–579.

Anastacio, J., B. Gidley, et al. (2000). *Reflecting Realities: participants perspectives on integrated communities and sustainable development*. Bristol, Policy Press.

Atkinson, P. (1990). *The Ethnographic Imagination: Textual Constructions of Reality*. London, Routledge.

Bahro, R. (1994). *Avoiding Social and Ecological Disaster*. Bath, Gateway Books.

Barnes, H., P. North, et al. (1996). *LETS on Low Income*. London, The New Economics Foundation.

Bennington, J. (1986). 'Local Economic Strategies: paradigms for a planned economy?' *Local Economy* **1**(1): 7–44.

Bentley, G., A. Hallsworth, et al. (2003). 'The Countryside in the City – Situating a Farmers' Market in Birmingham.' *Local Economy* **18**(2): 109–120.

Berens, C. (1995). 'Generation X – Do-it-Yourself Politics.' *New Statesman*: 22.

Best, S. and D. Kellner (1991). *Postmodern Theory: Critical Interrogations*. London, Macmillan.

Birch, S. (1995). 'Frontlines.' *The Globe*. Manchester. September: 26.

Boddy, M. and C. Fudge, Eds. (1984). *Local Socialism*. London, Macmillan.

Bookchin, M. (1986). *Post-Scarcity Anarchism*. Montreal, Black Rose Books.

Bowring, F. (1998). 'LETS: an eco-socialist initiative?' *New Left Review* (232): 91–111.

Boyle, D. (1999). *Funny Money: in search of alternative cash*. London, HarperCollins.

Boyne, R. and A. Rattansi (1990). *Postmodernity and Society*. London, Macmillan.

Brechter, J., T. Costello, et al. (2000). *Globalisation from Below: the power of solidarity*. Cambridge, Mass., South End Press.

Buber, M. (1949). *Paths in Utopia*. London, Routledge and Kegan Paul.

Burgess, R. (1984). *In the Field*. London, Routledge.

Cahn, E. (2000). *No More Throw Away People*. London, HarperCollins.

Callinicos, A. (1989). *Making History: Agency, Structure and Change in Social Theory*. Cambridge, Polity.

Capra, F. and C. Spretnak (1984). *Green Politics*. London, Hutchinson.

Carter, J. and D. Moreland, Eds. (2004). *Anti-Capitalist Britain*. Cheltenham, New Clarion Press.

Castells, M. (1986). *The City and the Grassroots*. London, Edward Arnold.

Chambers, R. (1990). *Putting the last first*. Toronto, Griffin House.

Clavel, P. (1986). *The Progressive City: Planning and Participation 1969–1984*. Brunswick, New Jersey, Rutgers University Press.

Clavel, P. and R. Kraushaar (1998). 'On being unreasonable: progressive planning in Sheffield and Chicago.' *International Planning Studies* **3**(2): 143–162.

Cochrane, A., J. Peck, et al. (1996). 'Manchester Plays Games: Exploring the Local Politics of Globalisation.' *Urban Studies* **33**(8): 1319–1336.

Cohen, J. and A. Arato (1992). *Civil Society and Political Theory*. Cambridge MA, MIT Press.

Coleman, D. (1994). *Eco-politics: Building a Green Society*. Brunswick, New Jersey, Rutgers University Press.

Cox, L. (1996). 'From social movements to countercultures: steps beyond political reductionism.' *Alternative Futures and Popular Protest II*. C. Barker and M. Tydesley. Manchester, Manchester Metropolitan University.

Croall, J. (1997). *LETS act locally: the growth of Local Exchange Trading Systems*. London, Calouste Gulbenkian Foundation.

Dauncey, G. (1988). *Beyond the crash: the emerging rainbow economy*. London, Greenprint.

Della Porta, D. and M. Diani, Eds. (1998). *Social movements: an introduction*. Oxford, Blackwell.

DFEE (1999). *Jobs for all*. Nottingham, Department of Education and Employment Publications.

Diamond, J. (2001). 'Managing change or coping with conflict? Mapping the experience of a local regeneration partnership.' *Local Economy* **16**(4): 272–285.

Diani, M. (1992). 'The Concept of Social Movement.' *The Sociological Review* **40**(1): 1–25.

Dobson, A. (1990). *Green Political Thought*. London, Harpercollins Academic.

Douthwaite, R. (1996). *Short Circuit: Strengthening local economies for security in an uncertain world*. Totnes, Devon, Green Books.

Draper, H. (1992). *Socialism from Below*. London, Humanities Press.

Eisinger, P. (1973). 'The conditions of protest behaviour in American cities.' *American Political Science Review* **67**: 11–28.

Ekins, P., Ed. (1986). *The living economy: a new economics in the making*. London, Routledge and Kegan Paul.

Engels, F. (1844). *The condition of the working class in England*. London, Penguin.

Eyerman, R. and R. Jamison (1991). *Social Movements: a Cognitive Approach*. Cambridge, Polity.

Fielding, N. (1993). Ethnography. *Researching Social Life*. N. Gilbert. London, Sage, pp. 154–171.

Foucault, M. (1980). *Power/Knowledge*. London, Harvester Wheatsheaf.

Foweraker, J. (1995). *Theorising Social Movements*. London, Pluto.

Gamson, W. and D. Meyer (1996). The framing of political opportunities. *Comparative Perspectives on Social Movements*. D. McAdam, J. McCarthy and M. Zald. Cambridge, Cambridge University Press, pp. 275–290.

Geras, N. (1990). *Discourses of Extremity*. London, Verso.

Gibson-Graham, J. (1996). *The end of capitalism (as we knew it): a feminist critique of political economy*. Oxford, Blackwell.

Giddens, A. (1979). *Central problems in social theory: action, structure, and contradiction in social analysis*. London, Macmillan.

Giordano, B. and L. Twomey (2002). 'Economic transitions: restructuring local labour markets.' *City of Revolution: Restructuring Manchester*. J. A. K. W. Peck, Eds. Manchester, Manchester University Press.

Gledhill, J. (1994). *Power and its Disguises: Anthropological Perspectives on Politics*. London, Pluto Press.

Glover, P. (1995). Ithaca Hours. *Investing in the common good*. S. Meeker Lowry. New York, New Society Publishers.

Goffman, E. (1974). *The presentation of self in everyday life*. London, Penguin.

Gramsci, A. (1971). *Selections from the prison notebooks*. London, Lawrence and Wishart.

Granovetter, M. (1973). 'The Strength of Weak Ties.' *American Journal of Sociology* **78**(6): 1360–1380.

Greco, T. H. (1994). *New Money for Healthy Communities*. Tuscon, Ariz., Self-published.

Greco, T. H. (2001). *Money: Understanding and creating alternatives to legal tender*. White River Junction, VT, Chelsea Green.

Greenwood, B. (1995). 'How Green is our Local Agenda?' *City Life* **279**(May): 10.

Hall, T. and P. Hubbard (1998). *The Entrepreneurial City: Geographies of Politics, Regime and Representation*. Chichester, John Wiley.

Hammersley, M. and P. Atkinson (1983). *Ethnography: Principles in Practice*. London, Tavistock.

Hardt, M. and A. Negri (2000). *Empire*. London, Harvard University Press.

Hardt, M. and A. Negri (2005). *Multitude*. London, Hamish Hamilton.

Harvey, D. (1992). *The Condition of Postmodernity*. Oxford, Blackwell.

Harvey, D. (1996). *Justice, Nature and the Geography of Difference*. Oxford, Blackwell.

Harvey, D. (2001). From Managerialism to Entrepreneurialism: the transformation in urban governance in late capitalism. *Spaces of Capital*. D. Harvey. Edinburgh, Edinburgh University Press, pp. 345–368.

Haslam, D. (1999). *Manchester, England: the story of the pop cult city*. London, 4th Estate.

Hastings, A., A. McArthur, et al. (1996). *Less than equal? Community organisations and regeneration partnerships*. The Policy Press, Bristol.

Hines, C. (2000). *Localisation: a Global Manifesto*. London, Earthscan.

Hoggett, P., S. Jeffers, et al. (1994). 'Reflexivity and Uncertainty in the Research Process.' *Policy and Politics* **22**(1): 59–70.

Holloway, J. (2002). *Change the world without taking power: the meaning of revolution today*. London, Pluto.

Houriet, R. (1973). *Getting back together*. London, Abacus.

Imeson, J. (1993). 'Swap Shop.' *Marketing Business* (April 1993).

Jackson, M. (1995). 'Helping Ourselves: New Zealand's Green Dollar Exchanges', available from the author markj@redgum.bendigo.latrobe.edu.au.

Jonas, A. and D. Wilson (2000). *The Urban Growth Machine: Critical Perspectives Two Decades Later*. New York, State University of New York.

Kantor, R. (1972). *Commitment and Community: Communes and Utopia in Sociological Perspective*. Cambridge MA, Harvard University Press.

Klandermans, B. and S. Tarrow (1988). Mobilisation into social movements: synthesising European and American approaches. *International Social Movement Research Vol 1*. B. Klandermans and S. Tarrow. New York, JAI Press Inc.

Lang, P. (1994). *LETS Work: Revitalising the local economy*. Bristol, Grover Publications.

Lapavitsas, C. (2003). *Social Foundations of Markets, Money and Credit*. London, Routledge.

Lee, R. (1996). 'Moral Money? LETS and the social construction of local economic geographies in Southeast England.' *Environment and Planning A* 28(8): 1377–1394.

Lee, R. (1999). Local money: Geographies of autonomy and resistance. *Money and the space economy*. R. Martin. Chichester, Wiley, pp. 207–224.

Lee, R. (2002). '"Nice maps, shame about the theory'? Thinking geographically about the economic.' *Progress in Human Geography* 26(3): 333–355.

Levitas, R. (1990). *The Concept of Utopia*. London, Philip Allan.

Linton, M. and A. Soutar (1994). *The LETSystem Design Manual*. Courtenay, British Columbia, LCS Ltd.

Logan, J. and H. Molotch (1996). The City as Growth Machine. *Readings in Urban Theory*. S. Fainstein and S. Campbell. London, Blackwell.

Mackintosh, M. and H. Wainwright, Eds. (1987). *A Taste of Power: the Politics of Local Economics*. London, Verso.

Mansbridge, J. (1980). *Beyond Adversary Democracy*. Boston MA, Basic Books.

Mayo, M. (1997). 'Partnerships for regeneration and community development.' *Critical Social Policy* 17(3): 3–26.

McAdam, D., J. McCarthy, et al., Eds. (1996). *Comparative Perspectives on Social Movements*. Cambridge, Cambridge University Press.

McAdam, J., J. McCarthy, et al. (1988). Social Movements. *Handbook of Sociology*. N. Smelsner. London, Sage.

McCarthy, J. and M. Zald (1977). 'Resource mobilisation and social movements: a partial theory.' *American Journal of Sociology* 82(6): 1212–1241.

McKay, G. (1996). *Senseless Acts of Beauty: Cultures of Resistance since the Sixties*. London, Verso.

Melucci, A. (1989). *Nomads of the Present*. London, Hutchinson Radius.

Melucci, A. (1992). Frontierland: Collective Action between Actors and Systems. *Studying Collective Action*. M. Diani. London, Sage, pp. 238–257.

Melucci, A. (1996). *Challenging Codes: Collective Action in the Information Age*. Cambridge, Cambridge University Press.

Morris, A. and C. Herring (1987). 'Theory and research in social movements: a critical review.' *Annual Review of Political Science* 2: 137–198.

North, P. (1996). 'LETS: a tool for empowerment in the inner city?' *Local Economy* 11(3): 284–293.

North, P. (1999). 'Explorations in Heterotopia: LETS and the micropolitics of money and livelihood.' *Environment and Planning D: Society and Space* 17(1): 69–86.

North, P. (2005). 'Scaling alternative economic practices? Some lessons from alternative currencies.' *Transactions of the Institute of British Geographers* 30(2).

North, P. and I. Bruegel (2001). 'Community Empowerment: Rethinking Resistance in an era of Partnership'. *Rebuilding Community: Policy and Practice in Urban Regeneration*. J. Pierson and J. Smith. London, Palgrave, pp. 174–188.

Notes-from-Nowhere, Ed. (2003). *We are everywhere: the irresistable rise of global anticapitalism*. London, Verso.

Offe, C. and R. Heinz (1992). *Beyond Employment*. Cambridge, Polity Press.

Pacione, M. (1997). 'Local Exchange Trading Systems as a Response to the Globalisation of Capitalism.' *Urban Studies* **34**(8): 1179–1199.

Pacione, M. (1999). 'The other side of the coin: Local currency as a response to the globalisation of capital.' *Regional Studies* **33**(1): 63–72.

Parkinson, M. (1985). *Liverpool on the brink: one city's struggle against Government cuts*. Hermitage, Berks, Policy Journals.

Parkinson, M. and F. Bianchini (1993). Liverpool: a tale of missed opportunities. *Cultural Policy and Urban Regeneration: the West European Experience*. F. Bianchini and M. Parkinson. Manchester, Manchester University Press, pp. 155–177.

Pearson, R. (2003). 'Argentina's Barter Network: New Currency for New Times.' *Bulletin of Latin American Research* **22**(2): 214–230.

Peck, J. and A. Tickell (1995). 'Business goes local: dissecting the 'business agenda' in Manchester.' *International Journal of Urban and Regional Research* **19**: 55–78.

Peck, J. and K. Ward, Eds. (2002). *City of Revolution: Restructuring Manchester*. Manchester, Manchester University Press.

Pickvance, C. (1995). Social Movements and the transition from State Socialism. *Social Movements and Social Classes*. L. Maheu. London, Sage.

Pile, S. and S. Keith, Eds. (1997). *Geographies of Resistance*. London, Routledge.

Polanyi, K. (1944/1980). *The Great Transformation*. New York, Octagon.

Powell, J. (2002). 'Petty Capitalism, Perfecting Capitalism or Post-Capitalism? Lessons from the Argentinean barter experiments.' *Review of International Political Economy* **9**(4): 619–649.

Primavera, H., C. De Sanzo, et al. (1998). *Reshuffling for a New Social Order: The Experience of the Global Barter Network in Argentina*. Enhancing People's Space in a Globalising Economy, Espoo, Finland.

Putnam, R. (1993). *Making Democracy Work: civic traditions in modern Italy*. Princeton, Princeton University Press.

Putnam, R. (2001). *Bowling Alone*. London, Simon and Schuster.

Quilley, S. (1994). 'Manchester's "Village in the City": The Gay Vernacular in a post-industrial landscape of power.' paper presented to Conference 'The Politics of Cultural Change, University of Lancaster, July.

Quilley, S. (1999). 'Entrepreneurial Manchester: the genesis of elite consensus.' *Antipode* **31**(2): 185–211.

Quilley, S. (2000). 'Manchester first: From municipal socialism to the entrepreneurial city.' *International Journal of Urban and Regional Research* **24**(3): 601.

Quilley, S. (2002). Entrepreneurial turns: municipal socialism and after. *City of Revolution: Restructuring Manchester*. J. Peck and K. Ward. Manchester, Manchester University Press.

Raban, J. (1974). *Soft City*. London, Flamingo.

Randall, S. (1995). 'City Pride – from "municipal socialism" to "municipal capitalism"?' *Critical Social Policy* **43**: 40–59.

Robson, B. (2002). Mancunian Ways. *City of Revolution: Restructuring Manchester*. J. Peck and K. Ward. Manchester, Manchester University Press.

Rucht, D., Ed. (1991). *Research on Social Movements: the state of the art in Western Europe and the USA*. Boulder, CO, Westview Press.

Schumacher, E. F. (1973) *Small is Beautiful: A Study of Economics as if People Mattered*. London, Blond and Briggs.

Schwedler, J. (2002). 'Social movements in politics: A comparative study.' *American Political Science Review* **96**(2): 446–448.

Scott, I. (1990). *Ideology and the New Social Movements*. London, Allen and Unwin.

SEU (1998). *Bringing Britain Together: a national strategy for neighbourhood renewal*. London, Social Exclusion Unit.

Seyfang, G. (2001). 'Community currencies: small change for a green economy.' *Environment and Planning A* **33**(9): 975–996.

Seyfang, G. (2003). '"With a little help from my friends". Evaluating time banks as a tool for community self help.' *Local Economy* **18**(3): 257–264.

Silo (1994). *Letters to my Friends – On Social and Personal Crisis in Today's World*. San Diego, Ca, Latitude Press.

Simmel, G. (1978/1908). *The Philosophy of Money*. London, Routledge.

Smith, D. (1987). *The rise and fall of monetarism*. London, Pelican.

Snow, D. and R. Benford (1992). Master Frames and Cycles of Protest. *Frontiers of Social Movement Theory*. A. Morris, J. McClerg and C. Mueler. London, Yale University Press.

Snow, D., E. Rochford, et al. (1986). 'Frame alignment processes, micromobilisation and movement participation.' *American Sociological Review* **51**: 464–481.

Solomon, L. (1996). *Rethinking Our Centralised Money System: the Case for a System of Local Currencies*. London, Praeger.

Spradley, J. (1979). *The Ethnographic Interview*. London, Holt Reinhart and Winston.

Stanley, L. and S. Wise (1993). *Breaking Out Again: Feminist Ontology and Epistemology*. London, Routledge.

Strange, S. (1986). *Casino Capitalism*. Oxford, Blackwell.

Taafe, P. and T. Mulhearn (1988). *Liverpool, a city that dared to fight*. London, Fortress Books.

Tarrow, S. (1998). *Power in Movement: Social Movements and Contentious Politics*. Cambridge, Cambridge University Press.

The Ecologist (1993). *Whose Common Future?* Vol 22/4.

Thorne, L. (1996). 'Local Exchange Trading Systems in the UK – a case of re-embedding?' *Environment and Planning A* **28**(8): 1361–1376.

Tilly, C. (1978). *From Mobilisation to Revolution*. London, Addison Wesley.

TimebanksUK (2005). 'newsletter.' **19**(March).

Tindall, D. B. (2003). 'From structure to dynamics: A paradigm shift in social movements research?' *Canadian Review of Sociology and Anthropology-Revue Canadienne De Sociologie Et D Anthropologie* **40**(4): 481–487.

Touraine, A. (1981). *The voice and the eye: an analysis of social movements*. Cambridge, Cambridge University Press.

Touraine, A. (2001). *Beyond Neoliberalism*. Cambridge, Polity.

Tye, R. and G. Williams (1994). 'Urban Regeneration and Central-Local Government relations: the case of East Manchester.' *Progress in Planning* **42**: 1–97.

Wainwright, H. (1987). *Labour: a tale of two parties*. London, Chatto and Windus.

Wall, D. (1990). *Getting There: Steps to a Green Society*. Totnes, Devon, Greenprint.

Ward, C. (1988). *Anarchy in Action*. London, Freedom Press.

Ward, K. (2000). 'From Rentiers to Rantiers: "Active Entrepreneurs", "Structural Speculators" and the Politics of Marketing the City.' *Urban Studies* **37**(7): 1093–1107.

Ward, K. (2003). 'Entrepreneurial urbanism, state restructuring and civilizing "New" East Manchester.' *Area* **35**(2): 116–127.

Weston, D. (1992). Delinking Green Pounds from the Big System. *New Economics*.

Williams, C. C. (1995). Trading favours in Calderdale. *Town and Country Planning*.

Williams, C. C. (1996a). 'Local Currencies and Community Development: an evaluation of Green Dollar Exchanges in New Zealand.' *Community Development Journal* **31**(4): 319–329.

Williams, C. C. (1996b). 'Local Exchange Trading Systems: a new source of work and employment?' *Environment and Planning A* **28**(8): 1395–1415.

Williams, C. C., T. Aldridge, et al. (2001). *Bridges into Work: an evaluation of Local Exchange Trading Schemes*. Bristol, The Policy Press.

Williams, G. (1998). 'City Vision and Strategic Regeneration – the Role of City Pride.' *Cities, Economic Competition and Urban Policy*. N. Oatley. London, Paul Chapman Publishing, pp. 163–180.

Index